The Social Process of Lobbying

Despite a wealth of theorizing and research about each concept, lobbying and norms still raise a number of interesting issues. Why do lobbyists and politicians engage in cooperative behavior? How does cooperative behavior in lobbying affect policy making? If democratic participation is good, why do we view lobbying as bad?

Lobbying engenders debate about its effects on the political process and on policy development. Sociologists and other social scientists remain concerned about how norms emerge, the content of norms, how widely they are distributed, and how they are enforced. Political scientists study how interest groups work together and influence the political process. Based on the experience of the author, a former lobbyist, this book looks at the social norms of lobbying and how such norms work in a general framework of other norms and legal institutions in the political process. In developing this argument, John C. Scott claims that:

Embedded social relationships and trust-based social norms underpin everyday interactions among policy actors.

These relationships and norms have concrete impacts on the policy making process.

Social relationships and norms inhibit participation in the political process by outside actors.

The investigation is conducted through an innovative theoretical framework, combining existing theoretical perspectives from different disciplines, and using a variety of data and methods, including longitudinal quantitative and social network data, interviews with lobbyists, activists, and policy makers, and anecdotal and historical examples.

The Social Process of Lobbying provides refreshingly new empirical evidence and theoretical analysis on how networks of trust are neither all good nor all bad but are ambivalent: They can both improve policy and fuel collusion.

John C. Scott is an Assistant Professor of Public Policy at the University of North Carolina at Chapel Hill. His research interests include social network analysis of political and social phenomena as well as social policies related to aging populations.

Routledge Research in American Politics and Governance

The Social Process of Lobbying
Cooperation or Collusion?

John C. Scott

Routledge
Taylor & Francis Group

NEW YORK AND LONDON

First published 2015
by Routledge
711 Third Avenue, New York, NY 10017, USA

and by Routledge
2 Park Square, Milton Park, Abingdon, Oxfordshire OX14 4RN

First issued in paperback 2016

*Routledge is an imprint of the Taylor & Francis Group,
an informa business*

Library of Congress Cataloging-in-Publication Data
Scott, John C., 1963–
   Social process of lobbying : cooperation or collusion? / by John C. Scott.
      pages cm. — (Routledge research in American politics and governance ; 19)
   1. Lobbying—United States.   2. Interpersonal relations—Political aspects—United States.   3. Legislation—United States.   I. Title.
   JK1118.S444 2014
   324′.40973—dc23
   2014030804

Typeset in Sabon
by Apex CoVantage, LLC

ISBN 13: 978-1-138-28734-1 (pbk)
ISBN 13: 978-0-415-72717-4 (hbk)

To Meredith, for your love and support during a long journey together. And to my parents for getting me started.

Contents

Acknowledgments

Many people helped me along what turned out to be a very long path. First, my former professional colleagues in Washington, D.C., many of whom consented to being interviewed, gave me a deep appreciation for the work that policy advocates do, and I have always appreciated their intelligence and good humor.

Several academic colleagues were helpful in the specific development of this book, which was originally my doctoral thesis. Victor Nee first suggested the topic when I was in graduate school, and Sid Tarrow, Doug Heckathorn and Richard Swedberg provided patient and critical advice at several points. Dan Gitterman at UNC provided a useful prod when I was struggling to get things done.

Several reviewers and commentators at conferences shaped the direction of this project in many ways.

The National Science Foundation provided a critical source of funding via the doctoral dissertation improvement grant (Award No. 0602388), and the Center for the Study of the Economy and Society at Cornell University also provided needed support.

Char Lloyd, Om Patel, and Jeff Summerlin-Long were very helpful in helping in collecting and processing the data.

My wife Meredith and my children Rosslyn and Lincoln were a constant source of love and support. Without them, it would not have been possible to do this.

Introduction

Americans continue to suffer from a notoriously short attention span. They get mad as hell with reasonable frequency but quickly return to their families and sitcoms. Meanwhile, the corporate lobbies stay right where they are, outlasting all the populist hysteria.

—Eric Alterman

A STORY

Mary, who is a lobbyist working for a trade association that represents large corporate employers, gets a call from Steve, who is on the staff of a congressional committee with jurisdiction over Mary's issues.[1] "Mary," says Steve, "as you know, we are working on some 204(h) legislation. We have a draft bill, and I wanted to know if your members could give some feedback."

The proposed legislation dealt with a sensitive topic for employers who sponsor retirement plans. As both Steve and Mary knew, many employers were in the process of reducing pension benefits, and how those reductions would be communicated to employees was a critical point of contention among different players on retirement policy: employers, unions, activists, and financial service providers. Steve's boss, Senator Blue, a liberal Democratic Senator who chairs the committee, wanted to introduce a bill that would increase the amount of information given to workers, including numerical examples of how the benefit cutbacks would affect individual workers.

Mary, who had known Steve for some time, said, "Sure, we'd be happy to get you some feedback," and the two discussed the specific issues covered by the bill, the kind of feedback requested, and the timing of the response. They did not discuss whether Mary could identify Steve as the source of the information, whether Mary could make the specific issues more public beyond her advisory group of member companies (who would be asked to keep the information confidential), or whether Steve would use the feedback from Mary's organization as an endorsement when the bill is introduced. Rather, Mary assumed, and Steve expected, that Steve's request would be handled in a manner in which confidentiality would be paramount. Both Mary and Steve knew that that bill would not be supported by Mary's trade association even if Steve implemented the suggestions of Mary's trade association members.

The picture gets a little more complicated a few weeks later. Senator Blue introduced the bill in the Senate, and Mary is on Capitol Hill with a few other lobbyists to lobby against it. Working together, the lobbyists have made appointments with many Senate staffers. On this day, they have an appointment with Sarah, who is an aide to Senator Redd. With Mary are Pat, who represents a small trade association similar to Mary's, and Rob, who represents a large, broad-based trade association. Pat, Rob, and Mary previously decided to form a steering committee for a coalition against Steve's bill. The group is loosely organized, with Mary's trade association and a few other trade associations taking the lead in setting up appointments with congressional staffers.

All three associations represented by Pat, Rob, and Mary have some overlap in terms of their members, and as a result there is some competition for getting credit and hence more membership dues. They do have some common goals, including this employee notification bill. But, Pat and Rob have more pressing issues that they would rather raise. To head off the potential problem of Pat or Rob going off on their own agenda during their meeting, Mary pulls Pat and Rob aside while they wait in the reception area. "I thought it might be easier if we divided up the presentation." Mary suggests that the other lobbyists each take some of the talking points about the bill.

Sarah, Senate Redd's staffer, comes into the reception area to meet the lobbyists and usher them into a conference room. Mary, as the person who set up the appointment, takes the lead: "Sarah, as you know, we are here today to discuss Senator Smith's bill that has just been introduced. We have more detailed information in our leave-behinds," Mary said, patting the folder in front of her, "but I thought I would take a minute to outline the bill's main provisions and why the employer community is concerned about it." Mary outlines the key provisions as well as some of the main arguments for and against the measure. Pat covers the practical problems of implementing the bill as his membership includes many financial services firms, and Rob discusses the effects on employer-employee relations as well as alternatives. The three lobbyists follow their scripts, which had been decided beforehand in the hallway outside, with Sarah asking clarifying questions. They also give accurate accounts of the reasons for supporting the bill but then give their take on these arguments. When they finish their brief presentations, Mary closes by asking for the support of Senator Redd if Senator Smith's bill makes it to the Senate floor for a vote.

At this point, Sarah asks more pointed questions. "What's wrong with giving employees more information, particularly when their pensions are being reduced?" "How much more trouble is it to produce a piece of paper that details the effects of a change on individual workers?" The lobbyists expected most of the questions, conceding that some ideas in the bill were good but that industry should be given more flexibility. Other questions from Sarah are more strategic: "Is there a Senator out in front in opposing the bill?" "Can you find an employer in my boss's state who can speak to the bill?" The meeting closes with the lobbyists promising to follow up on Sarah's questions and highlighting the written materials in their 'leave-behinds,' including both material from individual trade associations and from the coalition fighting the Smith bill.

Suppose that a sociologist and a political scientist were watching these interactions in order to understand how lobbying works. The political scientist might ask, "Why would Steve call Mary if Mary's trade association would lobby against the bill after its introduction? Why would Mary agree to review a bill that her membership would vehemently oppose? What does each person get out of this exchange?" The sociologist might wonder, "How are these lobbyists connected to each other? Why do groups work together instead of pushing separate agendas? What were those expectations and assigned roles that the lobbyists followed in their meeting with Sarah? Why did they follow them instead of pursuing their own issues?"

MOTIVATIONS AND ARGUMENTS

The story provides both a glimpse into the practice of lobbying and an illustration of the issues that are driving this book. This volume is a study about lobbying, networks, and social norms. Lobbying engenders debate about its effects on the political process and on policy development. Political scientists study how interest groups work together and influence policy making. Sociologists and other social scientists remain concerned about how social norms emerge, the content of norms, how widely they are distributed, and how they contribute to order in a community.

These questions interact with each other, and that interaction is what this book is about. This book combines these two areas by looking at the social norms of lobbying and showing how such norms work in the political process. From the perspective of networked lobbyists who ascribe to their own social norms, I want to address these motivating questions:

- How does cooperation come about in lobbying work? How do relationships matter?
- How does cooperative lobbying affect policy making?

How Does Cooperation Emerge and Matter?

People have numerous opportunities for lobbying. Formal political processes often invite the opinions of individuals and groups such as when a congressional committee holds a hearing. However, formal procedures make up a relatively small part of the day-to-day work of official government business. The process of government is slow with many periods in which action on legislation comes to a standstill. These gaps in the formal institutions of government provide ample opportunity for informal interaction (Amenta, Carruthers, and Zylan, 1992).

As shown in the example that began this chapter, informal lobbying is an exchange of information and services. From their exchange, Steve and Mary each receive a benefit, one immediate and concrete, the other more abstract and distant. Steve expects that Mary's members will suggest technical improvements, and he will know which provisions will provoke the most opposition. Because of Steve's request to have Mary's association review his bill, Mary now knows which way a key legislator wants to go on a policy issue of interest to Mary's membership. This knowledge is something of value that Mary can use in a number of different ways, and Steve undoubtedly is aware of that fact. However, the exchange can be generalized in that Mary may feel more comfortable in later calling Steve on an unrelated issue. Mary never expects, much less suggests, an explicit *quid pro quo*, but Steve will remember the favor.

Such interactions take place in a complex environment and can be risky and costly. The policy making environment is dynamic with many groups continuously moving in and out of policy domains. The salience of issues frequently rises and falls. Information about the identity of interested actors, let alone their preferences, is sometimes incomplete or incorrect. In addition, the risks and costs of interaction are influenced by political institutions that shape the interests and interactions of actors. For example, public comment and criticism occurs late in the process, usually after the politician has taken a position on an issue. To reduce the risk of a negative reaction, politicians informally seek advance information and services from lobbyists, particularly those lobbyists or groups that the politician can expect to 'recur' in the policy space again and again (Milbrath, 1963; Chubb, 1983; Hansen, 1991). The politician may be seen as biased in favor of special interests, however, if these consultations become public. Steve's boss, Senator Blue, may not want to be publicly associated with the business lobby on the employee notice issue, so Steve hopes that Mary will treat their communications as confidential. And whereas it might appear that lobbyists would have every incentive to cooperate with the politician, there are risks to the lobbyist as well. In the story that opened this chapter, Mary may not want it broadly known that her organization provided review and feedback on a bill that would hurt her membership if the bill were to pass.

Moreover, politicians have decision-making power at several points in the political process, such as when they introduce or vote on a bill. As the focal point of lobbying before decisions are made, a politician may be able to play one lobbyist off against another, or perhaps more likely, a politician will discount the arguments of lobbyists who are acting alone or on their own behalf. Thus, lobbyists—like Mary, Pat, and Rob—will have an incentive to work together to offset their weakness at these decision points, but they may have to compromise their individual positions or preferences in order to adopt a consensus position (Holyoke, 2009). Joint activity also has logistical costs that flow from planning and coordination. Finally, coalition members may defect from the group position, behave opportunistically, or free-ride off the efforts of others. For example, Mary, Pat, and Rob may take the lead in setting up meetings with congressional staffers to discuss Steve's bill, but other members of the coalition may not make similar efforts to make appointments on Capitol Hill or may use these opportunities to pursue their own agenda.

Given the costs and risks for all parties, why do politicians risk the wrath of the public by cooperating with lobbyists? Why do competing lobbyists cooperate with each other?

Lobbying could be conceived as a bargaining situation in which actors exchange political resources in an arm's length transaction (e.g., Becker, 1983; Holyoke, 2009). Some economists have viewed the lobbying process as a market exchange in which lobbyists representing firms and industries receive policy outcomes in exchange for payments to policy makers (Stigler, 1971; Peltzman, 1976).[2] A number of political scientists use an exchange perspective on lobbying. Wright (1996), Hansen (1991), and Ainsworth and Sened (1993) generally argue that lobbyists exchange information for access to or influence of legislators who look for information that will reduce the legislator's uncertainty about the political environment. Wright in particular highlights the importance of strategic uses of information.

In contrast, some political scientists have recognized the importance of relationships in policy making. One attempt to explain lobbyist activities included the 'Iron Triangle' or subgovernment model, which claimed that small sets of political actors working in impermeable, long-term relationships set policy by consensus (Freeman, 1965; Cater, 1964). The subgovernment model might be still applicable in some cases, but scholars also recognize that policies result from an environment in which political relationships are more permeable, numerous, and transient than the subgovernment concept allows (Lowi, 1969; Heclo, 1978; Heinz, Laumann, Nelson, and Salisbury, 1993; Hula, 1999). The 'issue network' views interest groups as independent actors who move in and out of loose issue-based networks and without the presence of core players around which stable networks would attach (Heclo, 1978; Heinz et al., 1993). However, research has shown that lobbying groups that have a long tenure are often successful with bureaucratic lobbying because such a group will likely be of use to the agency in the future (Costain, 1978).[3] Informal social relationships in lobbying exist and can serve useful ends (Chubb, 1983; Milbrath, 1963).

This relational perspective points to a growing body of work by a number of scholars of politics who are incorporating network analysis in order to examine the role of recurring interactions and relationships in the political process. In these circles, there is a growing recognition that trust matters in these interactions (Berardo and Scholz, 2010; Heaney and McClurg, 2009).

I combine these exchange and network perspectives with the importance of trust and social norms as part of the study of policy making. When scholars model human interactions in the social sciences, they often assume that actors maximize self-interest such that any interaction is conducted in arm's length transactions. This assumption achieves parsimonious models, and such models are often tractable for quantitative analysis. So models of lobbyist-legislator interactions are quite formal in nature yet not quite realistic. However, instead of a model that assumes an arm's-length relationship between lobbyist and legislator, I argue that many such relationships are infused with social content that incorporates memory and history with an expectation of future interactions.[4] I see policy areas as interconnected relationships that give rise to expectations of behavior.

Cooperative exchanges among lobbyists and politicians make sense because they are underwritten by trust and trust-based norms that flow from close-knit relationships. Such close relations take the form of recurring interactions both among lobbyists and between lobbyists and policy makers. Close-knit relations and associated social norms provide actors with concrete benefits such as more credible and fine-grained information, and they reduce the costs to exchange by, for example, lowering an actor's exposure to opportunism.

This book is different from other interest group work in a couple of other ways. I focus mostly on lobbyist-to-lobbyist interactions rather than just lobbyist-to-client or lobbyist-to-politician. In addition, many popular books focus on the well-known or very powerful lobbyists, but these lobbyists account for only a fraction of the total interest group community. The perspective of this book is on the entire community of both long-term and episodic players.

The first argument is really a foundational statement: *Lobbying organizations that consistently work in a public policy are likely to have close-knit relationships among each other.* Perhaps another way to say this is that a policy domain consists of a core set of actors who know each other and who interact with each other based on their knowledge. If we can take a set of policy issues that are conceptually related to each other (retirement, pensions, Social Security, etc.), we should see (a) a stable set of policy actors with (b) a stable set of relations. This is not to say that some actors come and go; they do. However, in the ebb and flow of activity, a core of actors is more or less consistently present, recognizes each other, and establishes durable relations amongst themselves. Why? Some lobbyists do focus on different policy issues at different points in time. For-hire lobbyists are particularly prone to episodic participation either because of client turnover or because of changes in issues as a client's issues may change over time. But if the interests of actors are relatively stable over time, then the issues that they focus on will be relatively stable. Moreover, a focus on a smaller and similar set of issues is less costly; one can avoid repeatedly climbing the learning curve.

The second argument is that *close-knit ties increase the likelihood of joint activity.* Close-knit relationships develop over, and are characterized by, shared interests over time, and these shared interests over issues should then translate into joint activity and coalitions. But whereas lobbyists tend to work together on policy issues of shared interest, the question is whether shared interest alone generates this joint activity or do close-knit relationships play a role here as well?[5]

Organizations working in alliance with other groups face considerable moral hazard concerns because of the unpredictability of the behavior of partners and the costs from potential opportunistic behavior. Faced with uncertainty about a partner, actors adopt a more social orientation and resort to existing networks to discover information that lowers search costs and alleviates the risk of opportunistic behavior (Gulati, 1998; Wellman, 1988).

For a lobbyist to cooperate with other lobbyists, the net benefits from coalition work must be greater than the net benefits from lobbying alone. If the costs of coalition work are very high, then a coalition strategy will be unattractive. If an organization is more deeply embedded in a policy domain, joint activity seems more likely as sharing information and finding reliable coalition partners would seem easier, i.e., less costly, than if the lobbyist is not part of an embedded network.

In addition, the story that began this chapter suggests a positive outcome from interactions. Policies that are subject to deliberation and discussion will, on average, be better policies. Deliberation and discussion encourage more compromise and consensus as well as policy coherence (May, Sapotichne, and Workman, 2006). If politicians can get better and faster feedback on proposals through the relationships that underpin informal lobbying, then the final policy product—legislation and regulation—is likely to be better in the aggregate. In the story that opened this chapter, Steve's bill will be improved by input from people in Mary's trade association, who will look for technical flaws and suggest revisions. The suggestions are not offered to improve the bill's chances of passage, but if the bill were enacted, Mary's members would want the law to be workable in a 'technical' sense. In addition, there is less likelihood that the law will need corrections from subsequent legislation or regulation, which makes Steve and his boss look better.

Thus, a third argument is that *lobbying organizations influence other organizations and increase their reputation for influence when linked to a group network consisting of close-knit ties.* Embeddedness should have an effect on organizational outcomes; in the business context it might be survival or profitability (Uzzi, 1997). Superior network positions created through embedded ties create focal points of influence. Those lobbying organizations that are more central in the network have greater access to better information, and as noted previously, these positions are reinforced by participation in coalitions of lobbyists. In turn, such central lobbying organizations are able to transmit that superior information to policy makers. This makes the lobbyists more valuable and more influential with other lobbyists and with policy makers.

Fourth, lobbyists whose relations are characterized by close-knit ties are more likely to develop and maintain trust-based social norms that maximize group welfare. The problem faced by lobbyists is a collective action problem but not in the sense usually meant by social scientists. Many scholars think about this in mobilization terms: Can an association get members to contribute to a lobbying effort? But I consider the collective action problem to be one of coordination and sharing. Why help another lobbyist? Why share information? Why divulge strategy? Why write coalition letters when others will not help?

A key point of this book is that social norms act as an informal institution in the political process. Social norms are socially shared rules that are usually unwritten and are created, communicated, and enforced by members of the community outside of formal institutional processes.[6] To be sure, lobbyists work in a legislative and regulatory framework that is comprised of a host of formal institutions: legislative procedure, regulatory notice and comment, lobbyist registration and disclosure rules. The social norms that lobbyists follow and uphold complement the formal institutions of policy making

Trust forms the basis for repeated play among actors, and it does this through enhancing reliability and credibility and by invoking emotions that are the basis for sanctions. Norms of confidentiality, cooperation, and reciprocity that are based on trust, for example, stem from the thickness of the relational tie: As trust increases (or decreases), actors in turn modify their ties to make them 'thicker' (or thinner) by broadening (or restricting) the flow of information and stimuli over the ties. Trust, then, underwrites the social norms that generate cooperative behavior. Social norms must be shared by other people and partly sustained by their approval and disapproval (Homans, 1961; Blau, 1964; Elster, 1989).[7] What norms should we expect to see develop where lobbyists are generally inter-dependent? We would expect to see group norms that support those embedded relationships.[8] These group-specific social norms incorporate information about the prior interaction(s), about the other's expectations. Specific social norms of embedded lobbyists will be directed towards enhancing the welfare of group members as a whole rather than any one actor.

How can lobbyists be sure that other lobbyists will engage in cooperative behavior and maintain trust-based norms in the future? People know each other when they engage in repeated interaction with them. As interactions intensify, the opportunities for cooperation and generalized reciprocity increase. If people can recognize non-cooperators, they can simply refuse to interact with them. In many policy domains, a group of actors emerge who recognize each other and can decide to work with each other most of the time. So the collective action problem is not so much about what to do when your partner does not reciprocate; it's about choosing the right partner.

But lobbyists cannot always choose their partners. What keeps someone from shrugging off sanctions like ostracism and breaking commitments to reciprocate? When there is no third party enforcer, emotion may provide an answer to the commitment problem (Ridley, 1996). Emotions make credible commitments for us; shame, guilt, and anger lead to trust because one would feel shame or guilt if they let others down. Emotions that are based on past dealings and future expectations bring forward long-term costs that do not arise in short-term rational calculations.

Interconnected and durable relationships among policy actors lead to a second motivating issue:

How Does Cooperative Lobbying Affect Policy Making?

Why do some policies endure while others change? At the micro level of policy making, some researchers have looked at the role of 'policy entrepreneurs' who shop proposals and wait for windows of opportunity to arise (Kingdon, 1995). The policy diffusion literature focuses on learning effects and the process of attributing similarity to external events. At a more macro level, policy scholars have noted that areas of public policy are marked by long periods of gradual and incremental change that are occasionally punctuated by bursts of rapid and large-scale change (Jones and Baumgartner, 2005; Baumgartner, Berry, Hojnacki, Kimball, and Leech, 2009). The sources of what is known as 'punctuated equilibrium' are not well known and are likely varied.

Networked relations and associated social norms may play a role in these accounts of policy stability and change. For example, a process of influence may cause a group of policy actors to adopt a common agenda of issues. However, one source of change occurs when durable relationships come under outside pressure that invalidates those trust-based social norms. When scandal or crisis erupts, politicians forego established 'folkways' and react quickly; when the pressure lessens, old patterns re-emerge. If trust and trust-based norms matter within, and indeed demarcate the boundaries of, the insider community, they can collide with outside pressures.

But there may be other, less desirable effects. In 1897, *The Atlantic Monthly* related the following exchange:

> When Henry M. Whitney was examined in 1890, at the West End investigation, by the House committee of the Massachusetts legislature, he was asked the following question: "Do you state, then, that your corporation, as an applicant for legislation here at the State House, finds such a condition of things that a regular body of men, known commonly as the lobby, stands between the legislature and applicants for legislation, and that, in order to avoid having opposition in the legislature, it is necessary to retain them?" To which he replied: "That was my view of

the case entirely." Mr. Whitney testified further that he believed that the employment of those men was necessary in order to give his corporation that fair standing before the legislature which it ought to have and that if he could have presented his arguments to either the Senate or House he should not have felt obliged to employ the lobby.

(Bridgman, 1897: 156)

This quotation illustrates a central issue of whether the very function of lobbying inhibits participation in the political process. This concern was more implicit than explicit in our 'Mary and Steve' story. Mary and Steve are insiders in a community of lobbyists and politicians characterized by durable and long-lasting ties. This community is set off from others by the social norms by which they abide, and the strength of the community—its solidarity—reflects the level of commitment to the norms particular to the group of insiders.[9]

In contrast, the outsiders are those actors who are not a part of the community and who do not have the relationships that underpin interactions within that community. 'Outsider' can mean the broad public, the media, or other lobbyists. For example, the term 'outsider' could include social activists who are concerned about the same issues as the insider lobbyists but lack the relationships that exist among insider-lobbyists and politicians.

If close-knit relationships are likely to influence the actions of insiders in the political process, what are the implications for political outsiders who are trying to change policy? For example, Bachrach and Baratz (1962) raised the issue of the 'second face' of power, which is the ability to set the agenda and specifically to keep items off a policy agenda. Informal lobbying with its emphasis on trust-based interactions, and the inability of outsiders to reach this inner circle of interaction, would suggest that the public is effectively blocked from getting issues of broad importance on the political agenda except in rare cases. In the 'Mary and Steve' story, such outsiders are not mentioned, but the confidentiality of their exchange reflects the shadow of the outsider.

In addition, Olson (1982) argued that collusion among special interest groups leads to less efficiency in the economy, more divisive politics, and greater complexity in government. The concern here is that even if relationships and norms increase the efficiency of the policy process and improve legislation, groups of like-minded lobbyists and politicians will actively work together to promote their own shared, narrow interest at the expense of the public interest. Thus, close-knit relations among lobbyists and politicians may lead to real collusion that benefits only a small segment of the population.

THE REST OF THE BOOK

First, let me provide a brief note on data and methods. Much of the book uses data that I collected on retirement policy covering a 7 year period, and this data consist of information from various sources: lobbyist disclosure reports, interviews, organizational websites, news outlets, and congressional information. In some parts of the volume, I have augmented the core data with data from other areas of policy as well as from historical accounts or studies of lobbying. The analysis of the data relies on social network analysis but is supplemented by traditional statistical analysis and qualitative methods. To make the book as approachable as possible, I have used a technical appendix at the end of the book that focuses on the data.

In terms of the chapters, the book is laid out as follows: Chapter 1 addresses these questions: What is lobbying? Where did it come from? How has it developed in the U.S.? The chapter opens with a stroll along K Street. This chapter provides context for the rest of the book by placing lobbying within a historical, cultural, and social context. Lobbying as an activity predates the Constitution, and the etymology developed not long after. Lobbying evolved from an individual, part-time enterprise to a profession whose practitioners are often employed in corporations, consulting firms, and law firms. The manifestations from the stroll along K Street are reflected in the scholarly threads that have studied lobbying, from the hopeful promise of pluralism to the pessimism of elite theory. Lobbying in these studies and anecdotes is about ambivalence: democratic access and backroom haggling; public disdain and demand for access; cooperation amidst competition; fragmentation and uncertainty while interest groups in diverse policy domains work towards consensus.

Chapter 2 of this volume discusses the foundational assumption that lobbyists work in a close-knit community. That is, before I can show the existence and workings of social norms and practices, I need to show the existence of community in the form of durable and long-lasting relations organized around a set of policy issues. How do communities or social relationships emerge? The developments in the external world of politics and formal political institutions have created arenas that bring parties into policy debates and that become incubators for developing trust and common ground for legislative proposals. If there is community, we should find a set of actors who have participated in the policy domain for a long period of time as the most central or prominent in the policy domain network. These network positions can exist at different levels of relationships such as common issues, common organizational membership like a trade association, contractual relations as when one an organization hires another to represent it, and/or when two organizations engage in joint activity such as a coalition. Despite a lot of fluidity and dynamism in policy domains, individual lobbyists know each other pretty well. "[A]s a set of actors grappled with core issues over a period of years, the policy community developed what has been described elsewhere as a 'polity of discussion' or 'culture of cooperation.'"[10]

Why do lobbyists work together? Do strong relationships matter for coalitions and group activity? In Chapter 3 of this volume, I make two arguments. First, inter-organizational activity between long-term organizations in a policy domain will be more stable over time as compared to short-term organizations. Interest groups tied to other organizations by embedded ties are more likely to work together in common interest. Prior coalition work also increases the likelihood of coalition participation. Organizations leverage that prior coalition experience into further joint activity. Second, lobbyists follow particular patterns of joint activity that likely enhance efficiency and effectiveness. For example, lobbyists often make visits to congressional offices in groups, and each member of a group plays a particular role.

Chapters 4 and 5 of this volume focus on influence. Chapter 4 is concerned with the emergence of the lobbyist agenda: By what process do interest groups select the issues on which they lobby the Congress? Do relationships matter for interest group agendas? Specifically, do the choices of one lobbying organization affect the choices of another organization? Any one policy area often has dozens or even hundreds of proposed bills and equally as many interest groups and stakeholders. As a lobbyist is boundedly rational, he or she may have difficulty deciding on, or even knowing about, which piece of legislation she should lobby. In a crowded and competitive environment, lobbyists may look to other lobbyists in their policy area when selecting issues for monitoring and lobbying as a way to lower their search costs. Agenda setting is in part a social process in which interest group organizations influence each other in a complex and dynamic environment.

The lobbyist's reputation for influence is the subject of Chapter 5. How do certain lobbyists come to be known as influential? Is a reputation for influence a cumulative process, or do hot issues make hot lobbyists? The central idea of this chapter is that lobbying organizations increase their influence when embedded within a network. For long-term players in a policy domain, the churning of short-term players creates a need for trusted relations with other groups that can be expected to stay for the long term. Long-term players thus connect to other long-term players. In addition, those organizations that hold the most ties become more central and are better able to engage in brokerage and representation within the policy domain. The accumulation of ties and entrenchment of position enhances the reputed influence of these favored organizations.

How do these interactions and relationships, described in the prior chapters, work? Why do lobbyists cooperate in the absence of a central, organizing authority? Prior chapters imply that long-term relationships lead to trust and thence to cooperative norms. Trust and norms are the themes of Chapters 6 and 7. Chapter 6 engages the lobbyists themselves as they describe how trust emerges and the importance of trust in everyday lobbying. In Chapter 7, lobbyists whose relations are characterized by close-knit ties are more likely to maintain social norms that provide concrete, everyday benefits. Such norms include general calls for cooperation, and they also include more particular expectations such as "provide both sides to an argument," "be a straight shooter," "don't speak for others without permission," and others. When actors are self-organized, trust and cooperative norms are mechanisms that make policy interactions possible over a long period of time and across a diverse and dynamic policy area. These everyday norms facilitate exchange and interaction by reducing risk and enabling joint problem solving. Moreover, lobbyists will use norms that minimize not only the amount of 'deadweight losses' from failures to cooperate but also the transaction costs related to maintaining relations and cooperation.[11]

The concluding Chapter 8 summarizes the argument and the evidence as laid out in the prior chapters, critiques the central idea that informal practices and norms improves policy making, and suggests new avenues for research and teaching about the importance of informal institutions in a broader study of political institutions. The preceding chapters walk the reader through the common, everyday social interactions of lobbyists. Underlying these interactions is a series of norms that guide behavior, and the argument is that these norms improve not just the workaday business of policy advocacy but also the making of policy. Both advocates and decision makers, as boundedly rational actors, use such norms and practices to find information efficiently, to weight information according to credibility and trustworthiness, and to smooth group action. Such norms operating across a network of lobbyists and policy actors help solve collective action problems in policy environments that are dense and information-rich. Moreover, advocates use their position in close-knit communities of lobbyists and politicians for strategic and entrepreneurial action.

The concluding chapter also asks whether the fact that embedded lobbyists work within informal norms is good for policy making and democracy. In some senses, the answer is yes, as noted previously, because of the efficiencies in finding and processing information. In other ways, the answer is no. Such norms work in close-knit policy communities whose members have relationships that have a history and a belief in future repeated interaction (low discount rates). The practices and interactions within the community became shibboleths, which are difficult for someone outside of the community to understand or learn. For the citizen or activist who is not part of such a community, such practices reduce the effectiveness of their message or block it all together. Whereas outsiders have the freedom of speech and advocacy, that freedom is disabled by their outsider status.

I conclude with a call for more theory and research. Social networks and social processes are more than just interesting pictures and abstract concepts, but they are tools that can help us understand the ordinary work of politics that affects policy outcomes.

NOTES

1. The account is taken from personal observation, but the names of the people, organizations, and issues have been changed in order to preserve confidentiality.

2. One model is a lottery in which the probability of success for the lobbyist is a function of the lobbyist's expenditures relative to total expenditures, and another is an auction model in which the highest expenditure wins the policy 'prize' given policy makers' preferences (Fang, 2002; Besley and Coate, 2001; Tullock, 1975, 1980).

3. In contrast, a number of organized interests are known best for their outsider reputations as either dissidents or non-specialists. "These groups appear to contribute little of direct value to specific policy decisions because the costs of making their proposed policy changes are very high" (Browne, 1989).

4. Ainsworth (1997) does mention the importance of social context and mutual dependence in these relationships.

5. I want to distinguish between coalitions and embedded relationships as the two might be but are not necessarily identical. Mary may have long-term and durable relations with certain other lobbyists in the policy domain, but even if they share common interests, they might not form a coalition.

6. See, e.g., Helmke and Levitsky (2004).

7. Sociology has not always been adept at developing coherent theories of social norms. Functionalist schools of thought (Durkheim [1893] 1984; Parsons, 1951; Merton, 1968) held that social norms serve to promote the survival of the group. Whereas the functionalist approach has many issues associated with its analysis—tautology and the difficulty of translating evolutionary biology to social systems among them—the idea persists that social norms develop and exist because they provide a benefit of some kind. Another approach has been Marxist and other interest group theories that hold that the most powerful groups in society exploit norms in order to further their own interests. Thus, the idea of false consciousness in Marxist thought would hold that social norms encourage proletarians to engage in behavior that does not question or challenge the pro-capitalist social order. The difficulties here are in proof: For example, how does a neutral social norm like reciprocity reflect the dominant capitalist order?

8. Although I expect that social norms develop in smaller groups rather than larger groups, I do not think group size is the important criterion. As Olson (1965) notes, keeping the group small is one path to overcoming the collective action problem so we expect that community-oriented norms are more likely to develop in smaller communities than in larger communities, which is so because we have a limit on the number of relationships that we can maintain. Therefore, embedded relations, and associated social norms, are more likely to be found in smaller networks of embedded relations. The focus here, however, is on a network of embedded relations and not a particular group size.

9. This issue is related to, but still distinct from, the issue of the role of business unity in influencing policy, which is often explored in research involving interlocking directorates (see Mizruchi, 1992).

10. Oliver and Paul-Shaheen (1997: 740, citations omitted). On the same page the authors continue:

    > These cases serve as a reminder ... there is much connective tissue in contrast to the 'hollow core' and fragmentation ... Even as the an issue generates wider visibility and participation, the information and interests in health policy remain concentrated in a small network of leaders and stakeholders. Their shared assumptions, knowledge, and history of interaction help determine whether a 'decision subculture' will emerge, allowing an issue to move from the systemic agenda of government toward formal action.

11. See Ellickson (1991: 174).

1   Lobbying

> But I had a client come up to me. I was talking about, I gave a little
> speech about lobbying reform and how it's not getting done. It's pretty
> unbelievable it's not getting done given what happened earlier this year.
> And the guy came up to me afterwards and said—now I represent his
> association—he said to me, "I guess since you represent our associa-
> tion, I assume you are one of the good lobbyists, not one of the scum
> lobbyists." I said, "Yeah, that's me." "And why aren't people like you
> lobbying to get lobbying reformed?" And I almost had to say, "Because
> no one's paying me to do lobbying reform."
>
> —Interview with the author

A WALK ALONG K STREET

A short walk along K Street in Washington, D.C., is as good a place as any
to begin a chapter on lobbying. Standing on the corner of K and 10th Streets,
the first thing one would notice would be the construction activity as new,
gleaming high-rise office buildings with lots of chrome and glass were being
constructed in several places. Many of these buildings will be occupied by
lobbying organizations—more on that in a bit. But after acclimating one's
senses to this bustle, one would also notice a small retail and office building
at 1001 K Street. The building, which was built in 1926, was the former
headquarters of Local 132 of the United Brotherhood of Carpenters &
Joiners. Many unions established their headquarters or significant offices in
Washington, D.C., for the purpose of attaining legal recognition of the right
to organize, bargain, and strike over working conditions. In 1935, during
Franklin Roosevelt's New Deal administration, Congress passed the Wagner
Act, which was the first major federal law permitting union organizing on
a large scale. In the decades that followed, Congress, the courts, and the
executive agencies generally expanded the rights of organized labor. But
unionized industries began their decline in the 1970s, and a Reagan administration hostile to the unions limited the rights and gains of organized labor.
Looking at the Painters' Union building now, it is perhaps symbolic that the

Figure 1.1   Carpenters Union Building at 1001 K Street, Washington, D.C.

current resident is a tourist trinket shop that sells many items made overseas. The only evidence of its prior history is the cornerstone (see Figure 1.1).

Heading west, the Asbury United Methodist Church is on the southwest corner of 11th and K Streets. Founded in 1836 by seventy-five free and slave African Americans, Asbury is one of the oldest African American churches in Washington, D.C., and has counted many of the city's community and civil rights activists among its members. Churches like Asbury formed the backbone of many movements, from women's rights to civil rights to peace movements, and these church-based activists used their proximity to the hallways of Congress and executive branch agencies to press their claims (see Figure 1.2).

Figure 1.2 Asbury United Methodist Church at 11th and K Streets.

Another stop a few blocks away is at 1625 K Street, the site of the notorious 'little green house.' The little green house was the Washington, D.C., apartment and entertainment center of Attorney General Harry Daugherty in the Harding administration (1921–1923). Daugherty, a political crony from Harding's home state of Ohio, often entertained the president, members of the cabinet, and other Ohio political and business associates—known colloquially as the 'Ohio Gang'—with all-night poker and drinking at 1625 K Street. At these sessions, Daugherty was reputed to have colluded with political loyalists in the sale of pardons and immunities from prosecution. The intimacy of this setting also enabled Albert Fall, Secretary of the Interior, to convince President Harding to transfer large tracts containing oil reserves in the Western states from the Department of the Navy to his own Interior Department. Oil company interests then were able to lease these reserves at little cost in exchange for bribes to Fall, Daugherty, and others in the Harding administration in what became known as the Teapot Dome scandal. The little green house, which today has been replaced by an office building, probably gave birth to the impression of K Street as a den of corruption. More recent scandals refer to the street: The 'K Street Project,' for example, was an arrangement in the 2000s in which Republican congressional leaders pressured lobbying firms to hire Republicans, who in turn contributed to the campaign funds of GOP members of Congress.

All along our walk, we have passed existing modern office buildings or new ones in the process of construction, which we first noticed when we started from the former Carpenters Union building. Washington, D.C., has seen a veritable building boom in office space in the downtown area. As a real estate analysis notes, office space in downtown Washington, D.C., is more expensive than in Lower Manhattan and Los Angeles on a per-square-foot basis (Brooks, 2012). Of course, not all the office space is reserved for lobbying organizations as there are a large number of private firms that supply services to the federal government. However, as I will discuss later in the chapter, the boom in construction activity is matched by a boom in the number of lobbyists at the federal level (see Figure 1.3).

Like any other urban street, K Street is a dense space of buildings, people, and infrastructure, but our walk showed a diversity and history related to lobbying. Our popular conception is of lobbyists as well-dressed professionals in new office buildings. But lobbyists are also, among other things, activists in pursuit of civil rights, advocates for labor rights, and self-interested actors solely seeking personal gain.

This chapter discusses the origins of, and context for, lobbying in the U.S. A central argument of this chapter is that lobbying is deeply rooted within American democracy as it complements the formal processes and

Figure 1.3   View of K Street construction.

institutions of government. In addition, the particular qualities of physical proximity and social relationships mark the process of lobbying.

The discussion begins with the question, what is lobbying? The next section focuses on the how lobbying came to be in its present form with a particular emphasis on institutional factors that facilitated lobbying as well as institutional responses to lobbying. Lobbying and indeed other forms of political participation are rooted in ancient political rights. Whereas lobbying is open to all and is constitutionally protected, the distinction between insider and outsider has mattered for influence purposes since the earliest days of the U.S. government. The chapter concludes with short overview of popular perspectives on lobbying that reinforce this insider-outsider distinction.

WHAT IS LOBBYING?

Lobbying is a process that encompasses a number of activities, some of which occur simultaneously. Principal elements include researching and analyzing legislation or regulations, monitoring and reporting on developments, attending congressional or regulatory hearings, working with coalitions interested in the same issues, and then educating not only public officials but also the media and general public as to the implications of various changes (Nownes, 2006).

If we were to ask Mary, our fictional lobbyist, what she did in a typical day, she might say, 'meetings.' After getting to her office around 9:30 a.m. and checking emails and voicemails, Mary will probably spend some time getting ready for the next meeting on her schedule. Mary spends a significant portion of her day setting up meetings with other lobbyists, her association's members, and with policy makers. She is then out at meetings or running conference calls from her office or the association's conference room. In between these meetings, she might stop to chat with other lobbyists or make some calls from the taxi on the way back to the office. At the end of the day, she writes up some talking points for an upcoming visit to Capitol Hill or a summary of a new bill that's been introduced that will be posted on the association's website. Or she might head back up to the Hill for a committee hearing, at which she will take notes, get a word in with a busy staffer, and trade gossip with other lobbyists.

Both in the descriptions and in my thumbnail sketch of Mary's day, there is the flow of communication. It is the job of lobbyists like Mary not just to stay on top of the flow but to direct it as well.

So, we have a broad range of activities, but how do we define lobbying? A number of definitions exist: Under section 308 of the Lobbying Disclosure Act of 1995, any person "who shall engage himself for pay or for any consideration for the purpose of attempting to influence the passage or defeat of any legislation by the Congress" must register under the lobbying disclosure rules.[1] According to the *Oxford English Dictionary* (2013), a lobby in a collective sense refers to those "who frequent the lobbies of the House [of Commons]" or, in the U.S., "the persons who frequent the lobby of the house of legislature for the purpose of influencing its members in their official action."[2]

As noted in the Introduction, no standard definition of lobbying exists in the academic literature (see the discussion in Baumgartner and Leech, 1998), but the various definitions are similar enough that we can choose one. Berry (2001: 9001) defines lobbying as "the effort of organized interests to inform policy makers and persuade them to choose particular policy choices." The term 'interest' is not simply any value but rather "arises from the conjunction between some private value held by a political actor—public officials, or groups thereof as well as private sector operatives—and some authoritative action or proposed action by government" (Salisbury, 1994: 12). Organized interests then engage in communication efforts: "The most general way to state the nature of the lobbyist's job is to note that he must in some way communicate with governmental decision-makers" (Milbrath, 1963: 115).

Influence is the other part to Berry's definition, and is part of many other definitions, but influence itself evades clear definition. In modifying Baumgartner and Leech's definition ("an effort to influence the policy process"), Nownes suggests that lobbying "is an effort designed to affect what the government does" (2006: 5). So, communication and intent to influence, but not actual influence, are both necessary and sufficient for a definition of lobbying.

Focusing on definitions casts a wide net on activities but still misses some key elements, and highlighting these elements necessarily narrows the focus of this book. One key element in lobbying is physical presence.[3] The term itself refers to one who is waiting outside the doors of the decision makers. Pasley (2002) picks up on this idea by defining lobbying as "when some group or individual, typically a private economic interest seeking benefits or protection, makes its case *personally* to government decision-makers, often but not necessarily through some sort of specially deputed emissary" (59, emphasis original). Nownes notes that lobbying is a complex phenomenon that takes a variety of forms. In illustrating these forms with four examples, he uses a common phrase—'meets personally'—in each example (Nownes, 2006: 2–3). The importance of personal presence is highlighted by the testimony of the lobbyist Sam Ward, speaking in 1875:

> To introduce a bill properly, to have it referred to the proper committee, to see that some member in that committee understands its merits, to attend to it, to watch it, to have counsel to go and advocate it before the committee, to see that members of the committee do not oversleep on

the mornings of important meetings, to watch for the coming in of the bill to Congress day after day, week after week, to have your men on hand a dozen times, and to have them as often disappointed; to have one of those storms which spring up in the Adriatic of Congress, until your men are worried, and worn, and tired, and until they say to themselves that they will not go up to the Capitol today—and then to have the bird suddenly flushed, and all your preparations come to naught—these, these are some of the experiences of the lobby.

(Byrd, 1991: 496–7)

The physical presence of lobbyists often translates into personal relationships that channel communication and influence. Rothman (1966) relates the following example from the Gilded Age: "Herbert Terrill, agent for the sugar refiners, explained that he discussed [tariff] rates only with friends; with others 'I presumed my views would not have had much weight'" (205). Corporations disliked high turnover in Congress, relates a senator in the 1890s, because their lobbyists could not form stable connections to members (Rothman, 1966).

Another element involves representation. Lobbying can be on behalf of one's self, such as when a person seeks a public pension or a position in government.[4] In the early Congresses, it was not unusual, as in the English manner, to receive petitions and then pass acts that implemented that particular petition.[5] But by the early to mid-nineteenth century, lobbyists more frequently were agents on behalf of other persons or interests as the floodwaters of requests to Congress continually rose.

Representation highlights the relationship of lobbying to the broader processes of politics and policy. Thompson highlights the importance of representativeness in her definition of lobbying, which is the process by which the interests of discrete clienteles are represented within the policy-making system: "Lobbyists, then, can be defined as representatives who act concurrently with, and supplement the capabilities of, those who are selected at the polls" (1985: 140). This idea will be discussed more further on, but lobbying is so durable in this democracy because lobbyists are representatives of cross-cutting affiliations, groups, and even of specialized knowledge. By the 1890s, for example,

Agents typically answered the inquiries of interested Senators, explaining the various proposals on the calendar and clarifying the pertinent but dull details of intricate bills. With regularity, they supplied information that only representatives of particular organizations could gather. Helping members of Congress to understand the increasingly technical issues that came before the chamber, lobbyists became the experts in an era of specialization.

(Rothman, 1966: 203)

Another aspect of lobbying is that it can be a profession or an occupation, which was noted in the latter part of the nineteenth century by one observer:

> The term includes both those who, since they hang about the chamber, and make a regular profession of working upon members, are called 'lobbyists,' and those persons who on any particular occasion may come up to advocate, by argument or solicitation, any particular measure in which they happen to be interested.
>
> (Bryce, 1910: 691)

Lobbying is not an occupation or profession in the classic sense—there is no regulating body like a bar association—because the process draws on political rights and values that are open to all. Lobbying as an occupation or profession arises out of the combined effects of time, personal relationships, and proximity, and these effects lead to expectations of behavior among those in the occupation.

Having discussed what is lobbying, the next section provides a background on the development of lobbying over time, which will shed additional light on what is the process of lobbying as well as amplify some themes of this study.

HOW DID LOBBYING COME ABOUT?

Where did lobbyists come from, and when did lobbying manifest itself? How has lobbying changed over time, and what accounts for these changes? The section presents a brief social history of lobbying, which gives an important context for the rest of the study. In order to keep the discussion necessarily brief, we can trace the development of lobbying over five critical periods: The first Congresses of the late eighteenth century to the Civil War; the immediate post–Civil War period known as the Gilded Age (circa 1865–1890); the rise of Progressive reform (circa 1890–1917); the two World Wars and the New Deal (1917–1960); and the Civil Rights era and beyond (1960–present). These are approximate identifications of historical periods that do not have clean divisions, but they provide a framework for viewing the development of lobbying.

Moreover, much of the following discussion concerns lobbying on behalf of business, which is appropriate in that much of this study involves lobbyists working on behalf of corporate employers and financial service firms. Moreover, the data and research on business lobbying are quite good relative to other interest groups, and intuition suggests that business groups are more stable. First, however, I want to discuss some of the institutional precursors to lobbying. That is, what are (or were) the rules of the game that influenced the rise of lobbying?

Institutional Precursors and Influences

The institutional context for lobbying comes from two complementary sources, the rights of petition and association; the former deals with making claims and the latter concerns social groups in civil society. These two rights are derived from the English common law rights of petition and assembly (Rice, 1962). The right of petition was exercised in the American colonies, most notably when colonists petitioned to King George III prior to the outbreak of the Revolutionary War (Rice, 1962).[6] The Constitution of the U.S. incorporated the right of petition in the First Amendment.[7]

The Supreme Court in 1961 determined that lobbying was an important means of petitioning government and is protected to an extent by the Constitution.[8] That decision involved the right of a group of railroads to wage a lobbying and public relations campaign against the trucking industry. The truckers sued the railroad association by charging a conspiracy to foster the adoption of laws and law enforcement practices destructive of the trucking business as well as to create an atmosphere of distaste for the truckers among the general public. However, the court stated:

> The right of the people to inform their representatives in government of their desires with respect to the passage or enforcement of laws cannot properly be made to depend upon their intent in doing so. It is neither unusual nor illegal for people to seek action on laws in the hope that they may bring about an advantage to themselves and a disadvantage to their competitors.
>
> (365 U.S. at 139)

The related rights of association and assembly reflect an institutional concern with groups in civil society, a concern that can be traced back to ancient Greece. Plato argued that a state needs to be unified in its beliefs, whereas Aristotle countered that such homogeneity was detrimental. Hume discussed the dangers of factions for government. These beliefs are reflected in the arguments of the framers of the Constitution, who were distressed by the narrow-minded politics that were dominating state governments in the new Republic. As discussed in Madison's Federalist Number 10, the new federal system contained a number of checks on the power of 'factions.' The lodging of supreme authority in a national government meant that interests would be aggregated and balanced out by each other. The use of representatives, who would be somewhat removed in a national capital, would help move debate above local self-interests. The different branches of government, each with its own set of powers and jurisdictions, would make capture of the government difficult for any one set of interests.

Legislative procedure in the early Congress also influenced early lobbying. An early institutional distinction was made between public bills, which affected society broadly, and private bills, which affected only one person or organization. Unlike the British practice of utilizing different procedures for each type of bill,[9] since the first Congress all bills regardless of scope have been handled in the same way.[10] Moreover, the Congress had jurisdiction over a wider range of issues and claims than the British Parliament.[11] The American legislative system brought in a large range of interests in a way that avoided other institutions like the courts.

The institutional structure in the U.S. system afforded many opportunities for lobbying as a number of points of access were opened up through the system of checks and balances. This is particularly the case as Congress organized the legislative process through semi-autonomous committees of jurisdiction. Moreover, the lodging of authority in a national government that was removed from the local level and the insulated nature of legislative interaction meant that lobbying activities could be shielded from the public view. Almost immediately with the opening of the first Congress in 1789, lobbyists were present.

The Early Republic: A Tale of Two Lobbyists

There are many indicators of lobbying in the early Congress, and these early anecdotes illustrate the themes of group boundaries and social expectations. For example, William Hull was hired by Virginia veterans of the Revolutionary War in order to lobby for additional compensation for their war service. In 1792, Hull wrote to other veterans' groups, recommending that they have their 'agent' or 'agents' cooperate with him during the next session to pass a compensation bill in an early attempt at coalition building (Byrd, 1991). During a debate in 1802 about moving the national capital back to Philadelphia, Representative Lyons of Kentucky argued against moving because if "we move to Philadelphia we shall have a commanding lobby" (Annals of the Congress, 10th Congress, 1st Session. 1852: 1536). Following Lyons' comment, according to Pasley (2002), other Representatives began to refer to lobbies more frequently and in a negative sense. It was not long before the actual term became common: H. L. Mencken (1931) finds that in 1829 there were 'lobby-agents' at Albany, and in 1832 'lobbying' had been extended to Washington.[12] The *Oxford English Dictionary*, which provides examples of the earliest written usages of defined words, finds usages of the verb, 'to lobby,' dated 1837, 1848, 1850, 1855, 1860, 1862, and 1864.

The idea of boundaries between insider and outsider was an important facet of early lobbying. Pasley (2002) argues that one's reputation in late eighteenth-century America was based on one's level of gentility and social refinement. For those who were recognized as genteel and refined, it was relatively easy to enter into the work areas and even lodgings of members of Congress, and their arguments were given more weight. As Pasley (2002) notes, "the access to the powerful that modern lobbyists must fight tooth and nail for, an eighteenth-century gentleman could walk into noiselessly and almost automatically" (90). Speaking of the Rev. Manesseh Cutler, a lobbyist who successfully persuaded Congress to ignore its own land laws and award ownership of several million acres of Ohio territory to his group of investors, Pasley remarks:

> Once acknowledged as a fellow gentleman, a lobbyist could not only see a congressman but join fully in their social life at the seat of government, providing all sorts of nonofficial settings where contacts could be built and sensitive business matters could be discussed discreetly and effectively. Gaining access was not always quite as simple as walking the walk and talking the talk. It helped to have evidence of gentility beyond one's personal qualities, such as a noble title, a well-known family name, or recommendations from other members of the club. Cutler took the latter route, bringing so many letters of introduction with him to New York [then the national capitol] that it takes an entire page of the published edition of his journal just to list it all. Admitted to the club, Cutler used his membership privileges to the hilt. Almost all his lobbying took place at private homes or social gatherings.
>
> (Pasley, 2002: 90–1)

In contrast, consider the case of the Quaker abolitionists, who lobbied Congress at roughly the same time as Rev. Cutler. Petitions for anti-slavery legislation were sent by Quaker Meetings in Philadelphia and New York, and nearly a dozen Philadelphia Quaker leaders spent several weeks in New York, then the temporary home of the Congress, engaging in a variety of activities designed to press their case (Pasley, 2002). The Quakers published pamphlets based on their petitions, they visited the meeting place of Congress, and they went to the lodgings of members of Congress. It was a highly organized, multidimensional effort that ultimately resulted in failure, and such a visible campaign was not imitated by other groups for some time.[13] These two lobbying experiences underscore the fact that being a 'member of the club' is important but membership requires adherence to certain expectations. Lobbying was then and is still largely an in-person activity that relies on personal connections and relationships.[14]

Post Civil War: The Professional Lobbyists

Lobbying would undergo significant change in the years following the end of the Civil War in 1865. It also was in the post–Civil War era that lobbying became part of the national consciousness. By 1884, a magazine profiling life in general in the nation's capital would write:

> There are professional lobbyists who go there in numbers every winter; their doings and their methods, with their restaurant dinners, their hotel life, their intrigues, and their secret conferences, can be traced by the

aid of a detective reporter; and the spectacle is by turns exciting and repulsive, instructive and indecent.

("The New Washington," 1884: 654)

Lobbyists became so numerous and overt in this time that the coining of the term 'lobbyist' is credited—inaccurately—to a story about President Grant.[15] But there was a reason for their heightened profile: "In the 1870s, when party did not superintend the course of Senate affairs, lobbying for the first time became a vital element in government" (Rothman, 1966: 192). Both economic organizations and the government fundamentally changed during the latter half of the nineteenth and early part of the twentieth centuries. Certainly the growth of large firms, particularly the railroads and vertically integrated firms, contributed to the use of lobbying (Porter, 1973).[16]

Three factors in particular made lobbyists practically necessary to the functioning of government (Thompson, 1985). First, unlike today, most members of Congress in the post–Civil War era did not think of their service as a career; even career politicians focused on local and state politics and viewed federal service as a necessary but temporary obligation to bring federal benefits to local communities. The result was a high rate of turnover in both the House of Representatives and the Senate. Second, members of Congress had no staff resources. At most, a member might have a secretary. Working at their desks in their respective chambers,[17] a Representative or a Senator did their own correspondence and legislative drafting.

Third, the Civil War erased the obstacles to a large, centralized, and powerful national government. The period saw a vast increase in the workload of the federal government and, hence, that of members of the legislature.

> As welfare agency, employment bureau, ombudsman with the bureaucracy for constituents, policy initiator, program implementer, political barometer and partisan testing ground, oversight watchdog, and self-styled (if only sometime) guardian of the public virtue, the House and Senate had assumed or been asked to handle a range of responsibilities that collectively and, in most cases, individually exceeded dramatically their normal pre-Civil War, peacetime workload.
>
> (Thompson, 1985: 50)

These factors exposed a flaw within the constitutional system of representation. That is, as the framers, dealing with a new system and justifying a framework that covered a large and diverse polity, envisioned a system of representation that would encourage reflection of the commonweal rather than parochial will. However, Washington, D.C., in the 1870s was not only the seat of government but it was "the center from which radiate the varied influences which affect every citizen of the Republic, from the millionaire to the man dependent on his daily earnings" (McCabe, 1873: 5). As opposed to constituencies, Thompson argues that clienteles arose, detached from geographically distinct districts, and that within each congressional district there were multiple and overlapping clienteles: "Seeing representation not as an unvarying and constant relationship between legislators and constituents but rather as a multidimensional interaction among numerous discrete and overlapping clienteles and their agents—who may or may not be members of Congress—illuminates both the context and complexity of the process" (Thompson, 1985: 137).

Thus lobbying in the post–Civil War era was filling a growing institutional void. As noted previously, the Constitution and its framers envisioned a particular version of representation that Congress was to fulfill, but this vision was predicated on certain assumptions that no longer held up in the post–Civil War era, if it ever did. The federal government expanded its jurisdictional purview, and the country expanded in terms of population, large economic organizations, and geographic size (Thompson, 1985). Due to the discrepancy between vision and reality, lobbyists grew in numbers in order to serve as representatives between an increasingly disaffected citizenry and an overwhelmed Congress.

In the face of such difficulties, lobbying was a representational device that provided flexibility and precision in handling distinct stakeholders in a way that was compatible with policy making processes (Thompson, 1985). "It must, therefore, operate in ways that foster cooperation from those within the process: by providing services that are beneficial to them, for instance, or by facilitating the execution of their representational responsibilities to heterogeneous constituencies" (Thompson, 1985: 139). Lobbyists could specialize and could afford to work in a bipartisan fashion. Because their work did not begin or end with the electoral cycle, they could be a source of continuity amidst turnover among lawmakers.

But this growth in government also strained lobbying. Lobbying remained a particularistic practice in Gilded Age Washington, D.C. For example, Rothman (1966) suggests that lobbyists were largely operating alone and in an uncoordinated fashion. Although information and statistics were certainly needed and requested from lobbyists, personal qualities of civility and gentility were what counted most. Consider the case of Sam Ward, the self-proclaimed 'King of the Lobby.' Ward was acknowledged to be the most important lobbyist in 1870s Washington, D.C., because of his superb social connections and lavish entertainment (Byrd, 1991).[18] Ward, an adventurer and diplomat, was the brother of the abolitionist and poet Julia Ward Howe and a close friend of the authors Oscar Wilde and William Makepeace Thackeray. Very well connected, he was able to enter government offices at will, even using the stationary of the Treasury Department or the Ways and Means Committee—whatever was at hand—to write notes or instructions. His knowledge of the Treasury's buying and selling of gold was invaluable at a time when currency issues were among the top issues for government action (Thomas, 1965). His influence was his person rather than that of a large organization or PAC.

The particularistic quality of lobbying in the post–Civil War era was also evident in the hiring practices of principals. Some firms hired dozens or even hundreds (in the case of one railroad) of lobbyists (Rothman, 1966). This practiced occurred because most lobbyists, in the absence of large-scale organizations like trade associations, had personal relationships with only a few legislators, and their influence was consequently limited. On the lobbyists' side, lobbyists accepted numerous and conflicting retainers because employers, having to hire many lobbyists, paid small fees (Rothman, 1966). So as lobbying became more important and more widespread, its effectiveness was hampered by custom and habit.

Given the rise of lobbying, it is perhaps not a coincidence that the Gilded Age also saw the first efforts to regulate lobbying activity. In 1876 the House of Representatives passed a resolution calling for lobbyist registration, but that resolution was effective only for that session of Congress and was not passed by the Senate. Some regulation of lobbying began to be seen, albeit in a limited and narrow scope, at the end of the nineteenth century. In 1879, members of the press galleries in Congress created rules of admission to the galleries that would bar all lobbyists posing as journalists, and they created a standing committee of correspondents to enforce the rules (Byrd, 1991). Earlier in the Gilded Age, members of Congress inundated the railroad lobbyists with requests for free passes, but the Interstate Commerce Act of 1887 prohibited passes for national lines (Rothman, 1966).[19]

The Progressive Era: The Lobbyist Is the Group, the Group Is the Lobbyist

Lobbying in the early twentieth century shifted from the individual-based approach to the group approach with the growth of regulation and expertise. Consider Figure 1.4, which provides the number of business associations both nationally and just those located in Washington, D.C., from 1865 to 1961. The figure focuses on business associations because of data availability and the likelihood that business associations would have more staying power over time than other types of associations.[20] One sees both an increasing number of business associations over time, but the acceleration in growth occurs at the end of the nineteenth century. Washington, D.C.-based business associations also show an upwards growth but not nearly as steep as for all business associations. If the Gilded Age was notable for reliance on individual lobbyists, the Progressive Era (circa 1890–1920) saw a change in the structure of lobbying. Historians have asserted that the Progressive Era constituted an 'organizational synthesis' for associations and a pivotal time when new interest groups flourished in the U.S. (Galambos, 1970).

One reason for this organizational shift was that political institutions changed. Wilson (1983) gives a succinct institutional comparison between the Gilded Age and the Progressive Era: From 1861 to 1900, the federal government expanded both in terms of staff (over 200,000 new employees) and

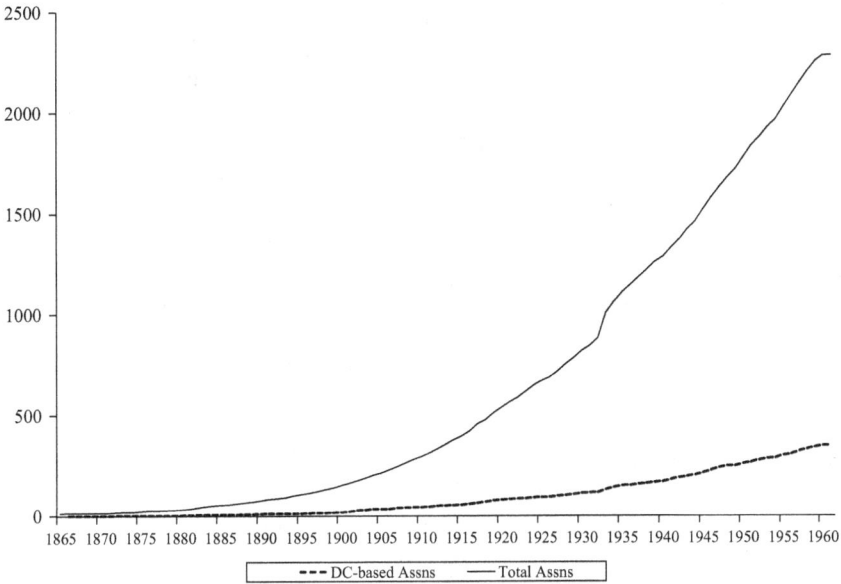

Figure 1.4 Total business associations and Washington, D.C.–based associations, 1865–1961.

agencies. The primary function of these early agencies—which included the Commerce Department, the Department of Agriculture, the Department of Labor, and the Civil War pensions bureau—was to provide services such as providing research, collecting statistics, dispensing federal lands, and distributing benefits. Crucially, as Thompson (1985) argues, Congress in the 1870s began to consider legislation that treated businesses, notably railroads, as a class in addition to so-called distributive legislation that awarded benefits, e.g., a subsidy, to particular firms. In 1887, the Interstate Commerce Commission was created, and its primary function was to regulate. Over the next thirty years, a number of new laws and bureaucratic organizations were created to regulate business as a class of activity.[21]

A likely consequence of these changes was that business became inclined towards joint activity. Previously, businessmen were inclined against overtly joint and coordinated responses to regulatory efforts because they believed that explicitly working together would lend legitimacy to Congressional regulation of economic activity that was inherently 'odious' and 'unnatural.' Moreover, business viewed as repugnant the thought of working in concert with one's competitors (Galambos, 1966).

And while common threats did eventually produce intra-industry discussion, business leaders also began a search for ways to make their business environments more predictable and certain in an expanding but highly variable nineteenth-century economy. In his wonderful study of business associations, the economic historian Louis Galambos (1966) discusses the transformation of informal business relations in the late nineteenth century to structured associations in the early twentieth century. Galambos characterizes the post–Civil War period association movement as the 'dinner club,' which involved informal meetings among business leaders within a particular industry. These 'dinner club' associations were marked by an ad hoc approach to issues and little leadership or administrative capacity. Around 1900, new entities that he calls 'service associations' began to emerge with the beginnings of a bureaucracy and a comprehensive political program (Galambos, 1966).

The trend toward associations was complemented institutionally. Progressive reformers pushed through many measures designed to curb the influence of the business lobby, including the direct election of senators in 1913, the increased use of public committee hearings in Congress, and high profile exposés of lobbyists' misdeeds. This new system called for more complex and vigorous forms of organized activity on the part of the manufacturer:

> If he was to make his voice heard, he had to have organizations which could operate effectively in this different context. He needed technically competent representatives to argue his case before commissions. He needed organizations that would be ever watchful for some new administrative ruling that might affect his interests. He needed trade groups that provided more services on a more continuous basis than did the older dinner-club associations.
>
> (Galambos, 1966: 50)

The total effect of the progressive movement was to break up the 'dinner club' model of the business lobby that had dominated American politics since the end of the Civil War (Galambos, 1966). "In its place there developed a new style of pressure-group politics which was more open, more responsive to public pressure. Personal influence became somewhat less important; well-organized group action and the appearance if not the reality of broad support became essential to political success" (Galambos, 1966: 49). The new governmental environment that the reform movement helped to produce, with the exception of the anti-trust laws, actually contributed to the spread of the associative concepts of stability, cooperation, and control (Galambos, 1966).

Finally, however, I cannot ignore the importance of social movements themselves as they agitated, without government assistance or encouragement, for various causes. The Progressive Era saw the rise of very large groups, such as the NAACP, that advocated for a variety of causes, including women's suffrage, immigration reform of various types, conservation, prohibition, and municipal reform (Skocpol, 1992; Clemens, 1997; Sanders,

1999). Thus, a constellation of factors all led to a shift away from the Gilded Age's particularistic lobbying and towards organizations and associations.

In contrast to earlier scandals involving individual lobbyists, scandals now involved associations. For example, press reports of lobbying excesses on the part of the National Association of Manufacturers launched an investigation by the House of Representatives, which produced a report recommending lobbyist registration. In 1919, Congress prohibited any lobbying effort with funds appropriated by Congress (Byrd, 1991). Congress again in 1928 attempted to enact lobbyist registration, but this time only the Senate passed a bill and the House declined.[22]

The rise of interest groups and associations is also reflected at this time in a shift in scholarship on politics and government. The previous nineteenth century scholarship focused on formal institutions and processes such as the Constitution and the structure of congressional committees, but the early twentieth century saw change in emphasis toward interest groups (Tichenor and Harris, 2002–2003). Bentley (1905) and Herring (1929) are both exemplars of this new scholarship.[23] Noting that there have always been various interest groups and minor parties in American political life, Herring comments: "More important still, they have become highly organized and are to-day conducted by shrewd and capable leaders. Now because of improved means of communication, these groups, no longer hindered by geographic limitations, are organizing on a national and even a world-wide scale" (Herring, 1929: 3). With a new focus on collecting data, Herring (1929: 19) conservatively estimates the number of organized groups in Washington, D.C., equal to at least 500 with over 1,000 individual representatives. But these numbers would seem puny compared to the growth in associations over the next two decades.

World War I, the New Deal, and World War II

To paraphrase Charles Tilly, it might appear that states make war, and wars make lobbyists. In less than thirty years, the U.S. fought two world wars and dealt with an economic calamity, and during these crises the government encouraged association-formation. In the case of World War I, the national government coordinated industrial production through the use of trade associations that linked industries and individual businesses that were scattered geographically (Tichenor and Harris, 2002–2003). Once the crisis of war was over, the associations continued their existence through the 1920s as group members realized the benefits of maintaining associational relations (Herring, 1929).

After 1932, the government of Franklin Roosevelt began a governmental expansion without precedent as it dealt with the Great Depression and, several years later, the specter of World War II. These efforts meant an overall expansion of regulatory scope and mission, budget, and employment as the government sought first to assert greater control over a moribund economy and then mobilize the economy for war.

For example, federal government outlays grew in constant dollars forty-four times over from 1901 through 1946. Government spending increased significantly in 1917 and never returned to its pre-war levels when World War I ended. The New Deal and World War II saw such growth of government spending that by 1945, the last year of the war, outlays are ten times the pre-war levels (Office of Management and Budget, 2006). An alternative view is examining the growth of the regulatory state in terms of the number of pages in the Code of Federal Regulations (CFR) from 1936 through 1946. Although data for the number of pages in the CFR are not available before 1936, by 1945, the last year of Franklin Roosevelt's presidency, the CFR was seven times its 1936 volume (Crews, 2002).

The upheavals of the 1930s and 1940s accelerated the institutionalizing of associations and lobbying, both in terms of encouraging the establishment of organized interests and in the regulation of such interests. Figures 1.5 and 1.6 illustrate the growth of business associations both nationally and in Washington, D.C. Figure 1.5 provides the year-by-year foundings of business associations for both non-Washington, D.C.–based associations and for those headquartered in Washington, D.C. The chart illustrates the slow growth of new associations through the Gilded Age until the Progressive Era (roughly around 1890), when there is a noticeable jump upwards. In 1917, when America entered World War I, there is a sharp increase, and a

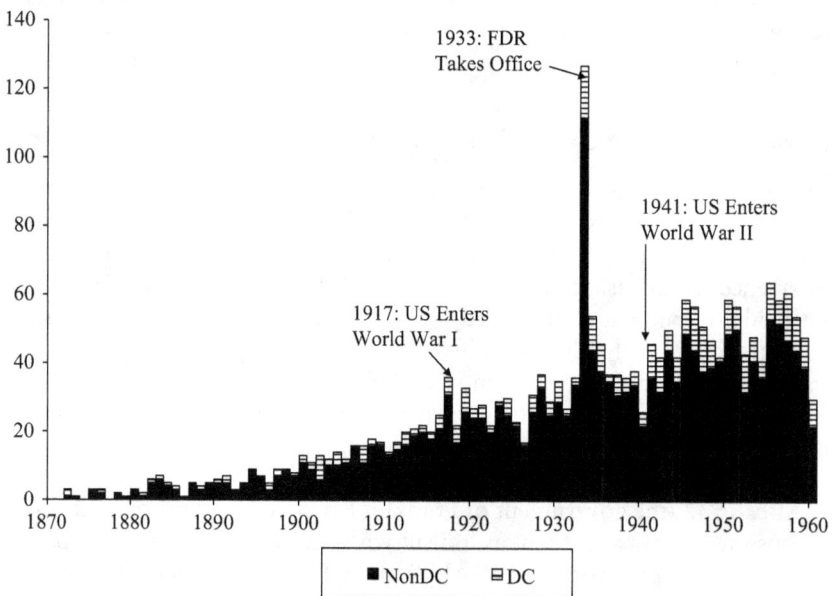

Figure 1.5   New business associations per year, in Washington, D.C., and outside Washington, D.C., 1870–1960.

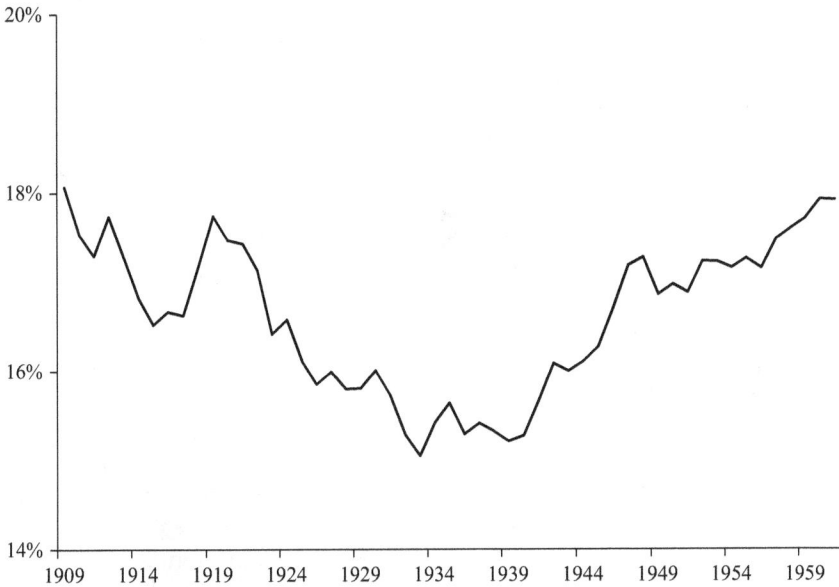

Figure 1.6 Ratio of Washington, D.C.–headquartered business associations to non–Washington, D.C., business associations.

higher level of new associations continues through the 1920s. But the New Deal drove the rate of new associations sharply higher as the Roosevelt administration encouraged association formation as a depression-fighting strategy, and this heightened growth continues through the 1930s and into the war years of the early 1940s. Interestingly, growth also continues into the 1950s, but the shift is moving towards locating association headquarters in Washington, D.C., by this time.[24]

Figure 1.6 confirms this Washington, D.C., bias as it provides the ratio of D.C.-based business groups to non–Washington, D.C., business groups from 1909 to 1960. Resembling a U-shape, clearly many new associations were being founded outside of Washington, D.C., during the 1920s, but the expanded role of government in the 1930s and beyond causes the trend to move in the direction of Washington, D.C.–based associations.

As the nation moved out of the immediate post–World War II period, the number of associations continued to grow. As in World War I, the process could be contagious: "Once the habit of associated activity was established under the stimulus of governmental encouragement, most such groups tended to persist and to invite imitation" (Truman, 1951: 55).

Although lobbyists were under criticism from scandals and exposés through the 1920s (including the aforementioned Teapot Dome scandal), little effort at regulation was made even when the inevitable scandal would erupt. For example, in the spring of 1935, lobbyists for an association of public utilities attempted to block passage of a bill that would have broken up utility holding companies into smaller entities. After Congress was deluged with hundreds of telegrams demanding that senators block the bill, congressional investigators determined that lobbyists impersonated constituents by dictating hundreds of unique telegrams. As a result, the Public Utilities Holding Company Act was amended to provide for registration of all company agents (Byrd, 1991). Senator Hugo Black, the future Supreme Court Justice and the lead investigator in the utilities lobbying scandal, introduced legislation for broad lobbyist registration, but the conflicting versions that passed each chamber could not be reconciled.

With World War II already underway in Asia, the first comprehensive reform was the Foreign Agents Registration Act of 1938 (FARA), which required that all agents of a foreign principal register their names, addresses, and the identities of foreign clients with the Secretary of State (Public Citizen, 2005). The enactment of FARA was followed in 1946 by the Federal Regulation of Lobbying Act of 1946 (FRLA), which again required registration and financial disclosure for lobbyists representing domestic interests, but the law did not regulate conduct. Anyone whose principal purpose was to influence the passage or defeat of legislation in Congress had to register with the Clerk of the House and the Secretary of the Senate and file quarterly financial reports. However, the law did not cover contacts with congressional staff, the executive branch, or a great deal of grassroots lobbying. Moreover, the phrase 'principal purpose,' which triggered the registration requirement, was not clearly defined.

While the Supreme Court ruled that the FRLA did not violate the rights of speech, press, and petition,[25] the Court also narrowed the applicability of the law by holding that it could only cover efforts to influence passage or defeat of a specific bill and for only those paid efforts in which lobbyists directly contacted members of Congress, not their staff. Persons who spent less than half their time contacting members of Congress on legislation were exempted from FRLA.[26]

As in the Progressive Era, scholarship continued to think in terms of groups, and the pluralist approach to politics reached its zenith with works by Truman (1951) and Dahl (1961). But the seeds of the pluralists' demise were being planted in this period as Mills (1956) and Hunter (1953) mounted a critique that focused on the overarching power of elites. As this critique went into full swing in the 1960s, a new cohort of interest groups came to the political scene.

The Civil Rights Era and Beyond

Despite the relative stability of the post-war era, lobbying continued to grow. Whereas the prior periods highlighted the importance of representation, groups, and expert information, the recent explosion of lobbying introduced the importance of uncertainty and complexity. Recall Thompson's (1985) functionalist assertion that lobbying grew in numbers and importance during the Gilded Age because the role of government changed but the resources of government, particularly the Congress, had not kept pace from pre–Civil War levels. What, then, accounts for the growth in lobbying organizations from the 1950s forward? Congressional staffs had expanded as had the bureaucracy during the Progressive Era as well as during the New Deal so the argument that lobbyists were filling vital functions seems weakened.[27]

Heclo (1978) notes two developments: One is that government expenditures continued to increase in an almost exponential form, which increase was nearly matched by the amount of regulations produced by the executive branch agencies. For example, Figure 1.7 provides a long-term view of regulatory page growth. One sees a drop in regulatory activity following the end of World War II, but then a steady rise occurs through the 1950s and early 1960s. Government spending accelerates with the Great Society and the Vietnam War in the late 1960s and early 1970s, but regulations really take off in the 1970s. In 1981, the number of pages of regulations reaches a peak of over 73,000. During the 1980s, the volume declines from this peak until 1986 when it again increases.

The second development noted by Heclo is that the level of federal employment remained virtually flat since the 1950s to the present. Combining these developments, the government is doing more with less. Part of the solution

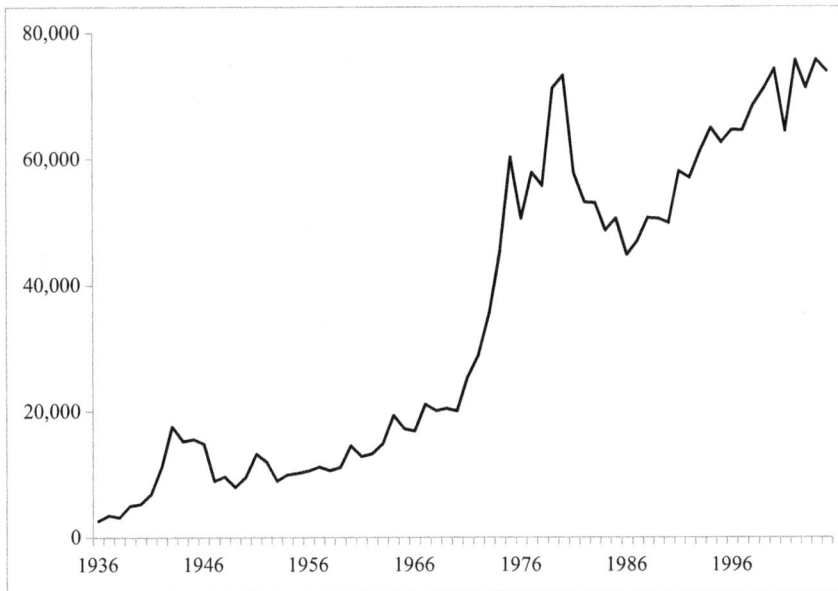

Figure 1.7   Growth of pages in the Code of Federal Regulations, 1936–2005.

has been to push responsibilities down to the states, but there also remains an opportunity for organized interests to advocate and provide information to Congress and the federal bureaucracy, as Thompson would have predicted.

At this point, it might be helpful to refer back to Figures 1.4 and 1.5, which illustrate the growth of business associations through 1960. It is striking to note that both Washington, D.C.–based and non–Washington, D.C., business associations continued to be founded after World War II and indeed the rate of growth was steadily upward through the 1950s. Clearly, the organization of business interests had taken hold generally and particularly with regard to establishing a presence in the nation's capital. Simple correlations show that a very positive relationship among outlays, pages of regulations, and associations (1 = perfect correlation):

- Outlays and total business associations (1901–1960): 0.777
- Outlays and Washington, D.C.–based business associations (1901–1960): 0.790
- Pages of regulations and total business associations (1936–1960): 0.450
- Pages of regulations and Washington, D.C.-based business associations (1936–1960): 0.451

The growth in business trade associations is closely matched by the expansion in the federal government.[28] As noted previously, business may in effect be lobbying for additional regulation, as Stigler (1971) postulates.

By the 1960s, the country experienced what Berry (1999) calls the rise of post-materialist advocacy. After the Progressive Era, lobbying was largely concerned with distributive concerns such as business regulation and labor rights. Beginning in the 1960s and continuing through to the present, new groups emerged—some out of the civil rights and anti-war movements and others inspired by them—to press for values and rights unrelated to materialist concerns such as jobs or industry. These values and rights included environmental concerns, recognition of new categories of peoples such as gays and Latinos, feminist issues, consumer protection, and others. In turn, the liberal movements of the 1960s and 1970s were matched by conservative counter-movements of the late 1970s and 1980s (Walker, 1991). In addition, the 1970s saw a tremendous expansion in the role of the federal government in terms of such post-materialist issues. Just considering environmental issues, the early 1970s saw the creation of the Environmental Protection Agency and the enactment of the Clean Water Act and the Clean Air Act, among others. The early twentieth century saw a number of conservation organizations formed as part of the broader progressive movement. But new environmental associations exploded in the late 1960s and 1970s and continued through the 1980s in response to the Reagan administration's conservative environmental policies.

As the number of lobbyists mushroomed, major lobbying reform finally became a reality. From the enactment of FRLA in 1946 until 1995, several agencies implemented ad hoc disclosure rules for lobbyists seeking government contracts, grants or loans, and federal employees were restricted from lobbying in certain circumstances. These efforts were not comprehensive but were a patchwork of mainly administrative rules. In general, the ineffectiveness of FRLA was made apparent in 1991 when it was disclosed that about 10,000 of the 13,500 individuals and organizations listed as lobbyists by the Directory of Washington Representatives were not registered under FRLA (General Accountability Office, 1991).

Passage of a comprehensive lobbying disclosure law came in the form of the Lobbying Disclosure Act of 1995 (LDA), which has been amended since then.[29] The LDA requires quarterly reporting, specific information on the issues on which the organization lobbied, financial disclosures, and personal information on the lobbyists working for an organization. The LDA has clearer definitions of lobbyist and lobbying, which includes the contacting of congressional staff and not just a member of Congress. The General Accountability Office in more than one study (e.g., 2013) finds that LDA compliance is relatively high.

In light of more recent scandals in the mid-2000s, commentators have noted a number of abuses within the system that are in need of reform. The following list (taken from Thurber, 2006) is not meant to be comprehensive but does indicate a number of issues:

- The use of earmarks has exploded in recent years. Much like private bills of old, earmarks are narrow provisions of law that are inserted secretly into legislation without public debate, notice, or attribution.
- The reliance on massive, unwieldy appropriations measures that become magnets for extraneous, special-interest provisions. Thus, the old 'public bills' versus 'private bills' distinction is merging as the institution of Congress is unable to cope with the flood of private requests.
- The use of closed rules, particularly in the House of Representatives, that restrict the right of the minority party to offer amendments has increased since the mid-1990s. Without debate or alternative bills being offered, substantive legislation is often hurried through. Other parliamentary procedures are increasingly relied on to shepherd legislation without challenge, such as the use of extended roll calls, self-executing rules, 'emergency' procedures, and reporting bills outside of normal hours.[30]

CHAPTER SUMMARY

This chapter had two goals. One goal was to give a working description and definition of lobbying mainly for readers who had little exposure to lobbying and interest groups. The point is that lobbying has different dimensions but this book emphasizes the personal, representational, and professional qualities. A second goal was to provide context for the research findings that follow in later chapters. This context was historical in nature, and I showed that the lobbying has developed into specialized areas of expertise; however, lobbying also finds itself in an environment of complexity and uncertainty. Today's lobbyist faces a number of challenges in trying to get her job done.

The next chapter will focus more narrowly on the data set of lobbyists that are studied in this book. I will detail the research sites—federal retirement and Medicare policies and North Carolina state government—in terms of institutional background, actors and their interests, and key trends. The next chapter will also provide the data analysis methods used for this study.

NOTES

1. There are some other technical requirements, such as the amount of time spent lobbying. The focus is on people who make lobbying a more or less full-time pursuit as discussed further on.
2. Thus, during an 1808 debate in Congress about moving the seat of government from Washington, D.C., back to Philadelphia, one member noted, "If we move to Philadelphia we shall have a commanding lobby" Annals of the Congress (1852: February 2, 1808, 1536).
3. By highlighting physical presence, I exclude other forms of lobbying such as grassroots activities, which are also characterized as 'indirect lobbying.'
4. "One of our fellow-travelers seemed to be a disappointed place-hunter, who had been lobbying the Houses of Legislature in vain for the whole session" (Lyell, 1855: 28).
5. For example, many Revolutionary War veterans or creditors of the army sent petitions for a pension or repayment for services rendered (Bowling et al., 1998).
6. The first American colonial treatise that codified the right of petition was the Body of Liberties by the Massachusetts Bay Colony Assembly in 1641 (Fatka and Levien, 1998).
7. "Congress shall make no law respecting an establishment of religion, or prohibiting the free exercise thereof; or abridging the freedom of speech, or of the press; or the right of the people peaceably to assemble, and to petition the government for a redress of grievances."
8. Eastern Railroad Presidents Conference v. Noerr Motor Freight, 365 U.S. 127 (1961).
9. In the United Kingdom, private bills are not assigned to a committee but are dealt with by a small judicial-like panel that only involves a few Members of Parliament and rules on private bills in a judicial manner, after permitting the introduction of evidence in support of or against the bill (Bryce, 1910).
10. "The lobbies of the legislative halls are filled with a class of men called agents, whose business it is, to work private bills through Congress, or public bills, in which, like the Morrill tariff, private interests are deeply concerned, by means of influence upon members" (Spence, 1862: 37).
11. For example, in England claims against the government must be brought before a law-court in the form of a Petition of Right (Bryce, 1910).
12. Mencken (1931: 97) argues that 'lobbying' and 'lobbyist' are particular examples of the unique brand of English spoken by Americans; in fact, in "two other familiar fields very considerable differences between English and American are

visible . . . They are politics and that department of social intercourse which has to do with drinking."

13. In fact, the editors of *The Documentary History of the First Federal Congress* write, "Congress took steps to prevent a repeat of that episode": Congress devised a gag rule in which all anti-slavery petitions were tabled automatically (Bowling, DiGiacomantonio, and Bickford, 1998: 314).

14. The importance of physical proximity for lobbying in the later antebellum era is also illustrated by newspaper correspondents who were then (but not now) permitted to sit on the House floor. For this privilege, reporters were required to pledge that they were not employed as agents to pursue any claim before Congress (Byrd, 1991). Yet an 1854 Congressional report found that such press reporters "are very generally regarded as the most efficient agents . . . we find that, in utter disregard of this pledge and its spirit, they have been employed in many of the railroad, patent, and other schemes which have engaged the attention of Congress" (Byrd, 1991: 493).

15. The story is that Mrs. Grant did not like President Grant's habitual drinking so Grant began going to the bar at the nearby Willard Hotel for a mid-afternoon whiskey. Men seeking an audience with the President soon learned that could approach him in the lobby of the hotel. Exasperated that he was running an ever-expanding gauntlet each day, Grant complained bitterly of all the 'lobbyists' who were getting in the way of his toddy (Smith, 1997).

16. For example, President Lincoln signed the Pacific Railway Act in 1862, in which the federal government spurred the construction of a transcontinental railway. Over the next fifteen years, railroads would compete for subsidies, construction loans, and lucrative land grants (Congressional Research Service, 1986).

17. Members of Congress did not have separate offices then; today, there are six large buildings dedicated solely to office space and meeting rooms in addition to leadership offices in the Capitol itself.

18. This is apparently no small claim. In later years, his biographer notes, Ward was recognized as America's authority on haute cuisine: "Largely because of the impetus he provided, the American understanding of what is proper to put into a human stomach was revolutionized: from the horrified Frenchman's 'country of fifty-two religions and one soup,' the U.S. became a land where a civilized man could dine" (Thomas, 1965: 409). This helped in lobbying as Ward heeded the axiom that "the shortest distance between a pending bill and a Congressman's 'aye' lies through his stomach" (Byrd, 1991: II:495).

19. The states were bolder in regulating lobbying. For example, Alabama amended its constitution in 1873 to make it a felony to lobby its legislature, and Georgia and California shortly followed suit. In 1890, Massachusetts enacted a disclosure rule, and in 1910 Wisconsin made solicitation of a legislator by a paid lobbyist a felony (Congressional Research Service, 1986).

20. I used the 1961 edition of the *Encyclopedia of Associations* for founding dates. Naturally, this is a flawed approach in that associations could have become defunct before 1961. However, I believe that the figures that follow will be useful even considering the shortcomings in the data collection.

21. For example, the Sherman Act of 1890, the Pure Food & Drug Act of 1906, the Meat Inspection Act of 1906, the Federal Trade Commission Act of 1914, the Clayton Act of 1914, and the individual and corporate income tax acts of 1914, to name a few.

22. The failure of lobbying reform may be due to the development of a trend of lobbying at this time: Lobbying became a common occupation for retired or defeated senators, who as a courtesy had the right to be on the floor of the Senate and mingle with old associates. It was proposed in 1897 that ex-senators

be barred from the floor of the chamber if they were representing some interest with business before the Senate. The Senate maintained its custom, however, and corporations continued to hire ex-senators (Rothman, 1966). With regard to lobbying in the Progressive Era, an observer could say that the "most dangerous men are ex-members, who know how things are to be managed" (Bryce, 1910: 694).

23. "Political evolution does not await the formal action of legislatures, nor is it bound by statutory codes and written constitutions" (Herring, 1929: 2).

24. The last year of the chart is for 1961, which shows a decrease in new business associations. However, this may be a result of data collection as the editors of the Encyclopedia of Associations often learned of new organizations a few years after their establishment.

25. United States v. Harriss, 347 U.S. 612 (1954).

26. Ibid.

27. Thompson acknowledges that the number of lobbyists has grown steadily since the 1870s and that such lobbyists in the 1980s would not be considered powerless. However, she argues that they face greater competition for and constraints upon their hegemony and their activities are different than in the Gilded Age (Thompson, 1985: 143, n.64). I discuss this point later in the chapter.

28. The current sample of business trade associations only extends to 1960, but it is my intent to extend the data through at least two more decades.

29. Public Law 104–65.

30. Speaker of the House Nancy Pelosi had proposed a number of lobbying reform initiatives, including: ban on gifts from lobbyists; a ban on all privately funded travel; ban on lobbyists attending or participating in congressional trips; disclosure of grassroots lobbying; increased disclosure in government contracting and tightening of government contracting laws; extending the ban on lobbying by former members of Congress to two years; extend the post-employment ban to senior congressional and executive branch staff; enact disclosure requirements for House members and staff negotiating for jobs in the private sector. See http://democraticleader.house.gov/pdf/houseprinciples.pdf.

2 Communities

Everybody in government is just like a bunch of ants on a log floating down the river. Each one thinks he is guiding the log, but it is really just going with the flow.

—Robert Strauss

During an interview, I asked one trade association lobbyist how well people knew each other. He laughed and said that everybody knows everybody: "It really shows how small we are . . . I send reporters down the line and, or the reporter talks to me, I can easily tell who they talked to before they talked to me even though they don't name them, then I tell them, 'You talked to so and so.'"

Do lobbyists view themselves as part of a community? What does community mean in the context of public policy? The lobbying world is a paradox in that some lobbyists belong to a group of long-term players who know each other well whereas policy areas can be characterized as dynamic and fluid with organizations and individuals flowing in and out on a regular basis. This paradox has implications for how lobbyists do their job and how they affect policy making.

Interest group representatives can—but do not always—belong to close-knit communities in which trust-based social norms operate to facilitate their policy work. But before we can talk about social norms or how their interactions affect lobbying, we need to establish the presence of community in which relationships are so close that they facilitate interpersonal trust. The goal of this chapter is to show that *lobbying organizations that consistently work on a similar set of public policy issues will likely have close-knit relationships with each other.*

The first part of this chapter provides a theoretical perspective on the notions of community and close-knit relations. The discussion then addresses the nature of the policy domain, which can contain a variety of policy organizations and relationships among those organizations. In the remaining portion of the chapter, I draw from research on retirement policy in order to show some evidence of community in the form of durable and long-lasting relations organized around a set of policy issues, and the evidence includes network and qualitative data. Despite a lot of fluidity and dynamism in policy domains, individual lobbyists know and interact with each other pretty well.

COMMUNITY AND RELATIONSHIPS

A dictionary definition of community means "a social group of any size whose members reside in a specific locality, share government, and often have a common cultural and historical heritage . . . a social, religious, occupational, or other group sharing common characteristics or interests and perceived or perceiving itself as distinct in some respect from the larger society within which it exists."[1] Applied to a group of policy actors, we look for identifiable actors who interact with each other within a bounded space, who recognize each other as members of that space, and who share common values with, and expectations of, each other.

The concept of the policy domain, area, or community has been defined and studied in various ways. As noted in the Introduction, political scientists once viewed policy communities as comprised of a small set of key actors— congressional committee chairmen, heads of agencies, and lobbyists for large trade associations—who exhibited tight relationships and who operated largely by consensus. But this so-called subgovernment or iron triangle model did not survive the explosion of government activity and growth of interest groups beginning in the 1960s onward.

Heclo (1978) provides an alternative view that viewed a policy community as a variety of actors oriented towards a common set of substantive set of issues but who exhibited varying levels of commitment to the community. The idea of a fluid network of actors provided a more stable foundation for later theoretical work. For example, Paul Sabatier's (1988) advocacy coalition framework views policy domains as fairly durable coalitions between long-term actors set in opposition to each other. But the networks exhibit some fluidity over time, and the actors regardless of specific conflicts between them have a shared understanding of the issues that comprise the policy domain. A different but similar approach was used by John Heinz and coauthors (1993) who rigorously mapped organizational networks in four policy areas, finding not a central, coordinating actor but a more decentralized grouping of organizations, whose representatives were beset by uncertainty stemming from complex issues and large numbers of interest groups.

Burstein (1991) notes at least three approaches to the idea of a policy domain. First, there is a focus on a set of issues that share substantive characteristics that have a certain logic and coherence. Second, policy domains encapsulate a set of organizations that are concerned about the set of substantive issues and that socially construct the logic and coherence of the issues. The social aspect of this approach notes that organizations take each other into account as they formulate and advocate on policy proposals. Over fifty years ago, Milbrath (1963) noted that lobbyists he interviewed were constantly aware of other lobbyists in their policy area. As one of his informants noted, "After you are up here for a while, you learn who is reliable and who is not" (Milbrath, 1963: 308). Third, a cultural approach considers how ideas and societal values shape the development of policy.

In addition, the shared knowledge group operates in an environment that is information-rich. Baumgartner and coauthors (2009) suggest a market metaphor in which information-armed policy actors—lobbyists and policy makers and others—compete with studies and interpretations, holding each other in check, which in turn contributes to the structure of the community and the policy equilibrium.

Although not directly disagreeing, I place a different spin on this explanation of policy equilibrium based on Herbert Simon's (1997) idea of bounded rationality. The problem in decision making is not information scarcity but attention scarcity. Because of our cognitive limitations and high cost of getting the right information in a complex environment, people and institutions often rely on bias and heuristics. Rather than a war of talking points and fact sheets that cancel each other out, policy actors repeatedly use the same people and organizations that are viewed as trusted or credible sources for information and interpretation. Whereas actors initially engage in a process of judging information from a source, once a source develops a reputation for credibility, actors get into the habit of going to sources again and again because that is the least cost or most efficient way of getting pertinent information. As William James (1981 [1890]) notes, habit simplifies the movements required to achieve a given result, makes them more accurate, and reduces fatigue by diminishing the conscious attention with which our acts are performed. This idea of repeated interaction that is almost unconscious forms the structure of policy communities and facilitates policy stability.

Recall the story that opened this book. Mary and Steve's personal relationship of exchange is emblematic of the larger domain of retirement policy. Just focusing for the moment on this dyadic relationship, social behavior is generally an exchange of activity, tangible or intangible, and more or less rewarding or costly, between at least two persons (Homans, 1961). The more often a particular action is rewarded, the more likely the person is to perform that rewarded action. For example, our congressional aide Steve is more likely to ask others for advice if he received useful advice in the past. On the other side, lobbyist Mary is more likely to give advice, give advice more frequently, or give more in-depth advice if her help was rewarded in the past. And the action is more likely to be repeated when the time between behavior and reward is short; long intervals between action and reward would lower the probability of repeated exchange. Moreover, rewarded action is repeated when the rewards are similar to those in the past. Thus, a process of generalization occurs in which actors tend to extend behavior to similar circumstances. In addition to the specific reward, an affective component to exchange often exists that makes the exchange relationship an expressive object that is valuable in its own right. Repeated interaction works through emotional processes to foster a sense that the exchange partners are part of something larger—an entity that the actors will take account of and nurture in future interactions (Lawler and Yoon, 1996).

As relationships of interaction and exchange increase, continue, and multiply, a social network perspective becomes relevant.[2] A network perspective is useful in getting at social reality in "dynamic, continuous, and processual terms" (Emirbayer, 1997: 281).[3] In this volume, I use both 'close-knit' and 'embedded' when describing relationships among lobbyists. Either term is meant to distinguish long-term, recurring, and durable relations that are thick with tacit knowledge and information transfer from those that can be characterized as short-term or arms' length in nature. Embeddedness means that social action and outcomes are affected both by paired or *dyadic* relations and by the overall network *structure* of relations (Granovetter, 1992).[4]

In terms of *dyadic embeddedness*, reciprocity is often unbalanced, differing in content and intensity, but actions are usually reciprocated in a generalized way (Wellman, 1988). Mary does not expect Steve to provide a favor when she gives her feedback, but she does expect him to remember that she gave feedback. In an interview with a congressional staffer, Zorack (1990) illustrates this idea: "Most staff members take a dim view of lobbyist who tries to make them believe they owe lobbyists something. Lobbyists must never even imply that staffs or Members are in any way obligated to them" (772).

Ties link network members indirectly as well as directly such that any tie between two actors must be defined within the context of the overall network.[5] Relational embeddedness typically has direct effects on individual action and leads to trust. Information from a trusted source is cheaper, richer, more detailed, and known to be accurate precisely because continuing relations often become overlaid with social content that carries strong expectations of trust and abstention from opportunism (Granovetter, 1985). Embedded exchanges make expectations more predictable and reduce monitoring costs. They also carry 'thick' information in the sense that the information exchanged incorporates tacit and proprietary know-how, and involves joint problem-solving arrangements that stress flexibility and feedback (Uzzi, 1997).

The cooperative relationship between Mary and Steve involves thick information such as technical revisions to legislative text, and it includes tacit know-how in the form of how the information is conveyed: They did not have to negotiate, for example, over whether Steve could use the name of Mary's trade association as an endorsement because Steve knew that Mary would not provide the feedback if her group was perceived as endorsing the bill.

In contrast to dyadic embeddedness, *structural embeddedness* takes a higher-level view of all these relations and typically has more subtle effects on action. The broad network of relations can provide multiple, independent paths that link pairs of structurally cohesive actors, which helps information flow among organizations in a way that facilitates politically similar activity (Moody and White, 2003).[6] Structural embeddedness, which arises from sharing one or more foci of activity with others, is less under the control of individuals and is more stable than any particular dyad (Feld, 1997).

The structural embeddedness seen in the involuntary nature of ties in lobbying stems from government institutions that create jurisdictional divisions by policy area. Issues in one policy domain (e.g., tax policy) generally are considered and debated in relative isolation from other areas of policy (e.g., defense policy).[7] So, lobbyists and policymakers are likely to specialize in a policy area or areas and have repeated contact with each other (Heclo, 1978).

Beyond relational and structural effects, embeddedness establishes markers of collectivities. Bourdieu (1985) stated that the relationships that provide social capital "are more or less really enacted and so maintained and reinforced, in exchanges" (249). For Knoke (2001), the basis for the social structure of mutual influences between networks and actors in a policy domain are those patterns of repeated interactions between actors. Exchange that is endlessly reproduced encourages and produces mutual knowledge and recognition: "Exchange transforms the things exchanged into signs of recognition and, through the mutual recognition and the recognition of group membership which it implies, reproduces the group" (Bourdieu, 1985: 250). Jordan and Taylor (2008) studied computer hackers and argued that hackers formed a social community in part based on interactions that provide support and services to each other and in part by constantly defining and redefining themselves relative to outsiders such as computer security professionals. Thus, those lobbyists and politicians—like Mary, Pat, Rob, Sarah, and Steve—who are part of the trust-based exchange network know each other, repeat their interactions, and reinforce the identity of their policy domain.

Moreover, relationships arise out of shared interests such that an increasing number of shared interests contributing to an increasing level of group-wide relationships. Thus, if Mary's coalition partners have a number of issues on their monthly agenda for discussion, their ongoing relationships are likely stronger than if they just had a couple of issues to discuss. Markovsky and Lawler (1994) identify 'reachability' as an essential idea to group embeddedness; that is, we should be able to trace a path from any group member to any other member. As new relations develop out of shared interests, multiple and independent paths between two lobbyists can be traced through the group (Moody and White, 2003: 106).

Close-knit or embedded relations are multilevel. Relations among lobbyists can include shared issues, common membership in a trade association, jointly participating in a coalition, and a host of other social actions. The point is that as a group becomes more close-knit in nature, ties or relations expand within any dimension, such as increasing numbers of shared issues, and across different dimensions.

Time is an important part of this relationship-building process. Steve goes back to Mary again and again for feedback; they are frequently in touch. Part of this ongoing interaction is because the policy process itself takes time: Many bills in Congress, for example, languish and die at the end of a Congress, only to be reintroduced, with some modifications, when a new Congress reconvenes following an election. As I noted in Chapter 1, lobbying reform has been repeatedly proposed since 1876, but the only meaningful reforms were passed in 1946 and 1995. Usually, focusing on any issue is a long-term commitment. When we see the same lobbyists working on a number of shared issues over time, we could say that they occupy a set of positions within a web of close-knit relationships. Therefore, those lobbyists who operate in one policy area over time increasingly develop a stable set of shared interests with other, similarly situated lobbyists relative to lobbyists who do not work consistently in a policy area over time. That is, ties tend to replicate and reproduce themselves.

How does this process work? First, issues and interested actors are funneled via jurisdictional rules to congressional committees, agencies, and key decision makers. This sorting process throws actors together. Second, politics is largely an in-person process. Despite grassroots advocacy and advances in technology, most institutional actors work in a face-to-face environment that is facilitated by geographical proximity and concentration. So the funneling process is as much physical as it is based on interests. Key actors bring people together. Congressional staffers or bureaucrats, by virtue of their central positions, connect interested parties who learn to recognize and interact with each other. This is a first stage reproductive process, but a second, more common stage process occurs when lobbyists go back to each other based on past interaction. This is business as usual. The same lobbyists get together periodically to swap information and strategies. Lobbyists find more similarities in interests and tactics, and relations become more stable.

So, based on the previous discussion, what should we expect to see if we look at a particular policy domain? The first argument for this chapter is that a *policy domain will consist of a set of lobbying organizations that consistently lobby on the same set of issues over time and that recognize each other as members.* From a social network perspective, any particular pair of lobbying organizations will vary in terms of their specific strength of ties to each other, but the larger network of ties has a unique level of cohesion (i.e., structural embeddedness) that should persist. From a qualitative perspective, the long-term players recognize and interact with each other.

Much like business firms within a particular market (White, 1981), lobbying organizations are sending signals to each other about which issues are important, which issues are moving, and which are not. Signals from established organizations are more credible and more likely to be acted upon than those from organizations that only occupy space in the policy domain for a relatively short period of time. Longevity and stable relations thereby translate into better information, which in turn translates into more centralized network positions with more freedom of action. The stable set of actors within a policy domain forms a core around which more temporary actors positions themselves. "Lobbyists arriving in Washington must either compete with those who already have access and proven track records or tie themselves to experienced lobbyists who are known and trusted" (Zorack, 1990: 642). That core is itself stable and replicates itself.

These conditions suggest that we should see differences in the quality of relations between the stable actors relative to actors that come and go: *Compared to short-term players, relationships among long-term organizations in the policy domain are more stable, and long-term organizations tend to be more central in the policy domain.*

THE RESEARCH SITE

I explore these arguments focusing on a case study at the federal level. The research site for this project is federal retirement policy using data from 1999–2004. Lobbying in this area covers issues related to Social Security, federal pensions, private sector pensions, executive compensation, and related employee benefits topics. Much of the activity relates to tax and labor laws that govern the private sector retirement plans. Private pensions are encouraged through tax incentives such as tax deductions for employer pension contributions as well as non-recognition for income tax purposes (at least until distribution) of worker contributions and earnings on pension assets. Along with health care and the home mortgage interest deduction, this is one of the largest tax subsidies as, for example, private pensions accounted for $142 billion in lost annual revenue to the government for the 2011 fiscal year (Office of Management and Budget, 2010). Not coincidentally, assets in private pension plans have seen tremendous growth since 1985 when total assets equaled $2.2 trillion (in 2004 dollars), but that rose to $5.7 trillion by 2006 (U.S. Department of Labor, 2008). The growth in assets, primarily in defined contribution plans, has been fueled by investments in equities, and in turn the increase in Washington, D.C., plan assets has propelled the growth of the mutual fund industry. For example, mutual funds accounted for 5 percent of all retirement assets in 1990; however, by 2005, the mutual funds' share of the retirement market reached 24 percent (Investment Company Institute, 2006). In turn, the retirement market became more important for the mutual fund industry over time. In 1990, the retirement plan market made up 19 percent of all mutual funds; however, by 2005, this proportion rose to 39 percent (Investment Company Institute, 2006).

The nature of retirement policy has opened the domain to a variety of groups. Since 1998, when more stringent lobbyist disclosure reports were required through 2004, a cumulative 392 organizations indicated that they lobbied on retirement issues at least once, either on their own behalf or on behalf of other organizations; however, during any one period, the figure is much lower, ranging from 97 organizations in 1998 to a high of 198 in the first half of 2004. Of these 392 organizations, 50 or 13 percent were long-term players; that is, organizations that lobbied in all prior seven years (1998–2004) while organizations that lobbied only one or two years made up approximately 35 percent of the sample. The implication of these numbers is that during the early 2000s new groups moved into the retirement policy domain in greater numbers, crowding the policy environment.

Why did this influx occur? Long-term trends and short-term events contributed to heightened interest in retirement policy issues among interest groups. As is well known, the American population is aging, and although an aging population puts pressure on prominent programs such as Social Security and Medicare, it also affects employers' decisions about providing retirement plans and other benefits to workers. This demographic trend combined with the decline of the unionized workforce has enabled corporate sponsors of pensions to switch from defined benefit plans, in which the risk of funding and investments are borne by employers, to defined contribution plans, in which workers are the primary decision makers concerning contributions and investments. Long-term budget politics have also put private retirement plans under pressure as Congress has periodically sought to adjust the tax incentives in order to raise revenue. These long-term trends became more pronounced in the early 2000s as the recession of 2001 put great pressure on employers to fund their remaining defined benefit pension plans. The Congress also passed major tax legislation in 2001 and 2003, and a Republican Congress and Executive Branch were receptive to employer and financial interests in expanding tax incentives and corporate flexibility with regard to retirement policy. In summary, various trends and events created heightened interest in retirement issues and a more crowded policy domain.

DATA AND METHODS

Data Sources

I provide a summary description of the data sources in this section, but the Appendix to this volume provides a more detailed description of the data sources and analysis. The population of lobbyists is derived from publicly available disclosure reports required by the Lobbying Disclosure Act (LDA) that were filed by lobbying organizations on a biannual basis with the U.S. Congress[8] over seven years for a total of fourteen time periods. These reports indicate the issues and bills on which organizations lobbied, policy domains in which the organization was active, lobbying expenses/income, and basic organizational information.

The LDA does not cover all possible interest group activity or even all face-to-face lobbying. Lobbying for registration purposes only includes informal contacts between lobbyists and policy makers (Furlong, 1998) and as such does not cover other activities such as public relations campaigns. LDA expenditure minimums may exclude groups using volunteers or that are active only for a short time or on a single issue (Baumgartner and Leech, 2000). So in terms of sample selection, I am not capturing every actor or group, but the LDA nonetheless is an appropriate source for this study. The LDA reports provide detailed organizational and legislative data, and I have a complete sample of lobbyists, which is important for social network analysis. Table 2.1 provides some descriptive statistics for the retirement policy sample.

Table 2.1 Descriptive Statistics for Retirement Policy Organization, 1999–2004 (*n* = 392)

	Mean (%)	SD	Min.	Max
Private employers (%)	0.43	0.50	0	1
Financial services (%)	0.24	0.43	0	1
Labor (%)	0.09	0.29	0	1
Total time in six-month increments	5.40	4.29	1	14
Number of staff	2.74	2.60	1	20
Number of coalitions	1.09	2.36	0	20
Average issue similarity	0.08	0.07	0	0.25
Average expense per policy domain	60,720	93,367	5,000	9,532,482
Average number of policy domains	7.16	5.45	1	39.75
Association	0.32	0.47	0	1
Represents other organizations	0.33	0.47	0	1

Source: Author's compilation of LDA data.

Networks

The data permits different types of relationships, and I will discuss these different networks as they are used in the book. In this chapter, a big focus is on how lobbyists are connected to each other via common issues. The data from the LDA reports for each time period was entered into matrices in which the rows represent lobbying organizations and the columns represent different legislative issues. These organization-by-issue matrices were transformed by matrix algebra into organization-by-organization networks in which common issues serve as ties between organizations.

Another set of networks come from association memberships that was created by looking up membership lists of the associations that had lobbying organizations as members. Whereas most organizations had longitudinal data on their membership, some did not, so I only used the most recent membership data within the time period to create a static membership network. For relationships in which a client organization hires lobbying firms, information was obtained from the LDA reports. I merged the association-level and for-hire level networks in order to get a comprehensive map of which organizations are paying others for membership or representation services—I refer to this as the 'membership network.'

Coalitions are the final network level. As noted in Chapter 4 of this volume, in which I define coalitions, not all joint activities are coalitions. I collected data on coalitions that were visible and had an identifiable membership. I researched various websites related to retirement policy and finding information produced by coalitions devoted to retirement policy.[9] I also used qualitative information from interviews as well as from Internet archives (www.archive.org) for this search and was able to identify thirty-one coalitions from 1998 to 2004 for which membership information was available. As with the issue network, the organization-by-coalition network was transformed into an organizational network in which individual actors are connected through common coalition participation.

Variables

An organization's position in the policy network is a critical concept in analyzing the arguments of this chapter. First, an organization's position relative to its peers may affect access to resources and its visibility and credibility among its peers. Second, an understanding of the broad pattern of inter-organizational ties and positions enables an understanding of the policy domain, the overall nature of embedded relations, and their sources and consequences.

I identify an organization's network position over both issue and membership networks using two measures, centrality and constraint.[10] In general, centrality is a measure of network prominence and this study uses a particular measure known as betweenness centrality.[11] Betweenness centrality measures the proportion of ties linking all actors in a network that pass through that particular actor.[12] In general, betweenness centrality measures information control (Borgatti et al., 2002), which is particularly apt for a study of lobbyists.

The constraint variable measures the extent to which an actor is invested in other actors who in turn are invested in each other. If I have ties to a group of people, and those people only have ties to each other, I will be highly constrained in my network. Conversely, if I have ties to different groups who are not tied to each other, I will not be constrained in my actions but would instead have the flexibility to engage in a number of actions such as a brokerage, gatekeeping, or representation.

A measure somewhat distinct but still related to network position is issue overlap, which is a measure of the number of issues two organizations have in common divided by their total set of issues. The measure provides an index ranging from 0 to 1. An organization that has a high issue overlap number averaged over all organizations therefore is representative of all the issue preferences of active lobbying organizations. In addition, a high issue overlap measure may indicate an organization's expertise in the policy domain.

The LDA reports also provide information about the organizations. The reports indicate whether the organization is representing itself or a different organization. It also provides the amount spent on lobbying, the number of individual staff, and the number of policy domains on which the organization is working.

I also gathered data on whether the organization was a membership association and the number of coalitions in which the organization was participating during the period under study—more information on coalition data can be found in Chapter 3 and in the Appendix of this volume.

Methods

In arguing that durable relations among long-term policy actors constitute a policy domain, I draw upon methods that are largely descriptive in nature. A descriptive approach is not too surprising in that the arguments of the chapter are largely a depiction of a community of relations and as such provides a foundation for the explorations in following chapters. After providing some simple social network visualizations of the policy domain, the quantitative analysis centers around simple statistics and proceeds in three basic steps. We should see a correlation between longevity within a policy domain and overall centrality and importance in the policy network in terms of betweenness centrality, agenda overlap, and structural constraint. Therefore, the more an organization lobbies within the retirement policy domain, the more central will be its position. Moreover, the more an organization lobbies within the retirement policy domain, the greater its agenda overlap with other long-term organizations. In addition, I would expect that long-term participants in the policy domain would be less constrained by ties to other actors.

If networks are stable, their structure should correlate over time. To examine network stability, I use quadratic assignment procedures (QAP). The QAP analysis (Hubert and Baker, 1978; Baker and Hubert, 1981) provides Pearson correlations of network structures such that we can identify in a statistically significant way whether one network structure is similar to another. In general, QAP indexes the probability that the similarity between two matrices can be explained as a random permutation of the rows and columns of either matrix—the lower the probability, the more likely it is that the two matrices are in fact similar (Walsh, 1994).

Finally, qualitative interviews provide individual perspectives on the idea of community: Do people know and talk to each other? The interviews provide information on the nature of the interactions, relationships, and mechanisms of social norms within each policy domain.

COMMUNITY IN POLICY

One of the first qualities to note about retirement policy is its dynamic nature. The histogram in Figure 2.1 is presented in terms of six-month increments, tracking the reporting intervals for the lobbyist disclosure reports. Figure 2.1 shows a fairly fluid policy area through a distribution

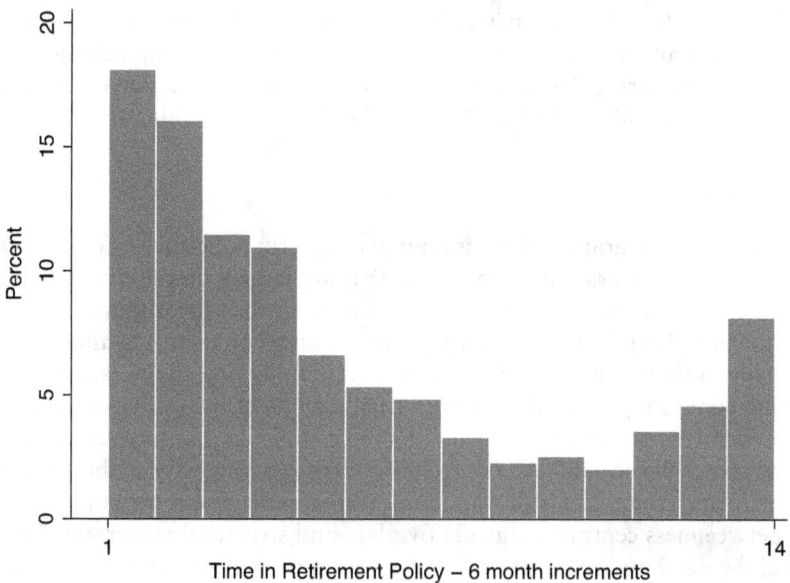

Figure 2.1   Time spent lobbying on retirement policy, 1998–2004 (six-month increments; $n = 392$).

of the interest group organizations in terms of total time spent lobbying. The vast majority of organizations are short-term participants, as nearly 40 percent spend only six months to a year working on retirement policy. At the other end of the scale, almost 10 percent of organizations were consistently working over all periods on retirement policy. In other words, we see a small core of organizations around which a large number of organizations are flowing.

I found a similar pattern in other quantitative data from other policy areas that will be used to compare and contrast with retirement policy. Figures 2.2 (top and bottom) are taken from the federal Medicare & Medicaid federal policy domain and the North Carolina lobbying data, respectively. Like retirement policy, these areas show a smaller core of long-term players—approximately 10 percent—and a much larger percentage of short-term actors.

The complexity of lobbying comes not just from the substance of the issues but in part from this fluidity of the policy environment. At the same time, however, many organizations are connected to each other in different and sometimes multiple ways.

Figures 2.3 visually represent the different social networks in the retirement policy domain for the second half of 2004. Different shapes indicate the types of organizational representation (triangles represent membership organizations like trade associations and unions, circles are used for self-represented [or non-membership] entities like corporations and public interest groups, and squares indicate for-hire organizations like law firms and consulting firms). In all figures, the size of the node (representing an organization) is proportional to the total amount of time (in terms of six months increments) that the actor has spent in the policy domain from 1998 to 2004. In addition to shape size, the number of shared interests is indicated by the thickness of the line that connects any two nodes.

Figure 2.3 (p. 55, top) shows the network of actors who are affiliated by shared retirement policy issues in the time period of July to December 2004, which is the last period in this study. Most of the actors[13] are connected to each other in terms of shared issues, but a single triangle labeled AICPA (the American Institute of Certified Public Accountants, a professional association) is the sole connector between two large clusters of organizations. In the lower right area of the figure, two separate clusters of unions and public interest groups are tied to each other in terms of shared issues in which no other organization has an interest. In general, long-time members of the policy domain tend to cluster among a thick set of issue-based relations.

Figure 2.3 (page 55, bottom) is a map of relations by membership in associations and unions, and here the ties have arrowheads on them to reflect the direction of membership: An arrow pointing from A to B means that A is a member of B. The figure shows that the organizations cluster into two large groups that are not connected to each other. In the upper left part of

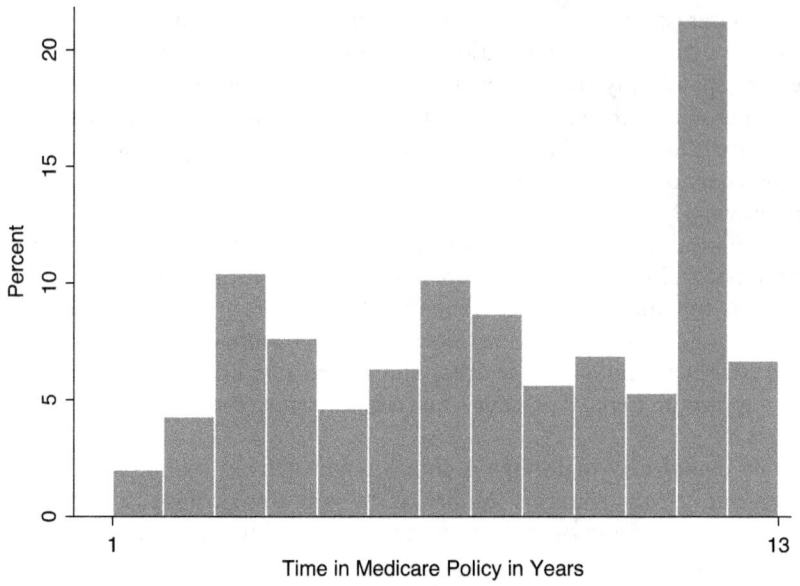

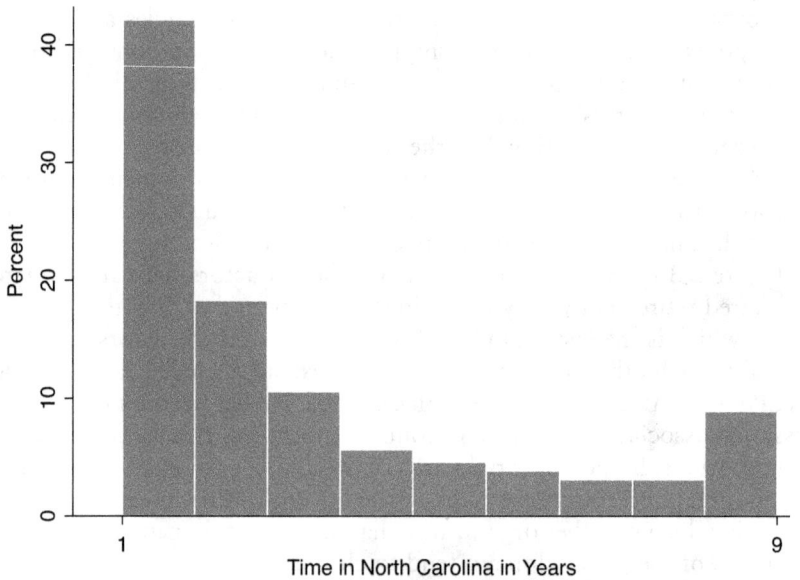

Figure 2.2 Time spent lobbying on Medicare policy (top) and in North Carolina (bottom), in years.

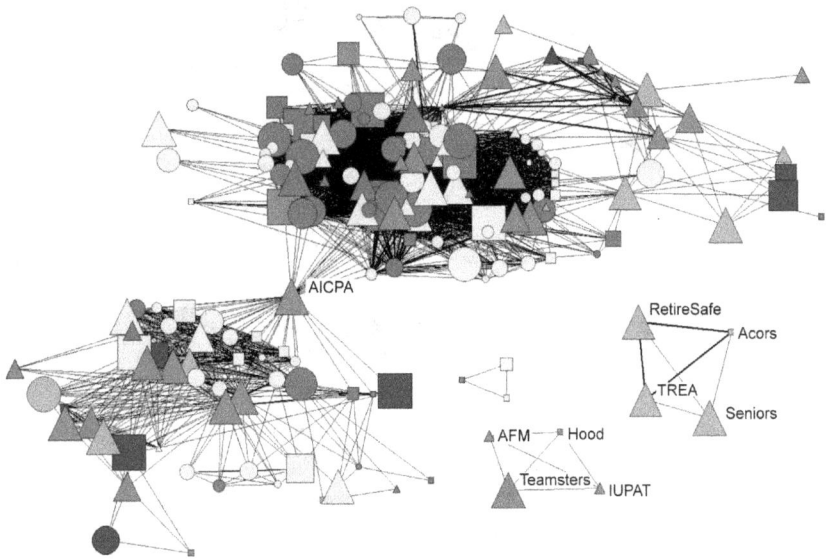

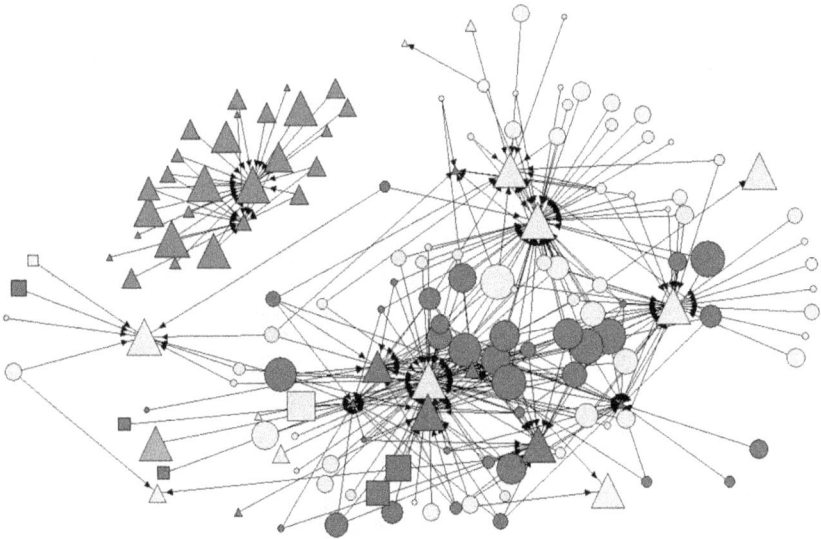

Figure 2.3 Networks of retirement lobbyists, July–December 2004, by interest (shading), time (size), and relational (shape) types: shared issues (top figure) and common memberships (bottom figure).

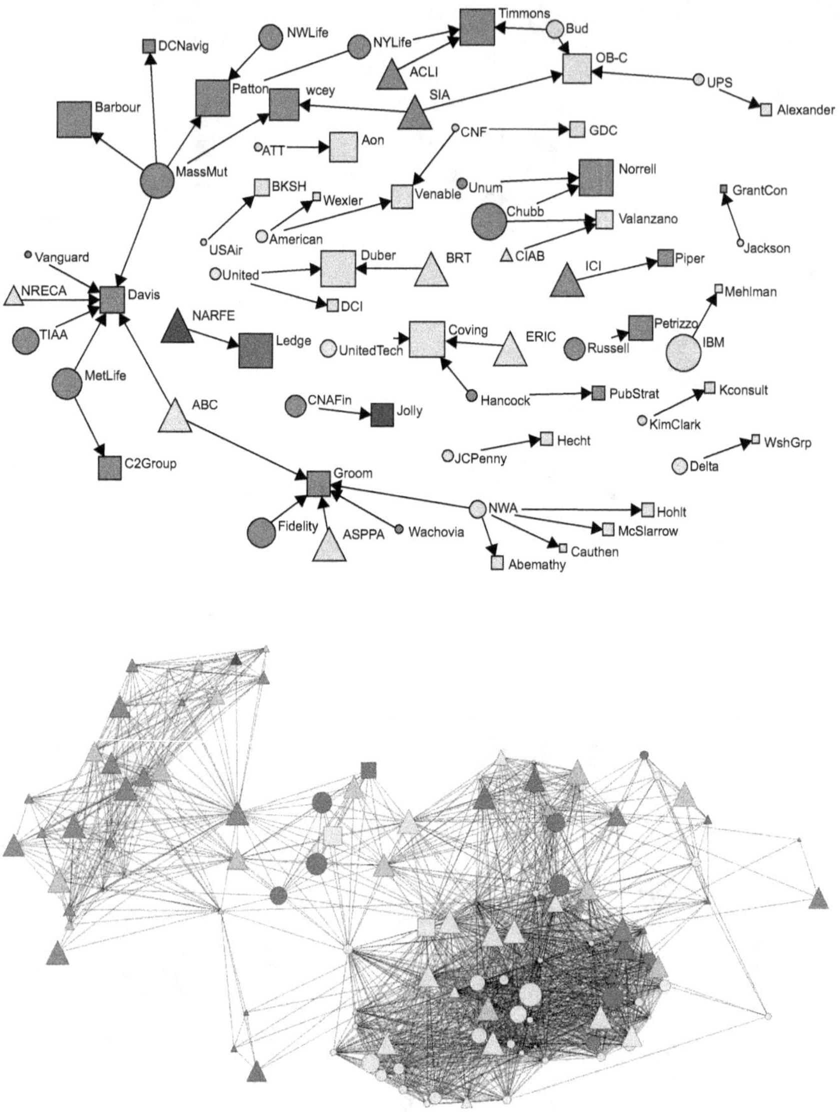

Figure 2.3   (Continued) For-hire relationships (top figure) and common coalition memberships (bottom figure).

the graph, there is a cluster of labor unions that are chiefly the constituent unions of the AFL-CIO. The other, larger cluster is a collection of management and financial services trade associations and their members. In this case the relations are not nearly as dense as in Figure 2.3, and it is apparent that a handful of long-serving trade associations and unions are the recipients of the vast majority of incoming ties and links; the shorter-termed organizations are mostly on the periphery. In the case of the management and financial services component, long-term, self-representing organizations (the circles) act as bridges among the major trade associations (see the area denoted by a yellow dotted-line oval). This central position among a dozen or so organizations may serve as a coordinating function among the different trade associations.

Figure 2.3 (page 56, top) provides a map of for-hire relationships at the end of 2004. This social network map also is directional in nature: An arrow going from A to B indicates that A has hired B. The map shows a sparse network of small, disconnected groups: Relatively few firms are hiring, and the hired firms only represent one or two organizations. However, because some organizations will hire more than one lobbying firm, one can see a chain of thirty organizations that create a large 'C' shape in the figure with a node Abernathy at one end and Hohlt at the other end. A significant number of organizations are linked, at least in this time frame, through hiring practices. Here, long-term organizations are often key links in the chain.

Finally, Figure 2.3 (page 56, bottom) illustrates the network of coalition membership. This situation is not like the membership network where labor and management/financial service clusters were completely separate from each other. Why would organizations on opposite sides of many issues still find common cause? Some labor unions sponsor their own pension plans and thus have some interest similar to private employers, and some other unions are joint trustees with private employers of plans and therefore find common cause on some policy issues.

In these figures, organizations that participate in retirement policy over a long period of time appear to have dense ties to other actors. But are long-term organizations unique? Are organizations that spend long periods of time in retirement policy different from organizations with more short-term focus on retirement issues?

Tables 2.2 and 2.3 shed some light on this question by providing the results of *t* tests of group means on selected organizational and network measures. Table 2.2 examines differences in group means of selected characteristics of long-term organizations (at least six years in retirement policy out of a total of seven) versus both (a) short-term organizations (six months only) and (b) all organizations that are not long-term players. Relative to short-term organizations, long-term organizations will have more staff working on retirement policy (4.1 persons versus 2.2 for short-term organizations). Long-term organizations are more likely to be membership organizations, and they spend more with an average expense or income of $99,754 on a per policy domain basis as against $29,543 for short-term organizations. Long-term organizations also participate in more coalitions and are called more frequently to testify before congressional committees. Only 20.8 percent of long-term organizations are for-hire lobbying firms as compared with 45 percent of short-term organizations.

Table 2.2 t Tests of Difference in Means of Selected Variables by Short-Term versus Long-Term Participation in Retirement Policy ($n = 143$)

	Long-Term Organizations		Short-Term Organizations			All non-Long-Term Organizations		
	Mean	SE	Mean	SE	t Test	Mean	SE	t Test
Staff	4.111	0.455	2.169	0.225	-3.808***	2.437	0.117	-5.098***
Self-Represented	0.222	0.049	0.267	0.052	0.627	0.387	0.027	2.661***
Association	0.569	0.058	0.281	0.053	-3.610***	0.259	0.025	-5.277***
Hired Gun	0.208	0.048	0.450	0.059	3.170***	0.353	0.026	2.378**
Expense	99,754	16,323	29,543	4,479	-4.123***	51,937	4,327	-4.001***
Policy Domains	9.459	0.853	4.915	0.446	-4.700***	6.638	0.269	-4.046***
Coalitions	2.972	0.501	0.225	0.067	-5.396***	0.662	0.075	-8.105***
Hearings	1.347	0.347	0.014	0.014	-3.809***	0.103	0.022	-7.277***

***Probability that ($|T| > |t|$) < 0.01.

Notes: The t test is evaluating the null hypothesis that the difference in group means is not different from 0. For the test using short-term organizations, the degrees of freedom equal 141. The groups are short-term organizations that lobby in retirement policy for only six months and long-term organizations that lobby in retirement policy for more than five years (out of a possible seven). For the test for all non-long-term organizations, the degrees of freedom equal 390. The groups are long-term organizations that lobby in retirement policy for more than five years (out of a possible seven) and all other organizations.

Table 2.3 t Tests of Difference in Means of Selected Variables by Long-Term Participation in Retirement Policy

| | 2001–2002 (n = 238) | | | | | | | 2003–2004 (n = 247) | | | | | | |
| | Long-Term Organizations | | All Other Organizations | | | | Long-Term Organizations | | All Other Organizations | | | |
	Mean	SE	Mean	SE	t Test		Mean	SE	Mean	SE	t Test
Issue Overlap	0.119	0.007	0.111	0.005	−0.846		0.129	0.010	0.107	0.007	−1.668*
Issue Centrality	0.241	0.040	0.048	0.007	−6.699***		9.183	2.234	2.971	0.671	−3.521***
Membership Centrality	0.312	0.113	0.033	0.007	−3.716***		0.362	0.139	0.071	0.014	−3.159***
Membership Constraint	0.545	0.054	0.728	0.031	3.112***		0.328	0.045	0.527	0.033	3.353***

*Probability ($|T| > |t|$) <0.10 **Probability ($|T| > |t|$) <0.05 ***Probability ($|T| > |t|$) <0.01

Notes: The t test is evaluating the null hypothesis that the difference in group means is not different from 0. The degrees of freedom equal 236 for 2001–2002 and 245 for 2003–2004. The groups are long-term organizations that lobby in retirement policy for more than five years (out of a possible seven) and all other organizations.

Long-term are not significantly different from short-term organizations in terms of whether they are self-represented, that is, whether they have their own in-house lobbyist. Focusing on the difference between long-term organizations and all other organizations, the results are much the same: Long-term organizations have larger staffs, are membership organizations, spend more money, work in more policy domains, join more coalitions, and testify more often. They are less likely to be self-representing and be a for-hire lobbying firm.

For-hire lobbying firms, the so-called hired guns, are present but only episodically. They go where the clients pay them to go but usually no further. Long-term organizations are more stable because either they are representing themselves or have a membership base. In all likelihood, stability is a function of selection: Members and clients are attracted to long-term actors because of the specialization and expertise. Stability translates into larger resources that can be thrown at an issue. More stable actors also have a broader focus in terms of the number of total policy domains, not just in retirement policy, in which they lobby. Short-term organizations, perhaps befitting the presence of for-hire firms who are hired with a limited budget, are more narrowly focused.

How do long-term participants do in terms of network position? Table 2.3 compares the network positions of the long-term organizations relative to all other organizations. Because network position may change from year to year, I present two separate t tests of group means analyses for the 107th (2001–2002) and 108th (2003–2004) congressional periods.[14] Long-term organizations are more central for both issue and membership networks. They are less subject to constraint at the membership level, which means that long-term organizations have more diverse networks. In terms of issue overlap, there is no significant difference between long-term organizations and all other organizations in 2001–2002, but in 2003–2004, long-term organizations have greater issue overlap on average than other, more short-term organizations.

The discussion thus far suggests that time matters in terms of position and prominence within the retirement policy network. Certain, but not all, lobbying organizations possess dense ties with other lobbyists partly as a function of time spent in the field. The next section examines the degree to which the structure of relations changes over time.

Stability of Network Structures

How much change occurs in the networks of lobbyists over time? A structure of networks should be reproduced over time such that there should be positive and statistically correlations between any two networks. Tables 2.4 and 2.5 provide results of the Quadratic Assignment Procedure (QAP) correlations for agenda overlap. As noted above, QAP correlations are correlations of entire network structures. Much like a standard statistical table of

Table 2.4 QAP Correlations between Issue Network Structures Using QAP Analysis, 1998–2004

	m98	e98	m99	e99	m00	e00	m01	e01	m02	e02	m03	e03	m04
m98													
e98	0.502												
m99	0.285	0.472											
e99	0.299	0.525	0.698										
m00	0.166	0.287	0.378	0.507									
e00	0.237	0.307	0.405	0.591	0.699								
m01	0.198	0.189	0.322	0.320	0.402	0.423							
e01	0.212	0.229	0.294	0.316	0.284	0.370	0.469						
m02	0.182	0.259	0.321	0.347	0.384	0.397	0.325	0.376					
e02	0.177	0.199	0.344	0.342	0.255	0.370	0.348	0.383	0.629				
m03	0.110	0.132	0.241	0.250	0.265	0.242	0.243	0.233	0.260	0.325			
e03	0.110	0.152	0.224	0.254	0.257	0.250	0.214	0.203	0.282	0.288	0.633		
m04	0.138	0.162	0.252	0.298	0.294	0.286	0.249	0.261	0.326	0.326	0.473	0.664	
e04	0.136	0.157	0.221	0.267	0.287	0.245	0.237	0.250	0.274	0.290	0.408	0.525	0.712

Source: Author's compilation of lobbyist registration reports.

Note: Each time period represents a six-month period corresponding to lobbyist reporting periods. An 'm' indicates a mid-year filing period while an 'e' represents an end-of-year filing period. For example, 'm98' is the period January through June of 1998 while 'e98' is the period July through December of 1998. Shaded areas indicate correlations of networks that occur in the same session of Congress. **Bolded** numbers indicate correlations of networks that occur between the end of one Congress and the start of a new Congress.

Table 2.5   Average QAP Correlations for Agenda Overlap Networks by Long-Term Organizations and All Other Organizations

	All Lobbying Organizations	Long-Term Organizations Only
All Time Periods	.338	.391
Within Congress	.559	.598
Immediate Inter-Congress	.421	.525

Source: Author's compilation of coalition data from various sources.

Note: Long-term organizations are those lobbying organizations that lobby on retirement policy more than five years out of the total seven years for this study (1998–2004). There are a total of seventy-two long-term organizations.

correlations, Table 2.4 should be read as the correlations for each network listed in the column label and each successive network reading down (all correlations are statistically significant). Looking at the first column of results, for example, the correlation between the network in the first half of 1998 (denoted as 'm98') with the second half of 1998 ('e98') is 0.502. Moving down the column, the next correlation is between m98 and the first half of 1999 ('m99'), which is 0.285.

Turning our attention to general patterns, one can see that in each column of Table 2.4, the correlations generally decline the farther in time one gets from the initial time period. This decline makes sense, as we would expect that networks would change and become more dissimilar with the passage of time. However, all of the correlations remain positive throughout and statistically significant.

In addition, the correlations are higher within the same Congress as compared to correlations between different congressional sessions. A congressional term lasts two years until an election occurs and a new Congress comes into place. Any bills that are introduced during a prior session are dropped as the new Congress starts from scratch. Lobbying relationships are highly correlated within a particular session of Congress, as indicated by shaded results. For example, looking at the third column labeled 'm99,' the first three results are shaded indicating that they occurred within the 106th Congress (1999–2000). The correlations between the first half of 1999 ('m99') and the next three time periods are 0.698, 0.378, and 0.405, respectively. In general, the shaded results are higher than correlations between networks across different sessions of Congress. Thus, the network of interest affiliations tends to replicate itself over time, and the correlations evidence stability in the relationships.

Table 2.5 compares the average correlations against the same correlations for long-organizations only. In all categories, long-term organizations had higher correlations. Across all time periods, the correlation of agenda overlap for long-term organizations was 0.391 as compared to 0.338 for all others. Within each two-year congressional session, longer-serving organizations' agenda overlap correlation was 0.598 versus 0.559. And from the end of one congressional session through the start of a new Congress, the correlation for long-term organizations was 0.525 as against 0.421 for all other organizations.

Although not completely resolving the issue, the evidence presented so far indicates that this particular policy domain evidences durable and strong relationships over time, especially for long-term groups. But do these quantitative results actually mean something? Do they reflect reality? The qualitative interview data provide additional support.

Qualitative Evidence of the Community in Lobbying

For a community to exist, actors in a policy domain must know each other, must interact with each other, must share information with each other, and must give credibility to the information gained from other lobbyists. But are these perceptions and interactions actually present? Each lobbyist I interviewed had several years or more of experience in retirement policy such that they should be able to indicate the presence of community.

Interviews with retirement policy lobbyists confirm the statistical distribution of Figure 2.1. In terms of the flux of lobbyists, one remarked to me: "Jesus, when I started doing pension issues, there were probably like 25–20 people lobbying, if that many, maybe like a handful that were really good at it. Now it's just dozens of people. You have got like regular corporate lobbyists now lobbying pension issues. It's sort of insanity."

But most were clear that a core group existed. For example, when I mentioned to one lobbyist that I counted over 300 organizations working on retirement issues in recent years, he said, "Of the 300, it's probably the thirty to fifty organizations and lobbyists who do this week in and week out. There is sort of the community on retirement." Another lobbyist who held positions in the legislative and executive branches characterized the size of the pension community as small: "Now there are more associations who are interested, but having said that, like everything else in the world, there are only a few who do all the work. Twenty percent of people do 80 percent of the work."

As the story that opened this chapter illustrated, lobbyists know each other. And this has a particular feel to it, as one informant said: "The people are fascinating to me, really sharp people and whether they are adversary or you are allies they are, there is a, for the most part, some degree of congeniality because everybody has been sort of on the same campus and like there is a campus feel to it."

CHAPTER SUMMARY

The goal of this chapter was to apply the concept of embeddedness to lobbying activity. In particular, I focused on relational embeddedness due in part to the nature of the data but also because relational embeddedness gets to the heart of political life in which personal relationships are thought to be paramount. Using a unique longitudinal dataset of lobbyists in one policy domain, I constructed and used social network variables that, although somewhat correlated with each other, provide a somewhat different approach to the idea of embeddedness. In general, I showed that relational variables like agenda overlap, centrality, and prior work in coalitions are associated with political activity. Perhaps just as importantly, I also reaffirmed the importance of time in operationalizing embeddedness. Time spent in any field is critical to establishing relationships and building a track record of trust and cooperation.

We see long-term organizations that have stable and similar relations within the retirement policy domain. For the most part, long-term organizations have superior network positions in the policy domain relative to more short-term organizations, although the type of network is relevant. In addition, lobbyists recognize each other in a policy domain.

The results provided by this chapter suggest that a policy domain is more than just a collection of lobbying organizations that work on a set of related issues. In this case, we see a set of organizations within a broader field that not only work on the same issues but that have a consistent set of ties and positions.

What do close-knit relations among lobbyists mean for every day lobbying work? Burstein (1991) argues that a policy domain focus means that policy processes and outcomes are affected primarily by forces within each domain. The tension between stability and conflict that runs through these theoretical accounts has an implication for policy outcomes. As Baumgartner and coauthors (2009) note, "today's policy communities push Congress toward equilibrium" (65). In other words, the very structure of policy communities creates a status quo bias in policy making because the recurring interactions structured by policy communities and reinforced by shared knowledge, values, and ways of discourse foster negotiation and compromise. The next three chapters of this volume provide some quantitative evidence of the processes that occur within lobbying networks, and Chapters 6 and 7 expand on the ideas of trust and social norms via qualitative interview data.

NOTES

1. Dictionary.com, "community," accessed on July 18, 2013, and available at http://dictionary.reference.com/browse/community?s=t.

2. Social network theory and analysis has a long tradition in political research. For example, the resource mobilization approach uses the patterned links among interest groups to show the structure of coalitions, cleavages, and competitive relations among such groups and how political actors are linked to resources (Wellman, 1988; Knoke, 1990). Political process theory also draws upon network models in order to understand mobilization and claim making (Tilly, 1978).

3. "Instead of society, I thus use the term relational setting . . . As such, it is a relational matrix, similar to a social network" (Somers, 1994: 72).

4. Moody and White (2003) commented that the nature of embeddedness, particularly its duality of relational and structural, lends a certain imprecision in its usage in the research literature.

5. "In practice, many ties are with network members whom one does not like and with whom one would not voluntarily form a twosome. Such ties are involuntary in that they come as part of the network membership package" (Wellman, 1988: 41).

6. "In saying this I draw on the principle that to the extent that a dyad's mutual contacts are connected to one another, there is more efficient information spread about what members of the pair are doing, and thus better ability to shape that behavior. Such cohesive groups are better not only at spreading information, but also at generating normative, symbolic, and cultural structures that affect our behavior" (Granovetter, 1992: 35).

7. This is not to say that jurisdictions do not overlap; they do. Moreover, different policy-making actors and entities often compete for jurisdiction over issues, and some of the jurisdictional overlap is institutionally designed. As a general matter, however, policy work is often done through division of labor.

8. The website for the federal lobbyist registration reports, accessed at various times since 2006, is http://sopr.senate.gov/.

9. For example, a press release by a coalition would describe the coalition and its issue.

10. For social network measures, I use the social networks software program UCI-NET (Borgatti et al., 2002).

11. A number of network measures are also available, but they are not appropriate or duplicate the measures actually used. For example, betweenness and closeness centrality are appropriate for directed networks rather than the affiliation networks that I focus on here.

12. More specifically, let b_{jk} be the proportion of all paths linking nodes j and k, which pass through node i. The betweenness of node i is the sum of all b_{jk} where i, j, and k are distinct. Betweenness is therefore a measure of the number of times a vertex occurs on a geodesic. The normalized betweenness centrality is the betweenness divided by the maximum possible betweenness expressed as a percentage.

13. Isolated organizations are not shown in Figure 2.2 or the following figures. For Figure 2.2, an organization is isolated if it does not have an issue in common with any other organization. There are seven such isolates in the last half of 2004 out of a total of 190 organizations that lobbied during that time frame.

14. For Table 2.3, I only use organizations that actually lobby during the time periods in question. For that reason the observations in Table 2.3 is less than the overall sample size of 392 organizations.

3 Working Together

If you want to get along, go along.

—Sam Rayburn

Why do lobbyists work together? Do strong relationships matter for coalition formation and group activity? The prior chapter discussed the nature of relationships of lobbyists in a policy domain, and this chapter looks at how relationships affect joint activity among interest groups. In the Introduction I suggested that *organizations with close-knit ties are more likely to work together in coalitions*. Close-knit relationships develop over and are characterized by shared interests over time, and these shared interests over issues should then translate into joint activity. But why do close-knit relationships play a role in joint activity?

Cooperation in the form of interest group coalitions and alliances is difficult for a number of reasons. The interest group environment is crowded (Salisbury, 1992), competitive (Holyoke, 2009), and cuts across distinctions between institutional and non-institutional actors (Strolovich, 2007; Heaney and Rojas, 2008). Coalitions often occur within a dynamic policy environment in which many interest groups briefly participate and then withdraw. Organizations entering into alliances face considerable moral hazard concerns because of the potential for opportunistic behavior by coalition partners.

The broad argument here is that interest group networks matter for coalition participation. Networked relations among people or groups in other times and/or contexts serve as pathways to discover resources such as potential coalition partners. Anecdotal and empirical data suggest that coalition stability and durability are a function of actors' experience with coalition work and with other actors, and hence time and trust are underlying processes in coalition development.

Why? Policy actors that face uncertainty about possible coalition partners will be more socially orientated and resort to their existing networks to discover information that finds partners and reduces the risk that coalition partners will behave opportunistically. In other words, networks lower search costs. Relationships are filled with histories of past interactions, and this information helps solve the problem of identifying and assessing possible partners. An organization's network position within a dense network of actors can strongly influence collaborative activity in the network. Organizations that are consistently embedded in a policy domain are more central, they broker ideas, and they have more contacts. Within lengthy and extensive social and communication networks, they can easily identify the location and availability of political resources. As a result of these processes, these embedded and central organizations are the focal points around which joint action forms.

The chapter is organized as follows: I begin by summarizing some of the prior research on interest group coalitions and network approaches to collaborations. To answer the questions I raised above, I return to the federal retirement policy domain and employ a dynamic longitudinal network model of the relationship between coalition participation and issue networks and other independent variables.

INTEREST GROUP COALITIONS

In this discussion, the term 'coalition' encompasses similar terms about joint activity used in other works such as 'alliance.' Drawing from Levi and Murphy (2006), I define a coalition as a collaborative, means-oriented arrangement that permits distinct organizations to pool resources in order to effect specific policy change. A coalition has rules for resolving conflict and defining membership. There are, of course, a wide variety of coalition types, and coalitions are created for different purposes, with different configurations of actors and with different kinds of rules. Coalitions can be either short term or long term. Short-term coalitions often are created for a particular lobbying event or discrete goal. Long-term coalitions entail ongoing cooperation with chosen partners beyond a specific objective. This chapter considers both kinds of coalition, but particular attention is given to stability and durability of coalitions. In fact, little systematic attention has been paid to the persistence of interest group coalitions over time (Whitford, 2003).

Of course, a coalition is itself a set of relationships that can be close-knit in nature. So, I want to distinguish between coalitions and embedded relationships as the two might be but are not necessarily identical. Mary may have long-term and durable relations with certain other lobbyists in the policy domain, but even if they share common interests, they might not form a coalition. So for clarity of discussion when I state that increasing work on a set of issues within a policy domain leads to close-knit ties, I am not talking about coalition ties. Non-coalition ties can include simple awareness of others and informal interactions as well as membership in a trade association. The reason I distinguish these ties from ties that constitute coalitions is that joining a coalition is both voluntary and is an important hallmark of political life. In addition, coalition ties usually are posterior to the other kinds of ties that make up a policy domain. However, the coalition argument discussed here could be viewed as a special case of the policy community discussed in the prior chapter.

But why should coalitions persist or even come into being? As Hojnacki (1997) asks, are coalitions in an interest group's interests? Lobbyists are rational and seek some benefit like legislation, income from clients, and/or the social capital from enhanced reputation or new relationships. In pursuing this benefit, lobbyists can cooperate with others or they can work alone, but either choice incurs costs (Hojnacki, 1997). For a lobbyist to cooperate with other lobbyists in a coalition, the net benefit from cooperation must be greater than the net benefit from lobbying alone. Cooperation may provide concrete benefits such as more credible and fine-grained information, economies of scale in operations, credibility and legitimacy, and/or a more amplified voice, to name a few (Truman, 1951; Hula, 1999; Strolovich, 2007). But cooperation also entails costs, including:

- transaction costs such as scheduling meetings, compromising on individual positions in order to achieve a consensus position, preparing coalitional materials, arranging group meetings with congressional offices;
- the costs of maintaining relationships in the policy domain; and
- opportunistic costs, as happens when, for example, a lack of a credible commitment on the part of coalition members results in shirking responsibilities and other self-interested behavior (Ostrom, Gardner, and Walker, 1994).

The costs of working alone involve the standard lobbying costs as well as 'relationship' costs, the costs of maintaining relationships between the lobbyist and the politician.

An illustration of these terms might be helpful. The lobbyist who would choose to work alone either has some sort of pre-existing relationship with a key member of Congress or she is in such a position that she does not need the help of others. As to the former, it is not unusual these days to see former members of Congress, such as Dick Armey or Tom Daschle, work as lobbyists because they are trading on the personal relationships that they developed during their public service; in effect, converting their accumulated social capital. I call these people 'relationship lobbyists' because they are relying on preexisting relationships to politicians rather than other resources in order to influence policy. For example, Dick Armey, former Majority Leader in the House of Representatives, might be able to convince a former colleague to insert a small provision into a bill—the proverbial 'earmark.' However, such relationships are not cost-free: They must be maintained, such as through ongoing contacts and/or campaign contributions, because social capital erodes over time (Parker, 2008). A lobbyist or organization working alone may also be in a position that she does not need or want help.

For example, the AARP is so large that it does not often need to compromise on its positions with potential allies.

But this latter scenario does not represent the reality for thousands of lobbyists. For them, influence stems from their ability to put together working relationships like coalitions that, for example, signal broad support (or opposition) to a policy choice (Milbrath, 1963) or enable more Capitol Hill visits than one lobbyist working alone can undertake.

Just focusing on costs, if the costs of coalition work are very high, then a coalition strategy will be unattractive. When the costs of cooperation are low, however, cooperative action is more likely to emerge (Heckathorn and Maser, 1987). If the costs of 'relationship lobbying' are high (such as the difficulty in establishing a personal relationship with a Senator via campaign contributions), then a coalition will be more appealing.

For example, Holyoke (2009) focuses on competition in the interest group environment with a set of policy preferences that lead to conflict or cooperation. Holyoke developed an elegant model of coalition formation amid competition in which lobbyists bargain over a compromise position (through a coalition) that would maximize their net benefits. In this model, lobbyists respond to different audiences (clients, legislators) who provide incentives for taking particular positions. Comparing the model with empirical data, Holyoke found that lobbyists resolve conflicts among their clients by making trade-offs among available resources and the positions of their differing audiences.

Organizational attributes and interests also influence these tradeoff decisions. For example, purposive organizations might be less likely than corporations and trade associations to compromise their positions (Hojnacki, 1997). However, Mahoney and Baumgartner (2004) find that organizational characteristics had little impact on coalition participation. Their work suggests that coalition participation might be related to actors' reputations and group morale building.

Coalition decisions may also be a function of environmental conditions facing the interest groups as well as the attributes of groups within that environment. A classical example of an environmental factor is the number and fluidity of groups, based on David Truman's (1951) discussion of pluralism, in which a host of interest groups with little individual power constantly shift into and out of alliances as issues rise or fall. This imagery was captured in part by the *issue network* in which interest groups move in and out of loose, issue-based relationships without the presence of core players around which stable networks would attach (Heclo, 1978; Heinz et al., 1993). Loomis (1986) suggests that the atomization of groups in a policy domain pushes them towards a coalition strategy. Hula (1999) argues that government expansion and the growth of interest groups in Washington, D.C., are the most likely drivers of coalition membership. In such an environment, "policymakers welcome joint fronts and joint presentations because it means a 'saving of work and tension for him.' Lawmakers do not want to pick one group over another and would rather have groups hash out differences in advance of coming to the lawmaker" (Hall, 1969: 105).

Hula (1999) also finds that the depth-of-issue interest for an organization is a key factor in the intensity of coalition participation. Organizations with a high, yet general level of interest in legislation will be highly involved in coalitions and will be leaders. This intensity of interest factor suggests a couple of mechanisms in that organizations with broad agendas may need coalitions to help advance their views, and such organizations may have a wide range of ties on which to draw in developing coalition strategies. Organizations with a narrow set of issues might join coalitions to shape the agenda to their set of interests. Hojnacki (1997) connects a resource-based argument to policy domain activity, as organizations that focus on a narrow set of concerns are less likely to join a coalition than organizations with a broad range of policy activities. Narrowly focused groups will be able to use their resources best by working alone as opposed to groups with a broad view that perhaps need the expertise or legitimacy from coalition partners to be effective. This argument is consonant with Browne's (1990) *issue niche* and connects to the environmental discussion above as the assumption is that relatively few actors will be active in these niche areas.

POLITICS, NETWORKS, AND COALITIONS

Networked relations matter for political and policy cooperation in a number of ways (Chubb, 1983; Milbrath, 1963; Cho and Fowler, 2010; Heaney and McClurg, 2009). Networks have been used to study legislative cooperation on bill sponsorship (Fowler, 2006), party cooperation across competing factions (Grossman and Dominguez, 2009; Koger, Masket, and Noel, 2010; Schwartz, 1990), and social movement cooperation across coalition boundaries (Heaney and Rojas, 2007, 2008).

Networks reflect the patterns and histories of interaction among actors, thus suggesting their degree of familiarity with one another's habits and preferences, reliability, and character. Thus, the strength or weakness of ties in networks, as well as the patterns in which they are arranged, may make all the difference in overcoming barriers to collaborative activity (Gould, 1993; Heaney and McClurg, 2009).

The well-known social capital perspective suggests that collaboration is more likely for actors embedded in dense, overlapping relationships with like-minded others (Coleman, 1988; Putnam, 2000; Burt, 2000). For example, Hula (1999) finds that interest groups often form close associations in several different coalitions and through interlocking boards. McCubbins, Paturi, and Weller (2009) finds that an increase in the number of connections improves coordination even when payoffs are highly asymmetric. Increasing connectivity in a policy network can reduce transaction costs by improving information on communities from which a coalition may be formed with as well as facilitate monitoring of coalition partners to ensure that they behave appropriately (Burt, 2000; Coleman, 1988, 1990; Putnam, 1995). "Mobilization for collective action depends on the timely and trustworthy transmission of information within a domain of interest" (Laumann and Knoke, 1987: 206).

Different types of networked relations may provide alternative opportunities for organization. Social and communication networks identify the location and availability of political resources, including potential coalition partners (Knoke, 1990). Uncertain about potential coalition partners, lobbyists resort to their prior and existing networks for information (Gulati, 1998). If a lobbyist were deeply embedded within a network of lobbyists, sharing information and finding coalition partners seems easier than if the lobbyist did not have embedded ties.

Much of the discussion to this point suggest a game-theoretic process in which organizations are continuously evaluating potential partners and coalitions in a Bayesian-like manner, but a single comment made to me by an experienced lobbyist suggests an often-overlooked, yet important mechanism. She said, "When we wanted to start the [XYZ] coalition, we started with the email list from the [ABC] coalition." Perhaps more strongly, pre-existing or continuing ties among actors in a policy domain are likely to encourage reproduction of those ties over time, including ties within coalitions. Thereby, a process of network transfer might occur in which actor A creates a tie with actor B in network X because actors A and B have a pre-existing relationship in a different network Y (Mehra, Marineau, Lopes, and Dass, 2009). By repeatedly playing a game, these patterns of interactions provide the foundation for future games or games in other contexts (Giddens, 1979; Klijn and Teisman, 1997). These patterns are rules for the establishment and operation of coalition. By creating expectations of behavior for each other, actors lower the costs of generating and maintaining coalitions.

Networked relations also may provide a basis for establishing trust in coalition partners by reducing the opportunistic costs noted above. Trust-based relations are one way[1] through which coalition partners can make credible commitments to share resources and adjudicate disputes amicably within a coalition (Levi and Murphy, 2006). Trust enables interest groups to navigate a competitive and confused environment and reach a viable solution to problems of acting jointly. In such unstable environments, repeated interactions and durable ties of formal and/or informal relations provide the source of trust-based cooperation. Trust can derive from personal relations that provide knowledge of past actions and commitments. Agents of firms who trust one another, for instance, have less concern about selection of partners and have lower coordination costs (Gulati and Singh, 1998). When there is greater uncertainty, repeated interaction and a history of informal relationships further reduce barriers to cooperation (Gulati and Singh, 1998). Trust generated from repeated interactions builds credible commitment and reduces the hierarchical elements of joint ventures (Scholz, Berardo, and Kile, 2008). As noted in Chapter 2 of this volume, repeated interactions may come about in certain contexts. For example, Laumann and Knoke (1987) observe that stable coalitions exist when issues are both recurrent and oppositional, such as in labor policy. Prior relations appear to be important as Hojnacki (1997) notes that organizations are more likely to continue to work in coalitions with partners with whom they have had prior experience rather than with organizations with little experience.

My conversations with lobbyists working in retirement policy highlight some of the themes mentioned previously. Clearly common interests are an important condition for coalition activity: "We have similar goals. So we started to feel like that's a great group to ally ourselves with. And we will seek out other groups with common interest as well." But this sense of shared goals or interest is usually in flux or uncertain: "the ongoing relationship (is) that these are the same people who, you know, may be our adversary on this issue but they may be our allies on another issue." The result is that working relationships are not always smooth: "You may be allies of convenience because for whatever reason you are on the same page. But there is a little bit of distance and distrust sometimes."

Arguments to Be Tested

Prior or concurrent relations serve as a heuristic. Resources expended in prior periods in creating a coalition are not wasted or ignored, and prior decisions likely influence later decisions: Why recreate the wheel? Close-knit relationships are likely to make repeated coalition formation easier, particularly when the range of issues and interest levels vary even among groups that broadly share the same interests or ideologies. Actors will use methods that save resources, time, and effort in order to achieve desired ends. Relations from prior time periods and/or from other contexts therefore reproduce themselves in new time periods or contexts.

> The *influence* argument: an organization is more likely to participate in a coalition if that coalition has members with whom the organization shares existing ties to other coalitions.

On the other hand, network analyses suggest that collaboration is more likely for well-connected, centrally-positioned actors with extensive 'weak tie' relationships (Granovetter 1973) that span the structural holes between groups that otherwise do not communicate (Burt 1992, 2000). The key assumption here is that an increase in the density of ties within the policy community reduces, all else being equal, the costs of coalitional work. If an organization is more deeply embedded in a policy domain, joint activity seems more likely to form around that organization as sharing information and finding coalition partners would seem easier than if the organization was located on the periphery. Such centrally located entities could be entrepreneurs who are instrumental in coalition building, especially when actors have little or no basis for regarding each other as trustworthy. Entrepreneurs can be either brokers who offer incentives to join to two or more distinct, possibly unconnected and potentially mistrustful parties, or bridge builders who have preexisting linkages and trust relations with the parties they unite (McAdam et al., 2001; Tarrow, 2005).

For example, Heaney (2004) combines network brokerage positions, informal communication networks, and coalition participation in a study of the 2003 Medicare Modernization Act. Heaney found an integrated pattern of relationships in which coalitions and brokerage relations played a vital part. Groups that navigated informal communication networks, coalitions, and political parties obtained brokerage positions. The network position of an initial contributor combined with the overall network density can strongly influence the participation of others in the network (Gould, 1993). In addition, Carpenter et al., (2004) reanalyzing the Laumann and Knoke (1987) health policy data, find that brokerage relationships were key building blocks in the development of influence within the policy domain. Those organizations that are consistently embedded in a policy domain have superior network positions: They are more central, they broker ideas, they have more contacts, and they have more social capital. As a result of these processes, embedded and central organizations are focal points (Schelling, 1960) around which joint activities form.

> The *activity* argument: The greater the existing coalition ties of an organization, the higher the likelihood that it will join a new coalition.

In addition, well-known mechanisms of network change may encourage the growth of coalition-based ties over time. In the context of network development, the physics literature suggests a process of network change known as 'preferential attachment.' When choosing between two nodes, one with twice as many links as the other, the process of preferential attachment predicts that twice as many actors will link to the more connected node (Barabasi, 2003). In making decisions about joining a coalition, information about potential partners is crucial; however, if information is not available or is imperfect, an organization may be reassured if many others have joined that coalition. A coalition with many ties might become a focal point for other organizations because the number of ties serves to validate their reliability and legitimacy (Berardo and Scholz, 2010). Hojnacki (1997) asserts that coalitions are often formed and led by an enduring set of core organizations, which are typically the peak associations with a broad mandate to represent a sizable membership. In other words, coalitions that are popular because of their existing ties continue to attract new partners:

> The *popularity* argument: An organization is more likely to participate in a coalition as the number of other organizations participating in that coalition increases.

SUMMARY OF DATA AND METHODS

The Data

This section summarizes the data used in this chapter as well as the methods of analysis—a full discussion of data and methods is found in the Appendix of the volume. The data include all organizations that lobbied in the federal retirement policy domain over 1999–2004 using Lobbyist Disclosure Act (LDA) reports, which were described in Chapter 2 of the volume. This chapter provides a social network analysis of the development of lobbying coalitions using bipartite or two-mode networks, one mode consisting of lobbying organizations and the other mode being coalitions.

I gathered the coalition data from several sources: by researching various Web sites related to retirement policy, witness lists at congressional hearings, press releases produced by the coalitions themselves, qualitative information from my interviews with individual lobbyists, and going to organizational and coalition websites, including archived websites from the Internet Archives (www.archive.org). I was able to identify thirty-one coalitions that operated between 1999 and 2004, although not all coalitions operated continuously. The coalition data was converted into longitudinal network data such that when an organization indicates that it is a member of a coalition, a directional tie goes from the organization to the coalition. To illustrate, Figure 3.1 shows a map of these bipartite relations for the second half of 2004. Organizations are represented by the circles, and squares are

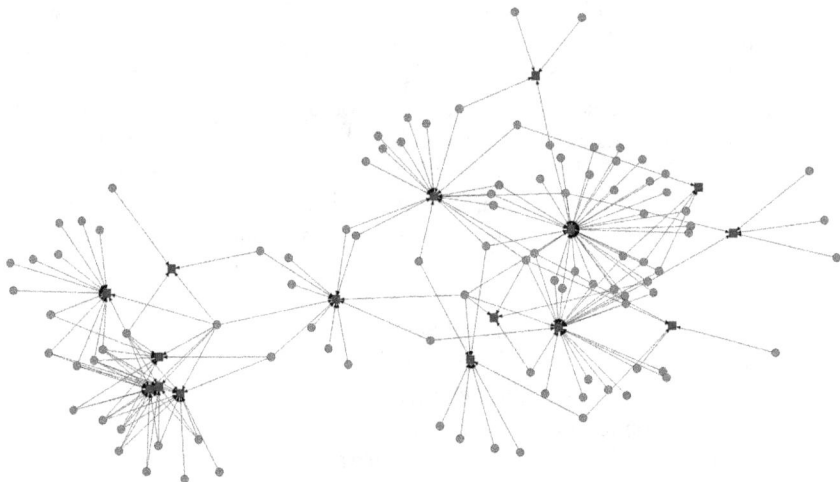

Figure 3.1 Network of lobbying organizations (circles) and retirement coalitions (squares), second half of 2004.

the coalitions. Figure 3.1 shows a pretty sparse network but one in which multiple organizations are connected via common coalition membership.

The analysis models changes to the network from one period to the next. The *outcome measure* is the set of lobbyist-coalition networks observed over time. Because working with large networks uses a lot of computational effort, a separate analysis is performed for each Congress: four networks each for the 106th (1999–2000), the 107th (2001–2002) and 108th (2003–2004) with each network representing a six-month time period.

Reflecting the influence, popularity, and activity arguments presented before, there are three main explanatory network effects. For the popularity argument, Figure 3.2a illustrates the network effect in terms of the number of a coalition's incoming ties.[2] The popularity effect is simply the number of lobbying organizations that are members of that coalition. As represented by the dotted line in Figure 3.2a, the effect predicts that an organization will select a coalition on the basis of its current popularity with other organizations.

The key network parameter for the influence argument is the 4-cycle effect. The 4-cycle effect looks at the effect of similar, prior choices made by any two organizations. If organization A belongs to coalitions X and Y and if organization B is belongs to X, the 4-cycle effect predicts that organization B will then join coalition Y because A and B both participate in X thereby creating a cycle of 4 paths. In Figure 3.2b the dotted line represents the predicted choice of the lobbying organization.

Similarly, the activity argument is represented by Figure 3.2c by the number of outgoing ties from an organization to coalitions. The activity predicts that the more outgoing ties an organization has, the more likely it is that the organization will add another outgoing tie to a new coalition.

As I have data on organizations and the issues on their lobbying agenda, I am also able to incorporate an effect for how, if at all, changes in the legislative issue network affect changes in the coalition network. Being connected to others through common issues likely influences the choice of coalitions. The legislative issue networks are also bipartite or two-mode networks, one

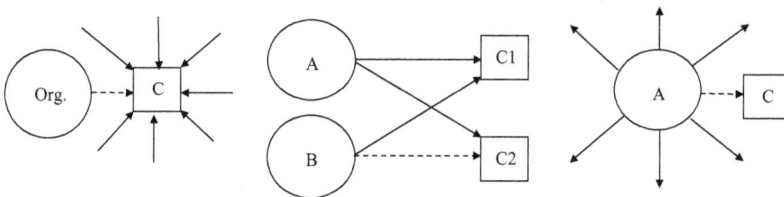

Figure 3.2 Structural effects for lobbyist-coalition ties, from left to right: (a) bandwagon (indegree); (b) influence (4-cycle); (c) activity (outdegree).

Note: Dotted lines indicate the predicated tie from organization to the coalition.

mode consisting of lobbying organizations and the other mode being legislative bills. When an organization indicates that it is lobbying on a particular bill, a directional tie goes from the organization to the bill. The legislative network effect examines whether increased legislative activity, that is, organizations listing legislation on their agendas, is connected to increased coalition activity.

Other explanatory effects include organizational attributes. Agenda choices may be associated with organizational attributes such as time and resources. I controlled for the organization's total time (in six-month reporting periods) spent on retirement policy over 1998–2004. I also controlled for the amount of an organization's lobbying expenses as a proxy for resources. The lobbying expense data come from the lobbying reports where an organization lists the total amount of lobbying expenses, which I divided by the number of policy domains listed on the LDA report to get an average amount spent on retirement policy.

Methods of Analysis

The analysis provides some descriptive information about the lobbying organizations and their coalitions. As in Chapter 2 of this volume, I use QAP analysis to see if coalition networks are fairly similar to each other from one time period to the next, and I also compare long-term organizations to other organizations.

To test these different arguments posed earlier in this chapter, I use longitudinal network modeling. As noted previously, policy domains are dynamic in nature with organizations entering and leaving in every period and new legislation being introduced continuously. During this flux, lobbyist-coalition relationships form, deepen, and dissolve with implications for the overall structure of relations (Heaney and Rojas, 2008; Powell, White, Koput, and Owen-Smith, 2005). "Choices made early on may strongly affect subsequent opportunities, but path dependence can be offset by a constant flow of new arrivals and departures" (Powell et al., 2005: 1136). Thus, the structure of interest group-coalition network changes over time.

To model changes in the organizational-coalition network, I used the stochastic actor-oriented model that represents network dynamics on the basis of observed panel network data and evaluates that data through statistical inference (Snijders, van de Bunt, and Steglich, 2010).[3] The Appendix of this volume provides a more detailed description of this method, and I summarize the main features here. In this model, each actor in the network evaluates the costs and rewards for that actor to be in a specific state (e.g., joining, leaving, never joining, or staying in a coalition) at one moment in time given the network structure, the changes made by other actors, and random influences. The model assumes that the actor is able to determine the immediate effects of currently contemplated actions. Therefore, each decision about an actor's network ties is associated with a change in utility.

When the expected change in its utility is approximately the same for all actions, the actor's choice will be more or less entirely determined by pure chance. However, if compared to other actions one action is associated with a relatively large increase in expected utility, the probability of choosing this specific action is also relatively large.

I estimated the different network effects on the probability of network change controlling for organizational and legislation-related effects. As noted previously, organizations move in and out of the policy domain and change coalition ties, and legislators introduce legislation throughout a Congress. The dynamic model can control for fluctuations in coalitions, organizations, and bills that are not available or that do not exist at a particular observation point. In this way, I can distinguish between coalitions that exist but not chosen from coalitions that do not exist and thus cannot be chosen.

RESULTS

Descriptive and Correlation Results

Figure 3.1 shows the coalition network during the second half of 2004. This figure only shows the groups that are part of the coalition network, but many organizations do not join coalitions. Figure 3.3 provides a den-

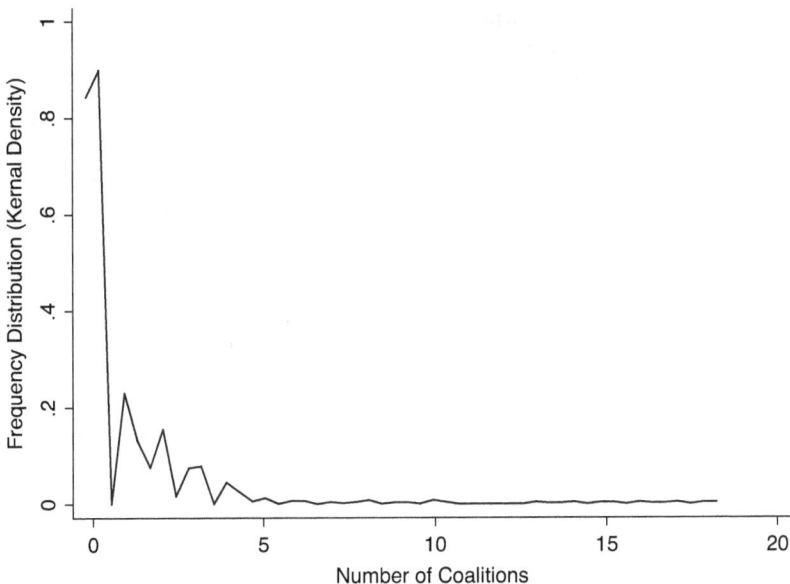

Figure 3.3   Density distribution of coalition participation for 1999–2004 (n = 392).

sity plot of the distribution of coalitions per organization cumulatively from 1999 to 2004. The figure presents a fat tail distribution with many organizations on one end not joining any coalition to a very small number of organizations on the other end joining multiple coalitions. The shape of the distribution is supportive of an activity process in which lobbying organizations that are active participants in coalitions remain active over time.

How much change occurs in the networks of coalitions over time? Coalitions should be reproduced over time such that there should be positive and statistically significant correlations between any two coalition networks. Tables 3.1 and 3.2 provide results of the QAP correlations for coalition participation. As with Table 2.4 in Chapter 2 of this volume, Table 3.1 should be read as the correlations for each network listed in the column label and each successive network reading down (all correlations are statistically significant). Looking at the first column of results, for example, the correlation between the network in the first half of 1998 (denoted as 'm98') with the second half of 1998 ('e98') is 0.740. Moving down the column, the next correlation is between m98 and the first half of 1999 ('m99'), which is 0.667. Turning our attention to patterns, one can see that in each column of Table 3.1, the correlations generally decline the farther in time one gets from the initial time period.[4]

As we saw with the issue networks in Chapter 2 of this volume, the correlations are very high when within the same Congress (the shaded area) relative to networks in different Congresses (the unshaded area). In general, the shaded results are higher than correlations between networks across sessions of Congress. Thus, the network of interest affiliations tends to replicate itself over time, and the correlations evidence stability in the relationships involving joint activity.

Does being a long-term actor in the policy domain make a difference in the stability of a coalition? Table 3.2 summarizes and compares the coalition network correlations for long-organizations versus all other organizations active on retirement policy. In all categories, long-term organizations had higher correlations. Across all time periods, the correlation of agenda overlap for long-term organizations was 0.752 as compared to 0.521 for all others. Within each two-year congressional session, longer-serving organizations' agenda overlap correlation was 0.843 versus 0.689. And from the end of one congressional session through the start of a new Congress, the correlation for long-term organizations was 0.888 as against 0.732 for all other organizations. In summary, coalitions tend to be durable over time, and coalition relationships among long-term organizations seem to drive this stability.

Table 3.1 QAP Correlations between Coalition Network Structures Using QAP Analysis, 1998–2004

	m98	e98	m99	e99	m00	e00	m01	e01	m02	e02	m03	e03	m04
e98	0.740												
m99	0.667	**0.942**											
e99	0.595	0.840	0.876										
m00	0.491	0.694	0.737	0.788									
e00	0.454	0.641	0.681	0.801	0.922								
m01	0.361	0.497	0.525	0.595	0.693	**0.696**							
e01	0.382	0.328	0.371	0.458	0.654	0.646	0.547						
m02	0.313	0.520	0.552	0.574	0.664	0.693	0.552	0.552					
e02	0.432	0.716	0.759	0.686	0.818	0.766	0.641	0.619	0.748				
m03	0.296	0.546	0.583	0.540	0.612	0.583	0.471	0.460	0.619	0.785			
e03	0.312	0.575	0.614	0.576	0.640	0.619	0.498	0.458	0.644	0.825	0.784		
m04	0.300	0.550	0.587	0.605	0.648	0.660	0.512	0.480	0.665	0.796	0.774	0.939	
e04	0.256	0.475	0.507	0.506	0.565	0.559	0.441	0.407	0.594	0.694	0.715	0.862	0.867

Source: Author's compilation of lobbyist registration reports.

Note: Each time period represents a six-month period corresponding to lobbyist reporting periods. An 'm' indicates a mid-year filing period while an 'e' represents an end-of-year filing period. For example, 'm98' is the period January through June of 1998 while 'e98' is the period July through December of 1998. Shaded areas indicate correlations of networks that occur in the same session of Congress. **Bolded** numbers indicate correlations of networks that occur between the end of one Congress and the start of a new Congress.

Table 3.2   Average QAP Correlations for Coalition Networks by Long-Term Organizations and All Other Organizations

	Long-Term Organizations	All Other Organizations
All Time Periods	0.752	0.521
Within Congress	0.843	0.689
Immediate Inter-Congress	0.888	0.732

Source: Author's compilation of coalition data from various sources.

Note: Long-term organizations are those lobbying organizations that lobby on retirement policy more than five years out of the total seven years for this study (1998–2004). There are a total of seventy-two long-term organizations.

Longitudinal Analysis

But coalitions do change over time. What drives this change? The longitudinal analysis presented in this chapter tests the main arguments posed earlier, namely the influence, popularity, and activity arguments. Table 3.3 provides a description of changes that occur from one time period to the next in terms of adding, dropping, keeping, and never having a tie to a coalition. Table 3.3 shows that many organizations do not join coalitions. Some informants mentioned previously in Chapter 2 of this volume that despite the flow of organizations through the policy domain, there is a core of organizations that do the heavy lifting. And whereas the table confirms the network correlations discussed above in terms of organizations keeping ties from one period to another, one can see a fair amount of adding and dropping ties over time.

Table 3.4 provides the results of the longitudinal modeling of the lobbyist-coalition networks. The table provides information about the following effects: the rate of coalition change, the coalition effects, organizational effects, and effects of changes in the legislation network including the rate of changes in the legislation network. Table 3.4 provides one set of results for the 106th Congress and two different sets of results each for the 107th and 108th Congress.

106th Congress

The first set of results is for the 106th Congress, which was in session from 1999 through 2000. The first three rows of results are the rate parameters that provide the estimated changes per organization from one period to the next, and these indicate an average rate of less than one tie change between the observation points.[5] The next row of results is the outdegree (density) parameter that is required in any model and serves as a control for the network density (Ripley et al., 2012). The fact that the coefficient is negative (–3.660) indicates that joining a coalition (as represented by a tie going 'out'

Table 3.3 Tie Changes in the Organization-Coalition Network between Observations, 1999–2004 (0 for no tie, 1 for a tie)

106th Congress	0 → 0	0 → 1	1 → 0	1 → 1	Distance	Jaccard
1st half of 1999 → 2nd half of 1999	1481	8	3	28	11	0.718
2nd half of 1999 → 1st half of 2000	1463	21	8	28	29	0.491
1st half of 2000 → 2nd half of 2000	1457	14	6	43	20	0.683
107th Congress						
1st half of 2001 → 2nd half of 2001	3442	42	29	57	71	0.445
2nd half of 2001 → 1st half of 2002	3428	43	25	74	68	0.521
1st half of 2002 → 2nd half of 2002	3449	4	43	74	47	0.612
108th Congress						
1st half of 2003 → 2nd half of 2003	6975	39	33	116	72	0.617
2nd half of 2003 → 1st half of 2004	6972	36	14	141	50	0.738
1st half of 2004 → 2nd half of 2004	6945	41	32	145	73	0.665

from an organization to a coalition) is costly such that organizations will join only if there are benefits to doing so. A density coefficient of –3.660 translates into a baseline conditional probability of choosing a legislative bill on which to lobby of 0.025 (equal to $1/(1 + e^{-(-3.660)})$). The remainder of the parameters test whether our arguments as conceptualized by the different network effects provide these benefits.

The significant effects are time and being a trade association. The coefficient for time is 0.214, which when added to the baseline density effect increases the probability of joining a coalition from 2.5 percent to 3.1 percent (equal to $1/(1 + e^{-(-3.660 + 0.214)})$). Not a very big change by itself! But the average amount of time (in six-month increments) spent by an organization in retirement policy is 8 periods. When we calculate the effect of time for the average organization, the likelihood of joining a coalition increases from 3.1 percent to 14 percent. The most dramatic effect is for trade associations, which have a coefficient of 4.073. This means that being an association increases the likelihood of joining a coalition to 60 percent.

Table 3.4 Dynamic Model of Changes in Ties to Coalitions, by Congress (1999–2004)

	106th		107th A		107th B		108th A		108th B	
	coeff.	SE	coeff.	SE	coeff.	SE	coeff.	SE	coeff.	SE
Coalition rate (periods 1 to 2)	0.212	(0.072)	1.024	(0.151)	0.880	(0.125)	0.638	(0.086)	0.623	(0.085)
Coalition rate (periods 2 to 3)	0.625	(0.150)	0.824	(0.151)	0.789	(0.134)	0.419	(0.066)	0.417	(0.062)
Coalition rate (periods 3 to 4)	0.377	(0.093)	0.791	(0.121)	0.800	(0.140)	0.662	(0.086)	0.649	(0.089)
Coalition network density	-3.660**	(0.689)	-6.355**	(0.863)	-8.624**	(1.260)	-4.464**	(0.294)	-4.547**	(0.275)
Time dummy 2			-1.546*	(0.735)	-0.013	(0.306)				
Time dummy 3			-4.936*	(2.172)	-2.484**	(0.526)				
Coalition 4-cycle (influence) effect	0.461	(0.231)	0.243**	(0.070)			0.162**	(0.030)		
Coalition indegree (popularity) effect	-0.027	(0.171)	0.505*	(0.209)	1.092**	(0.376)	0.060*	(0.029)	0.029	(0.029)
Time dummy 2			0.537*	(0.205)						
Time dummy 3			0.785	(0.579)						
Coalition outdegree (activity) effect	-0.554	(0.689)	0.305	(0.410)	3.004**	(1.017)	-0.219	(0.149)	-0.296	(0.155)
Coalition out-/indegree assortativity	0.241	(0.756)			-0.618	(0.326)	0.200	(0.152)	0.338	(0.154)
Time	0.214**	(0.068)					0.050	(0.038)	0.013	(0.039)
Association	4.073**	(1.072)	2.347**	(0.526)			2.233**	(0.387)		

	(1)	(2)	(3)	(4)	(5)
Private employer	1.901 (1.056)	0.456 (0.387)		0.961* (0.345)	
Time dummy 2		2.314** (0.721)			
Financial services	2.069 (1.039)				
Lobbying expenses (logged)				0.001* (0.000)	0.001* (0.000)
Labor				−0.590 (0.388)	
Association x 4–cycles			0.531** (0.136)		0.242* (0.116)
Private employer x 4–cycles					0.295** (0.145)
Labor x 4–cycles					0.082 (0.057)
Bill rate (periods 1 to 2)	2.395 (0.204)	1.690 (0.170)	1.701 (0.183)	2.272 (0.143)	2.274 (0.148)
Bill rate (periods 2 to 3)	3.093 (0.241)	2.829 (0.239)	2.844 (0.232)	2.772 (0.163)	2.777 (0.164)
Bill rate (periods 3 to 4)	2.422 (0.172)	2.844 (0.185)	2.841 (0.199)	5.052 (0.262)	5.050 (0.272)
Bill network density	−2.599** (0.059)	−3.021** (0.666)	−3.050** (0.440)	−2.413** (0.030)	−2.415** (0.031)
Time dummy 2	−0.410** (0.116)	1.950 (1.987)	2.029 (1.317)		
Time dummy 3	−0.198 (0.117)	1.796 (1.990)	1.881 (1.314)		
Bill outdegree on coalition activity	−0.099 (0.130)	−0.448 (1.097)	−0.504 (0.736)	0.252** (0.046)	0.249** (0.045)
Time dummy 2		2.922 (3.288)	3.119 (2.205)		
Time dummy 3		3.464 (3.288)	3.642 (2.218)		

Source: Author's compilation of lobbyist registration reports and other publicly available data. **$p < 0.01$; *$p < 0.05$.

However our arguments of activity, influence, and popularity find little support during this time period.

107th Congress

The results for the 107th Congress are split into two models, A and B, in order to capture some interactions in the B model. Under the column of results for model A, the coefficient for outdegree in model A is very large at −6.355, which means the baseline probability of joining a coalition is basically 0. When necessary, dummy variables for time change were added, and the time dummy variables for coalition network density were also negative.

Of the significant effects, the 4-cycle effect with a coefficient of 0.243, which is testing the influence argument, has a very small impact on the chances of joining a coalition.

The effect for coalition incoming ties, the popularity measure, has a larger effect: The baseline effect of a coalition having one incoming tie is 3.6 percent, but when we consider that the average number of ties for a coalition is 4.6, the likelihood of the average coalition adding a tie increases to 19 percent. In other words, the likelihood of an increase in ties to a coalition with the average number of members is 19 percent. Note that the coalition incoming time dummy for the 2001–2002 period has a similar effect.

Being an association has a large coefficient (2.347), but it only changes the likelihood from 0.2 percent to 1.8 percent. Interestingly, being an organization that represents private employers does not have a significant effect except for the time dummy for the period of the end of 2001 to the first half of 2002 (2.314). But this effect is small in terms of magnitude, moving the baseline probability from near 0 to 2 percent.

Model B for the 107th Congress is similar to model A in terms of the effect for coalition popularity: The baseline change (1.092) is small, and it remains small until the number of ties to a coalition passes 6. When ties reach 7 and higher, the probability is virtually 100 percent that another tie will be added to that coalition.

Unlike model A, model B shows a significant effect for organizational activity (3.004) but by itself is a miniscule change from the baseline. However, the effect of organizational activity on the likelihood of coalition participation increases by 6 percent when an organization has at least 2 ties to coalitions. Coalition activity begets more activity.

Finally, as to whether organizations influence each other in terms of overlapping ties to coalition, model B adds an interaction effect between being a trade association and the 4-cycle effect. Whereas this inter-association influence effect is significant, the effect is very small with a less than 1-percent increase.

108th Congress

The analysis for the 108th Congress is also split into two models, A and B. As in the other models, the coalition density effect is significantly and substantially negative for both models, indicating a baseline 1-percent probability of joining a coalition. In terms of significant effects, the 4-cycle effect in model A (0.218) invokes very little change—even at average number of 4 cycles (about 4), the likelihood only moves from 1 to 3 percent.

The popularity of a coalition (0.060) also has very little effect, with the probability of joining a coalition essentially unchanged at 1 percent. We don't really see the S-curve effect that we saw in the 107th Congress.

A few organizational variables were included in model A, and three showed significant effects on coalition participation. First, being an association increases the likelihood to 9 percent. Second, an organization that represents private sector employers increases the chance of coalition participation to 3 percent. Finally, lobbying expenses (logged) produce a 4.5-percent increase at the average level of expenditures.

A variable that is significant for the first time is the effect of legislative ties on coalition activity. Again, this effect is the link between the amount of legislation that an organization is lobbying on and joining a coalition. In the 108th Congress this is a significant effect (0.252), but it is modest by itself, raising the chance of joining a coalition from 1 to 1.3 percent. However, the average number of legislative ties per organization is 7.85, which increases probability of coalition participation to 7 percent for the average organization. As the number of issues increase for an organization, the likelihood of joining a coalition increases.

Model B for the 108th Congress is largely the same as A in terms of the outcomes: The coalition density effect is negative, and the coalition popularity and legislation activity effects are positive at roughly the same magnitudes as in A. But model B adds an interaction effect between trade association and 4-cycle. At the average number of 4-cycles per trade association, the probability adding a coalition increases to nearly 6 percent. Similarly, an interaction between the 4-cycle effect and private employer organizations increases the chance of coalition participation by 9 percent.

Finally, significant effects were again shown for the effect of legislative activity on coalition participation, and for the first time, there was a positive relationship between high activity organizations and popular coalitions (0.338). But in both cases, the effects are not strong.

In Summary

The longitudinal modeling provides some evidence for the importance of networked relations and coalition activity. The influence argument found support in the significance of the 4-cycle effect, but magnitude of this process was weak overall. A stronger case for influence occurred when the influence was between similar types of organizations; for example, association-to-association and between private employers. The popularity effect was stronger in the 107th Congress but was not a factor in other periods. The activity argument also found support in the 107th Congress but not elsewhere.

In addition, certain organizational attributes matter at least some of the time. Being a trade association boosts the likelihood of coalition participation, and this makes sense for a couple of reasons. Trade associations likely have the resources and staff to maintain and manage coalitions, they often have the prestige to front joint activity, and more often than not they tend to specialize in a policy domain (or have staff that specialize) and thus recognize issues in need of joint effort. In addition, organizations that tend to focus on more bills than other groups tend to be more active in coalitions.

CHAPTER SUMMARY

In this case study of coalitions in one policy domain over time, this chapter showed that coalition work exhibits certain patterns. Organizational participation is divided among those organizations that do a lot of joint work, others that do just a little, and the majority of organizations that do not join any coalitions. Perhaps for this reason, we also see that coalitions themselves are networks that are fairly stable over time, especially when long-term players in the policy domain are participating. This stability was reflected in the dynamic models of coalition change: It is costly to add coalition ties. Network-based arguments found some inconsistent support in these dynamic models, but clearly other reasons—some of which we cannot measure—come into play.

Much like prior and concurrent relationships, organizations with many coalition-based ties might have a reputation for coalition leadership or effectiveness that reduces uncertainty for new coalition members. This data did not contain information on coalition leaders or similar indicators such as membership in the steering committee or executive committee of a coalition. However, active players that usually have experience tend to drive coalition formation, which is suggestive of the importance of leadership and raises important questions for future research: Are network determinants indicative of coalition leadership? More central actors may indeed be leaders or coalition entrepreneurs, but central positioning may also indicate a passive monitoring role. From a network perspective, who manages the network that forms the basis for coalition generation or reproduction?

The next chapter moves to the issue of agenda development. This is the flip-side of this chapter, which looked in part at how legislative activity affected coalition activity. But Chapter 4 of this volume examines how lobbyists develop their agendas: In particular, how do networked relations affect the lobbying agenda of organizations, if at all?

NOTES

1. Levi and Murphy (2003) argue that a second way is through institutional arrangements and rules. For a coalition, even an event coalition, to survive, there must be institutional arrangements that ensure membership reliability through monitoring and enforcing compliance with the rules and norms of the coalition.
2. Social network analysis uses the term 'degree' for a tie, and in the case of directional relationships 'indegree' means ties coming into a node and 'outdegree' means outgoing ties.
3. I used RSiena version 4.0 (Ripley, Snijders and Preciado, 2012). A free copy of the latest version and documentation are available at http://www.stats.ox.ac.uk/~snijders/siena/.
4. All the correlations remain positive throughout and statistically significant in Table 3.1.
5. As Ripley, Snijders, and Preciado (2012: 92) note, the rate parameter "refers to unobserved changes, and that some opportunities for change lead to the decision 'no change,' and moreover some of these changes may cancel (make a new choice and then withdraw it again), so the average observed number of differences per actor will be smaller than this estimated number of unobserved changes."

4   Setting the Lobbying Agenda

> Power is always gradually stealing away from the many to the few, because the few are more vigilant and consistent.
>
> —Samuel Johnson

In 2001, President George W. Bush signed into law the massive tax reform bill with the ungainly title of "The Economic Growth and Tax Relief Reconciliation Act" or EGTRRA. EGTRRA was the key economic priority of the new Bush administration and included sizeable shifts in the income, capital gains, and estate tax policies. The law also made many significant changes to the rules for retirement plans, greatly expanding the ability of workers to save money in 401(k) plans and Individual Retirement Accounts. Many of the employer and financial groups active on retirement policy worked for these retirement law changes in collaboration with a small, bipartisan group of members of Congress. This was a persistent effort in developing the legislative proposals and attracting a number of interest groups who normally do not work on retirement issues to support the proposals as part of the broader tax bill. I spoke with a representative of an association that did a lot of work on retirement issues and whose membership included many powerful corporations and financial firms, companies like Microsoft and Fidelity Investments. The association had done a lot of work in developing the EGTRRA proposals, and I asked how long they had been pushing for these ideas. "Hmmm," she thoughtfully said, "we've been talking about this for a long time but our first white paper was produced in 1989." In astonishment, I said, "You're kidding; you've had these ideas out there for at least twelve years?" "Well," she said, "in our membership, it takes a while to reach agreement on issues, and then you have to get out there and work with other groups and the Hill."

This chapter of the volume, like the prior chapter on coalitions, examines a basic part of what lobbyists do: How do interest groups select the issues on which they lobby the Congress? Do relationships have an effect on how lobbyists pick issues to work on? Specifically, do the choices of one lobbying organization affect the choices of another organization? Any one policy area often has dozens or even hundreds of proposed bills and equally as many interest groups and stakeholders. A lobbyist may have difficulty selecting, or even knowing about, a particular piece of legislation she should lobby on.

In such a crowded and competitive environment, lobbyists may look to other lobbyists in their policy area when selecting issues for monitoring and lobbying as a way to lower their search costs. Politics is inherently social, and agenda setting is in part a social process in which interest group organizations influence each other in a complex and dynamic environment. In addition, when we view a policy domain as a network of actors who are choosing legislation, we see a skewed distribution: A handful of bills attract a great deal of interest whereas the vast majority of bills receive little attention. How does this pattern come about?

To address these questions, I use longitudinal data of interest group networks from retirement policy and their legislative choices, but I also look at interest groups working on Medicare and Medicaid issues for a contrasting view. To capture the social interdependence of the process, I study the evolution of a network consisting of organizations and legislative issues. I analyze these selections by using a stochastic actor-based dynamic model of network change that conditions changes in legislative choices on the choices of other organizations (Snijders, Van Bunt, and Steglich, 2010).

The discussion in this chapter begins with a review of prior work on lobbying and agenda setting, and I focus on possible social processes in the development of a lobbying agenda. Social processes suggest the importance of social capital, and I argue that interest groups provide information to each other to confirm the salience of one issue over another. Three processes are of particular interest. First, in the *bandwagon mechanism*, lobbyists will select bills to add to their agenda when they learn that other lobbyists are selecting that bill. Second, the *influence mechanism* suggests that a lobbyist will choose a bill that another lobbyist has chosen because they have other choices in common. Finally, there may be a *monitoring mechanism* in which certain groups may act as a clearinghouse for legislative issues.

I apply the dynamic network model to the retirement and Medicare policy areas over different congressional periods. The data and methods section discusses in detail the lobbying and legislative data sources as well as dynamic network model. In the analysis section, I provide quantitative evidence for these mechanisms in agenda development by looking at how the network of interest groups and bills changes over time. The actor-oriented dynamic model estimates the impact of different effects—including bandwagon and influence mechanisms—on observed changes in network ties. I conclude the chapter with a brief discussion on the implications of these results for understanding the development of policy agendas.

THE LOBBYING AGENDA

To be clear at the outset, I am talking about the lobbying agenda, which is distinct both from the agenda of members of Congress or other policy makers and from the public agenda or issues that are salient with the broad public (Baumgartner et al., 2009; Kimball, Baumgartner, Berry, Hojnacki, Leech, and Summary, 2012). Congressional agendas are those items that are up for a decision or vote whereas the public agenda includes those issues of most importance to the general public. The lobbying agenda, by contrast, are the issues that the lobbyist is following or pushing in their work. These different agendas are clearly connected to each other, but those connections are not the focus of this chapter. However, lobbying agendas both reflect intelligence about the congressional agenda ('what bills are moving') and signal the issues that lobbyists would like on or off the congressional agenda ('what bills I want to move or block').

Despite the plethora of studies on lobbying, there are few conclusions about the nature and processes of influence in this area (Baumgartner et al., 2009). Appropriately, much of the work on interest group influence uses a political or policy outcome such as roll call voting as the dependent variable, but such studies have not produced agreement on how interest group activities influence such outcomes (Smith, 1995). The next chapter's discussion on reputations for influence provides more background on these issues.

However, if legislators are influenced by interest groups at all, they are *least* likely to be influenced when votes are cast (Baumgartner and Leech, 1998). Instead, most scholars in both political science and political sociology "assume that agenda setting is the arena where advocacy organizations will have their greatest influence" as they use various methods to bring greater attention, raise awareness, and create urgency around their preferred issues (Andrews and Edwards, 2004: 492). As the lobbying agenda reflects lobbyists' preferences and opportunities, the study of the lobbying agenda's development contributes to the broader question of political influence.

According to Kingdon (1995: 5), an agenda is "the list of subjects or problems to which governmental officials, and people outside of government closely associated with those officials, are paying some serious attention at any given time." Agenda setting is a process in which certain public problems are identified, recognized, and defined, and specific solutions or alternatives are generated, considered, and attached to these problems. Due to the limited attention span and information-processing capacity of actors, the list of problems and solutions on any particular agenda is usually very short (Baumgartner and Jones, 1993; Kingdon, 1995). The critical issue, then, is in influencing the policy-making agenda, i.e., getting your issue on the decision-making agenda if it is not on it already. If certain issues are not even on the political agenda, groups interested in them have little chance to exert influence in the policy-making process. Moreover, groups will have little chance of defending their interests if they do not even know what is on the policy agenda. But we know little about the mechanisms for the hidden development of lobbying agendas.

At least twenty years ago, scholars noted the broad issue scope of interest groups as the number of groups rapidly expanded in Washington, D.C. (Heinz et al., 1993). As noted in Chapter 2 of this volume, most policy domains are comprised of a variety of issues and with varying complexity and coherence. We can think of policy space that runs on a continuum from a fragmented space with a diversity of interest groups seeking out their own issue niche to a space of coherence, dominated by a few interests who force attention to a more restricted set of issues (May, Sapotichne, and Workman, 2006). "The crowding of the issue space for a given policy area is not as important for policy coherence as is the degree to which attention is focused on a smaller set of issues" (May et al., 2006: 383; citing Baumgartner and Jones, 1993).

Heinz et al. (1993) noted that many interest groups face a great deal of uncertainty because of not just the number of groups but also the increasing number of proposals vying for attention, the difficulty in defining preferences, and the lack of a central set of mediators that could broker deals. Those authors concluded that many groups devoted substantial resources monitoring events and other interest groups. The uncertainty inherent in the policy-making process made groups dependent on information in order to reduce their uncertainty. In turn, groups may be reliant on certain sources of information that are perceived as highly credible such that their agenda choices are conditional on these sources. How, then, do lobbyists develop their lobbying agendas? I argue that the development of the lobbying agenda is a function of social processes.

Political activity is inherently social whether because of the need for alliances or because policy change can affect a wide range of interests (Baumgartner et al., 2009). The last chapter provided the example of the need for coalitions to help advance a group's views, and the discussion there connects to this idea of issue agenda development. Narrowly focused groups use their resources best by working alone as opposed to groups with a broad view that perhaps need the expertise or legitimacy from coalition partners to be effective (Hojnacki, 1997). This argument is consonant with Browne's (1990) issue niche and connects to the policy space discussion above because the assumption is that relatively few actors will be active in these niche areas. Holyoke (2009) focused on competition in the interest group environment, in which the set of policy preferences can lead to conflict or cooperation among participants.

But the study of the lobbyist's policy agenda requires a social orientation that goes beyond arm's length exchange in coalitions. As noted in Chapter 2 of this volume, Hugh Heclo (1978) made a key early contribution by noting the rise of issue networks, the critical characteristics of which are their fluidity of large numbers of actors who had varying levels of commitment to others and their social nature: "Network members reinforce each other's sense of issues as their interests, rather than (as standard political or economic models would have it) interests defining positions on issues" (Heclo, 1978: 102). Kingdon's (1995) policy entrepreneurs engaged in continuing interaction as they reviewed and shaped each other's proposed solutions: "Ideas are floated, bills introduced, speeches made; proposals are drafted, then *amended in response to reaction and floated again. Ideas confront each other (much as molecules bumped into one another) and combine with one another in various ways"* (117, emphasis added). Baumgartner and co-authors (2009) note a similar process:

> People inside and outside of government are constantly monitoring their peers to see which new studies are being received with credibility, which key actors are showing interest in which proposals, and which legislative vehicles may be taking shape. They want to be associated with initiatives that have a chance of passage, not to waste their time working on proposals (even ones they like) that are likely to go nowhere.
>
> (252)

The result of this process of monitoring others' positions and activities amidst uncertainty is that policy activity reflects a social cascade in which initial 'chaos' changes over time into an ordered state (Baumgartner et al., 2009), an outcome somewhat similar to the policy agenda coherence noted previously. Initially, lobbyists might have a wide variety of possible legislative proposals from which to choose, but over time and under certain conditions they focus on a much smaller set of initiatives.

But these studies do not provide an underlying process that explains the types of interactions that we see—let alone the lobbying agenda development. One possible process is similar to the theory of legislative subsidy as developed by Hall and Deardorff (2006). In this theory, a lobbyist is motivated to supply high quality information to a member of Congress not as an exchange but as a subsidy to the legislator's constrained time and cognitive budget. The legislator then uses these information subsidies to exploit the policy process in order to pursue legislative objectives that she shares with the lobbyist. We might apply this idea to the development of the lobbying agenda: In a complex environment characterized by differential knowledge, lobbyists with better information, more experience or deep expertise may provide information subsidies to other lobbyists in the policy domain as part of their agenda development.

This subsidy or information sharing idea suggests a social capital perspective in which connected lobbyists accumulate resources that are specific to their relationships (Coleman, 1988). As social capital inheres in relations and is not possessed by individuals, it enables the willingness both to give and to receive information that is not otherwise available. For social capital to work, trust or reciprocity must be present (Glanville and Bienenstock, 2009), a topic I will address in Chapter 6 of this volume.

To be sure, organizational resources or policy preferences matter. "Groups that seek influence must have the kind of costly resources that enable them to know, to attain, to frame, and to deliver the sort of political and policy information (and interpretations) that are relevant to the goals of those legislators who have the power to make decisions that affect policy" (Leyden and

Borelli, 1994: 443). However, resources can include social relations within the policy domain because such relations lower search costs and enhance credibility and influence (Uzzi, 1997).

As noted in the prior chapter, relationships and networks matter for politics and policy making in a number of ways, and the number of network-based political and policy studies is growing (Heaney and McClurg, 2009; Robbins, 2010). Network analysis may be particularly relevant in addressing interactions between interest groups. "Networks reflect the patterns and histories of interaction among actors, thus suggesting their degree of familiarity with one another's habits and preferences, reliability, and character. Thus, the strength or weakness of ties in networks, as well as the patterns in which they are arranged, may make all the difference in overcoming barriers to collaborative activity" (Heaney and McClurg, 2009: 729–30, citing Gould, 1993). The next section discusses specific networked-oriented mechanisms of lobbyist agenda development.

Bandwagon, Influence, and Monitoring Mechanisms

Dür (2008) distinguishes three broad approaches to measuring interest group influence: process-tracing, assessing attributed influence, and gauging the degree of preference attainment. With regard to preference attainment, "the outcomes of political processes are compared with the ideal points of actors ... the idea is that the distance between an outcome and the ideal point of an actor reflects the influence of this actor" (Dür, 2008: 566). For example, Mahoney (2007) ascertained the preferences of a sample of advocates over a sample of issues and assessed whether or not an outcome associated with each issue reflected the preferences of advocate sample.

Applying preference attainment to this study, I extend prior work on agenda choices (Scott, 2013) and look at whether organizations change their agenda choices in response to the choices of other actors as well as incorporating monitoring. Of course, agreement on what are the important issues is not the same as developing coordinated actions around those issues. Opponents can influence each other as to what is important even if they disagree on the merits, and groups on the same side of an issue influence each other even when they have different levels of interest or different ideas about tactics. I use the three processes from Chapter 3 of this volume—influence, bandwagon, and activity—but adapt them to the lobbying agenda context.

Bandwagons

Baumgartner and Leech (2001) found the skewed distribution of issues listed in lobbyist disclosure reports: a small handful of issues were listed by a large number of lobbyists, what they termed a 'bandwagon' effect, while most issues received very little attention and were 'niche' issues. But these results were largely descriptive in nature.

An issue that attracts interest or activity might become a focal point because such interest or activity signals the issue's importance and legitimacy (Berardo and Scholz, 2010). "The social nature of lobbying, with its sensitivity to context, can therefore be characterized by mimicry, cue-taking, and bandwagon effects" (Baumgartner and Leech, 1998: 140). An organization new to a policy domain may know the basics of an issue and where it stands on the issue, but it may not know about the merits and/or likelihood of a specific legislative proposal. Choices by other organizations may send signals about such legislative proposals. There even may be an underlying process of deference as new organizations look to organizations with more expertise or experience in the policy domain (Baumgartner et al., 2009). For example, some studies have shown that organizations that are more central in an information network or a resource network will have greater influence in their policy domain (Knoke et al., 1996).

Network scholars outside of the policy and political science disciplines have theorized as to the development of highly skewed distributions within networks, distributions that resemble skewed lobbyist-issue distribution noted by Baumgartner and Leech (2001). Such scale-free or power law distributions arise from two key forces: network growth and preferential attachment (Barabási, 2003). As new actors join a network, they do not randomly attach themselves to incumbent actors but are more likely to attach themselves to those incumbent actors that have the most ties with other actors. In other words, if a new actor has a choice between actors A and B, and A has twice as many ties as B, the new actor is much more likely to choose A over B. These conditions should hold in a policy domain with fluid participation by lobbyists and newly proposed legislation introduced over time. In other words, *an organization is more likely to lobby on a piece of legislation as the number of other organizations lobbying on that legislation increases.*

Influence

As noted previously, policy domains are social in nature in that organizations look to each other when orienting themselves to common issues. Homophily, a process of attachments based on social similarity (MacPherson and Smith-Lovin, 1987), might also affect agenda choices. But unlike other homophily studies that use similarity in terms of individual attributes, I use similarity in terms of choices. Again, two organizations on different sides of an issue may nonetheless agree on which bills are important. Organizations that have the same issues in common may make the same choices in the future. If a lobbying organization has a number of common issues with another actor, their ongoing relationship is likely to be stronger. As one of my informants put it,

> You tend to have a sense of how much a particular individual lobbyist's issue agenda for the company or their trade overlaps with your own just

by, because it's not that big of a community. You tend to have a sense of where there's a lot of commonality of agenda. And where there's a lot of commonality of agenda, you tend to feel more comfortable; where there's not as much commonality of agenda, you tend to feel less comfortable.

That is, *an organization is more likely to choose a piece of legislation that another organization chooses as the number of their joint choices on other legislation increases.*

Activity as Monitoring

Monitoring is the opposite of the bandwagon mechanism. Monitors collect information about what is going on in the policy environment either for their own internal consumption or to position themselves as a source or broker of information to others who are not able to collect information on a broad scale. Policy monitoring is a fairly common activity of lobbyists and interest groups, particularly by defenders of the status quo in a policy domain or even by those groups that are not trying to influence policy but just conform their behavior to changes in policy (Baumgartner et al., 2009; Salisbury, 1992). Monitoring may be a social process, at least not like the bandwagon and influence mechanisms, but it may be social in its effects if monitors share their information with others. *The monitoring argument states that legislative agenda choices are driven by monitors; that is, the more choices that a lobbying organization has made in the past, the more likely it is that it will make an additional choice in the future.*

This chapter tests these arguments by looking at longitudinal data of lobbying organizations and their legislative agendas regarding retirement and Medicare & Medicaid issues using a dynamic model of network change. The retirement policy area is the case study for this book, but the Medicare policy area presents a nice contrast for this chapter. For both policy areas, this analysis uses the organization as the unit of analysis. This is an appropriate level of analysis as the policy domain is a subsystem whose organizational members are identified by a criterion of common orientation (Laumann and Knoke, 1987). The following section provides background on policy areas and the time periods under study.

SUMMARY OF DATA AND METHODS

Data Sources

For both retirement and Medicare policy areas, the data sources are the LDA reports discussed in Chapter 3 of this volume, and the types of networks are the same for both policy areas.

Lobbyist-Bill Bipartite Networks

The focus in this chapter is on networks of lobbying agendas. The networks are bipartite or two-mode networks, one mode consisting of lobbying organizations and the other mode being legislative bills. When an organization indicates that it is lobbying on a particular bill, a directional tie goes from the organization to the bill. Figure 4.1 illustrates these bipartite relations in retirement policy for the second half of 2000 with blue squares representing bills and red circles representing lobbying organizations, and a line going from an organization to a bill indicates that the organization listed that bill on its LDA report.

The *outcome measure* is the set of changes in the lobbyist-bill bipartite networks observed over time. The analysis is broken into three parts for retirement policy: I use four networks for the four six-month time periods within each Congress (106th: 1999–2000; 107th: 2001–2002; 108th: 2003–2004). In the 106th Congress there were 190 lobbying organizations and 311 legislative bills, the 107th Congress consisted of 238 organizations and 285 legislative bills, and the 108th Congress had 247 organizations and 297 legislative bills. For the Medicare area, the analysis covers three-month time periods as the LDA reports became a quarterly requirement by 2009. The Medicare data consist of the first three quarters of 2009 with 1,149 organizational entries and 434 legislative bills.

The dependent network measure only includes the specific legislation (e.g., 'H.R. 3028') listed on the LDA report but not general descriptions of issues (e.g., 'savings'). This focus on specific legislation raises a couple of issues. Data from the LDA reports are self-reported and raises the issue of whether specific legislation is accurately reported. I collected all listings of

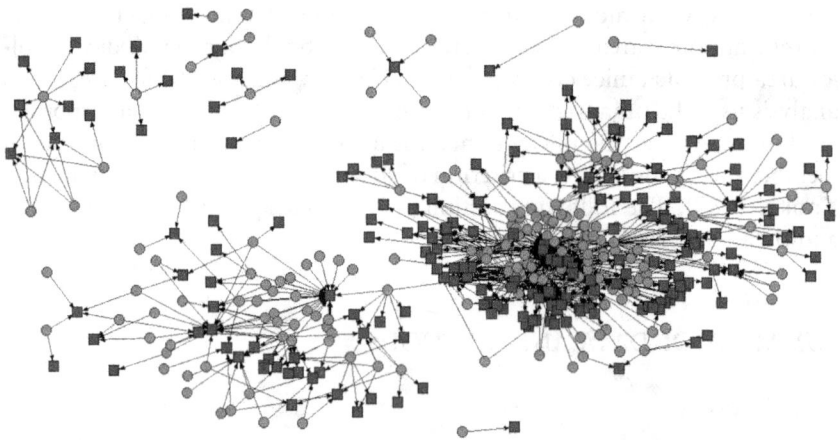

Figure 4.1   Bipartite network of lobbyist-bill ties in the retirement policy, second half of 2000 (main component only; circles are lobbyists and squares are bills).

issues no matter how vague or specific and inputted them into the dataset. In the retirement policy area, about 80 percent of the LDA reports listed identifiable legislation.[1] Interestingly, the percentage of specific bill mentions to all issues showed a gradual increase within each Congress. For example, at the start of the 107th Congress, 69 percent of issues were identifiable pieces of legislation and by the end the percentage rose to 81 percent. This makes sense because the choices for listing legislation in the LDA reports is more limited at the beginning of a Congress than at the end because legislation is introduced over time.

Even if it were possible to use both identifiable bills and non-bill issue descriptions, I was interested in seeing how concrete agendas developed over time. Specific legislation seemed a better indicator of actionable agenda formation than descriptions of non-bill issues. This is not to say that a reference that does not identify a specific bill is vague as some descriptions are very specific. However, even within fairly narrow sub-issues there are different approaches that are possible, and these approaches are captured by concrete legislation. Therefore, I focus on identifiable bills.

Explanatory Network Effects

As in Chapter 3 of this volume, the main explanatory network effects that test the bandwagon and influence hypotheses are illustrated in Figures 4.2a, 4.2b, and 4.2c. The key network parameter for the bandwagon hypothesis is the popularity (indegrees)[2] effect of a bill. The popularity or indegree effect is simply the number of lobbying organizations that selected a particular bill. If a bill has a lot of ties coming in from lobbying organizations, its popularity or indegree measure will be high, and the effect predicts that an organization will select a bill on the basis of its current popularity with other organizations. Figure 4.2a illustrates this effect with the dotted line representing the predicted choice of the lobbying organization.

The key network parameter for the influence hypothesis is the 4-cycle effect. The 4-cycle effect looks at the effect of similar choices made by any two organizations. If organization A is lobbying on bills X and Y and if

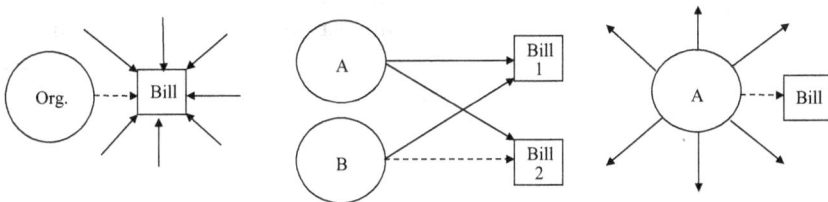

Figure 4.2 Structural effects for lobbyist-bill ties, from left to right: (a) bandwagon (indegree); (b) influence (4-cycle); (c) monitoring (outdegree activity).

Note: Dotted lines indicate the predicated tie from organization to bill.

organization B is lobbying on X, the 4-cycle effect predicts that organization B will then select bill Y for lobbying because A and B have both selected X. Figure 4.2b illustrates this effect with the dotted line representing the predicted choice of the lobbying organization.

The final network effect of interest is the outdegree activity effect, which represents the monitoring mechanism. The predicted activity of a lobbying organization A is a function of the squared outgoing ties to legislation or outdegrees of that organization. The more outgoing ties, the more likely that organization will select additional legislation, as shown by the dotted line in Figure 4.2c.

I also incorporate an effect for how, if at all, changes in the coalition network affect changes in the legislative bill network. As discussed previously, alliances and coalitions are visible social processes within policy domains, and being connected to others in a coalition likely influences lobbying agendas. Chapter 3 and the Appendix of this volume provide more information on the collection of the coalition data. I converted the coalition data into longitudinal network data in which the lobbying organizations are tied to each other if they share one or more coalitions in common.[3] The coalition data allowed me to include a coalition activity effect, which is the effect of the number of an actor's coalition ties on that actor adding a tie to legislation in the legislative network.

Explanatory Organizational Effects

Agenda choices may be associated with organizational attributes such as time and resources. I controlled for the organization's total time spent on retirement policy over 1998–2004 or on Medicare policy over 1999–2011. I use these extended time periods for the time variable in order to assess the effects of long-term actors on policy. Organizations spent about 3.5–4 years on average on retirement policy out of maximum of seven years, but as discussed in Chapter 2 of this volume, the standard deviations shown in Table 2.1 for both periods indicate a sizeable minority (about 20 percent) of organizations are consistent long-term players in retirement policy. For retirement policy, I also controlled for the size of an organization's lobbying staff as a proxy for resources, and for Medicare I was able to control for type of organization: device manufacturers, health professional groups, hospitals, insurers, pharmaceutical firms, public interest groups, and other groups. A quarter of the pairs are self-represented client organizations. Other organizational variables were considered, such as interests, but these variables were dropped during the model selection process, as I am about to discuss.

Explanatory Legislative Variables

Not all proposed legislation was created equal, and scholars have made a point of distinguishing among legislation (e.g., Mayhew, 1991). Legislation associated with a powerful sponsor or that have many cosponsors may attract interest group attention. In addition, lobbyists often speculate on which bills move through Congress as relatively few might make it out of committee. Therefore, for legislative bills I control for the (a) number of cosponsors for that bill, (b) whether the bill sponsor is the member of the committee of jurisdiction for that bill, and (c) the bill's ultimate progress in terms of an ordinal scale ranging from 1 (not reported out of committee), 2 (reported out of committee), 3 (approved by one chamber), 4 (reported out of committee in the second chamber), 5 (approved by the second chamber), to 6 (passed into law). Cosponsorship and bill progress are skewed as few bills have lots of sponsors or are enacted into law. About half of the bills in both Congresses are sponsored by members of committees of jurisdiction.

Table 2.1 in Chapter 2 of this volume provides descriptive statistics for the retirement policy area (descriptive statistics for Medicare policy are provided in the Appendix).

Longitudinal Network Modeling

To model changes in the organizational-legislative bill network, I again use the stochastic actor-oriented model that represents network dynamics on the basis of observed panel network data and evaluates that data through statistical inference (Snijders, van de Bunt, and Steglich, 2010).[4] I summarized the method in Chapter 3 of this volume and more detail is provided in the Appendix. As noted previously, the dynamic model can distinguish between bills that have been introduced but not chosen from bills that have not yet been introduced.

In general, the model simulates what happens between observations using the random utility model. The organizational actions that make the network develop are the core of the simulation procedure. The SIENA software program estimates the model based on a maximum likelihood estimator using the method of moments, implemented as a continuous-time Markov Chain Monte Carlo simulation. The model (a) calculates likely starting values for the parameters, (b) simulates the choice process according to the starting values, (c) compares the resultant simulated network with the observed networks, and (d) adjusts values to reduce differences between the observed and the simulated data. The model then uses a number of simulations to determine the frequency distribution of predictions, which then are used to calculate standard errors for the final parameter values.

I also tested the model for time heterogeneity. The basic model assumes that the effects on network changes do not vary over time, which is not the case with lobbying networks. When time heterogeneity is indicated, time dummy variables can be added to control for variance over time (Lospinoso, Schweinberger, Snijders, and Ripley, 2011).

RESULTS AND DISCUSSION

Descriptive Results

The retirement policy lobbyist-legislative bill network has a particular pattern. The average bill has about four or five ties from lobbyists, but the core-periphery structure shown in Figure 4.1 suggests that a skewed distribution of ties for both lobbying organizations and firms. Figure 4.3 shows the smoothed kernel density distribution of ties for lobbying organizations over each 6-month time period of this study. The distributions all show a 'fat-tail' such that a small number of organizations have a lot of ties. Most organizations focus on a small subset of bills, but a small group of lobbyists are actively pursuing and/or monitoring a larger set of bills. Shown in the figure by the changes in the line is that fact that many organizations initially do not make a selection as many bills have not been introduced, but over time new selections are made, also as shown in Table 4.2 (the discussion of which follows). Yet, the skewed pattern of legislative choices shown in Figure 4.3 persists.

In terms of the 4-cycle pattern, there are, on average, about eighty such relationships per organization over the whole 106th Congress, sixty-nine for the 107th Congress, and about forty-four per organization for the 108th.

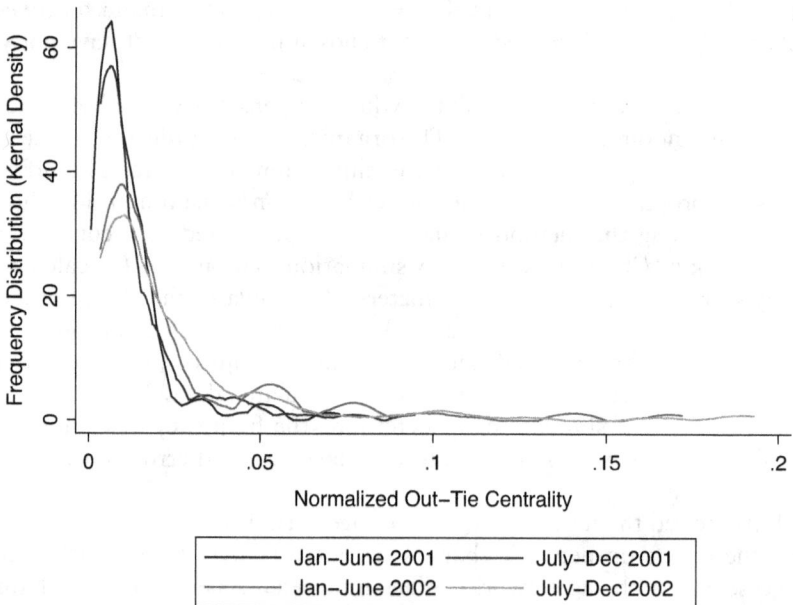

Figure 4.3   Distribution of ties for lobbying organizations (outgoing) and legislation (incoming), 1999–2000 and 2001–2002.

The presence of these 4-cycle relationships is driven by a small number of organizations and bills that are garnering the lion's share of the network ties.

In sum, we see a distinct pattern of relationships between lobbyists and bills, but what causes this pattern? The analysis provides the results of the quantitative modeling for bandwagon and influence mechanisms that likely generate the skewed pattern of ties between bills and lobbyists.

Dynamic Modeling of Lobbyist-Bill Networks

Table 4.1 describes the changes in the lobbyist-bill network over the observed time periods by Congress. Looking at the first column of results, No Bill $(0 \rightarrow 0)$, the vast majority of observations consist of non-ties, that is, a lobbying organization has not chosen a bill. The second column, labeled New Bill $(0 \rightarrow 1)$, indicates newly created ties when an organization adds a bill to its agenda. The third column, Drop Bill $(1 \rightarrow 0)$, gives the number of times an organization drops a bill from its agenda. The fourth column, Keep Bill $(1 \rightarrow 1)$, indicates when an organization keeps lobbying on a bill from one time period to the next. In summary, lobbying organizations' choices changed quite a bit. For example, between the first and second halves of 2003, 297 new ties to legislation were created while 127 ties were dropped by lobbying organizations and 333 legislative ties were maintained. Note that the number of unchanged legislative choices generally increased over time in each Congress.[5]

Table 4.2 provides the results of the longitudinal modeling of the lobbyist-bills network. To make what can be a technical discussion more accessible, I will show only at the outset how the coefficients from Table 4.2 translate into predicted results, but during much of this section I will provide a more qualitative discussion of what the results mean.

The first two columns of results are for the 106th Congress, which was in session from 1999 through 2000. The first three rows of results are the rate parameters that provide the estimated changes per organization from one period to the next, and these indicate an average rate of a little more than three tie changes per organization between the observation points.[6] The next row of results is the outdegree (density) parameter that is required variable in any model that controls for the density of ties in a network (Ripley et al., 2012). As noted previously, the fact that the coefficient is negative (−3.786) indicates that selecting additional legislation (as represented by a tie going 'out' from an organization) is costly such that organizations will select additional legislation only if there are benefits to doing so. A density coefficient of −3.786 translates into a baseline conditional probability of choosing a legislative bill on which to lobby of 0.022 or 2.2 percent (equal to $1/(1 + e^{-(-3.509)})$). The remainder of the parameters test whether our processes of interest capture these benefits.

The focus of this chapter is on social processes that affect agenda choices, and they are the 4-cycles effect for the influence argument, in which similar

Table 4.1 Changes in Lobbying Organizations' Ties to Bills, by Congress (106th through 108th)

Periods	No Bill	New Bill	Drop Bill	Keep Bill	Jaccard	Alternative
106th Congress	$(0 \to 0)$	$(0 \to 1)$	$(1 \to 0)$	$(1 \to 1)$	Index	Index
1st half 1999 → 2nd half 1999	58,389	254	124	323	0.461	
2nd half 1999 → 1st half 2000	58,188	325	181	396	0.439	
1st half 2000 → 2nd half 2000	58,189	180	188	533	0.592	
107th Congress						
1st half 2001 → 2nd half 2001	67,282	219	139	190	0.347	
2nd half 2001 → 1st half 2002	66,716	705	174	235	0.211	0.562
1st half 2002 → 2nd half 2002	66,604	286	291	649	0.529	
108th Congress						
1st half 2003 → 2nd half 2003	71,861	297	127	333	0.440	
2nd half 2003 → 1st half 2004	71,672	316	217	413	0.437	
1st half 2004 → 2nd half 2004	71,506	383	369	360	0.324	

Note: Sample sizes: 106th Congress: 190 lobbying organizations, 311 legislative bills; 107th Congress: 238 lobbying organizations, 285 legislative bills; 108th Congress: 247 lobbying organizations, 297 legislative bills. For the 107th Congress, I calculated an alternative index for the middle time period based on the fact that this time period is experiencing a period of growth.

organizations make similar choices; the indegree popularity for the band-wagon argument; and the outdegree effect for the monitoring argument. The 4-cycle effect is significant (0.029) and increases the chance of lobbying on a bill because of this 4-cycle effect from 2.2 percent to 2.3 percent—not a big change! But, there are, on average, eighty 4-cycles per lobbying organization so, on average, the 4-cycles effect results in a 9 likelihood in choosing legislation. One time dummy was added for the change in observations between the end of 1999 and the first half of 2000, and the coefficient (−0.22) is significantly negative and offsets the original effect for that period.

Table 4.2 Actor-Oriented Model Results for Retirement Policy Lobbyist-Bill Networks, by Congress (106th through 108th)

	106th (1999–2000)		107th (2001–2002)		108th (2003–2004)	
	Est.	SE	Est.	SE	Est.	SE
Rate Parameters:						
Year 1: 1st half → 2nd half	3.772	0.322	1.897	0.197	3.245	0.231
2nd half (Yr. 1) → 1st half (Yr. 2)	3.806	0.308	3.840	0.412	3.706	0.237
Year 2: 1st half → 2nd half	3.254	0.242	3.262	0.408	7.833	0.475
Outdegree (density)	-3.786***	0.105	-3.623***	0.412	-3.625***	0.126
Time dummy 2	0.348	0.223	0.562	0.403	1.430***	0.373
Time dummy 3	0.049	0.209	1.404	1.699	1.372***	0.369
4-cycles (influence)	0.018***	0.003	0.038***	0.010	0.037***	0.003
Time dummy 2	-0.022***	0.005	0.065***	0.021	-0.003	0.007
Time dummy 3			0.014	0.021	-0.020**	0.007
Indegree (popularity of bill)	0.059***	0.003	0.036***	0.007	0.026***	0.002
Time dummy 2					-0.018***	0.004
Time dummy 3					-0.013**	0.004
Outdegree (monitoring)	0.040***	0.006	0.010	0.081	0.105***	0.020
Time dummy 2	-0.051***	0.018	0.004	0.029	-0.221***	0.058
Time dummy 3	-0.040*	0.017	-0.156	0.232	-0.212***	0.058

(Continued)

Table 4.2 (Continued)

	106th (1999–2000)		107th (2001–2002)		108th (2003–2004)	
	Est.	SE	Est.	SE	Est.	SE
Coalition activity–bill activity	0.032	0.039	−0.035	0.116	0.040**	0.016
Time dummy 2			0.421	0.318		
Time dummy 3			0.943	0.557		
Total time in policy domain	0.094***	0.018				
Time dummy 2	0.027	0.045				
Time dummy 3	0.024	0.040				
Number of staff			0.153	0.100		
Bill progress			0.065	0.035		
Time dummy 2				0.096		
Time dummy 3				0.095		

Notes: Coalition rate and density parameters are omitted for space considerations. Time dummies control for heterogeneity across time periods such that the initial coefficient represents the change from periods 1 to 2, time dummy 2 controls for change from periods 2 to 3, and so on.

The indegree parameter evaluates the effect of a bill's popularity on the choices of lobbying organizations to select it. This, too, has a significantly positive effect (0.059), such that at the average amount of ties from lobbying organizations (about five) there is a 3 percent likelihood of an organization will select that bill. So if twenty organizations have selected a particular bill, the chance that another organization will select that bill increases to 7 percent. But this increase is not linear: If 100 other organizations select that bill, the chance of selection goes to 89 percent. That is, an organization's propensity to choose a bill accelerates as more organizations add that bill to their agendas. Thus, we can see how the 'bandwagon' effect or 'social cascade' that Baumgartner et al. (2009) mention can occur—some tipping point is reached when lobbyists flock to a bill. The time dummies are not significant.

The outdegree effect (0.040) is also positive and significant, but the magnitude of its effect is relatively light, even for outliers who are very active. The average number of ties for a lobbying organization is about 8, and this represents a chance of bill selection of 3 percent, not much different from the baseline 2.2 percent. Even for an active organization that is selection twice the average number of bills, the probability only goes to 4 percent. So the monitoring function is present but not very strong in the retirement policy community.

The other network effect of interest is the effect of changes in the coalition network on bill selection. However, the coalition activity-bill activity effect is not significant.

In terms of significant effects for organizational controls, total time in the retirement policy domain is significantly associated with adding legislation to one's agenda (0.094). If an organization is active over all time periods, the probability of selecting legislation increases from 2.2 to 8 percent. Being a long-term player in the policy domain may evidence an ability or interest in covering more issues as bills are introduced over the span of a Congress. Someone who has spent time on retirement policy knows who are the relevant policy makers, likely has good information about developments, and is best positioned to update their agendas as legislation is proposed. Long-term participants may also be acting as an information clearinghouse to which others can refer.

The results for the 107th Congress are similar to those of the 106th. The rate parameters for the next Congress are similar to the prior time period although the rate parameters increase from one time period to the next. The outdegree (density) parameter remains negative (−3.623).

We see similar results of significance, direction, and magnitude for the first effect of interest, the 4-cycles effect with a coefficient of 0.038. As the average number of 4-cycles per organization is sixty-nine, the probability of selecting legislation for the average organization rises to 27 percent. The indegree popularity measure (0.036) is again small but the effect increases as more organizations choose a bill, as we saw in the results for the prior Congress. For example, if 100 organizations have selected a bill, the probability for any other organization selecting that bill is 49 percent. Again, organizations look to choices of others when they already share similar preferences, and bandwagon and influence effects appear to be present.

The outdegree monitoring effect (0.010) is neither statistically significant nor large in magnitude. Although coalition activity had a negative effect on legislative choices (–0.035), the results were not significant. The control measures that were included in the model for the 107th Congress—number of staff and progress of legislation—were not significant.

Finally, the results for the 108th Congress are in general very similar to the prior congressional sessions. The 4-cycle effect for influence is positive and significant although the time dummies show a weak but negative effect that partially cancels out the initial positive finding. Similarly, the indegree effect for the bandwagon argument and the outdegree effect for the monitoring argument are both positive but slightly negative for the time dummies. The coalition activity effect on legislative choices is positive (0.040) and significant, but the impact is not very large.

In Contrast: Medicare and Medicaid

The previously discussed results suggest some significant and interesting influence and bandwagon mechanisms within the retirement policy domain. But do these network-based effects play out in every other policy area? Of course not, and to demonstrate this idea, I performed a similar analysis with data from the Medicare & Medicaid policy area. The Medicare and Medicaid data is somewhat different so I provide a brief policy background here (henceforth I use the term Medicare to cover both programs).

Medicare is the federal program that funds health care services for older Americans, and Medicaid provides health care for children and the poor as well as nursing home services for older persons and a host of other services. The federal government is the principal purchaser and payer for health services in the United States, and public funding sources as a share of total health payments increased from 29.3 percent in 1993 to 36.4 percent in 2010 (Centers for Medicare & Medicaid, 2012). Medicare accounted for 15 percent of the federal budget in 2011 (Kaiser Family Foundation, 2011). Medicare accounts for 29 percent of total national spending on hospital care and 23 percent of total spending on physician services (Kaiser Family Foundation, 2011). The program spends so much that at the highest level of aggregation, hospital payment politics becomes indistinguishable from macro-budgetary politics.

The composition of the organized groups in the Medicare policy space has changed over time. Whereas physicians once led the charge against government-provided health insurance, leadership on Medicare policy has passed to the insurance and pharmaceutical lobbies with the help of hospital organizations and large employers. Some of the change might be related to the general growth and complexity of Medicare and health care: Medical fields are increasingly specialized and services and products have proliferated. An interesting, if unstudied, collection of lobbying organizations is comprised of those firms that provide services—management, consulting, technology, and staffing—to the healthcare industry but not any healthcare services directly to consumers. Vladeck (1999) points out that Medicare spending engenders a 'Medicare-industrial-complex' such that multiple interest groups, including providers and suppliers, develop distinct and strong economic stakes in the program that have become entrenched over time. Indeed, Medicare is the largest single source of income for most regions' hospitals, physicians, and clinical laboratories. The Medicare program has spawned a host of providers whose services range across home health services, durable medical equipment, and therapy services (Vladeck, 1999).

In addition, Medicare managed care has made private health insurers more visible in the politics of Medicare and illustrates the emergence of the 'delegated welfare state' (Morgan and Campbell, 2011). Medicare's first risk contract program was created in 1982 (O'Sullivan, 2008). The Balanced Budget Act of 1997 (BBA) replaced the risk contract program with the Medicare+Choice (M+C) program, which eventually led to a broad range of managed care plans that are now known as Medicare Advantage (Lieberman, 2000; Oberlander, 2003). Overall, the healthcare industry has spent more than $5 billion on lobbying from 1998 to the present (Center for Responsive Politics, 2012).

Medicare Results

In order to spare the reader and save space, I do not show the results here but just describe them. A table of results is in the Appendix of this volume. The Medicare & Medicaid policy area is a big space with hundreds of organizations participating, but it is certainly plausible that similar influence and bandwagon effects would be present given the flux in both players and issues.

I gathered similar lobbying data for the Medicare & Medicaid policy area ('Medicare') for the first three quarters of 2009—reforms enacted in 2006 now require lobbyists to file quarterly LDA reports. Over the first three quarters of 2009, there were 969 organizations that were active on Medicare policy, some of which represented themselves while others hired a total of 286 external lobbying firms. In total, these entities listed 454 unique pieces of legislation. As with retirement policy, the distribution of the number of bills listed by organizations was highly skewed.

The stochastic actor-oriented model was used to analyze the Medicare data in a manner similar to the retirement, but I did not have coalition data for Medicare and certain attributes were different. I did include the structural effects—indegree popularity, 4-cycles, and outdegree activity—that were of interest in the retirement model, and these effects were statistically significant for Medicare policy while the magnitude of the effects were small. However, changes in the legislative bill-organizational network (from the first quarter of 2009 to the third quarter) were associated significantly and strongly with outdegree or monitoring effect. That is, changes in the lobbying agenda were driven by organizations that previously selected many issues: If you selected many issues in the prior period, you are likely to select additional issues in the next. I also looked at the types of organizations that tended to report lots of issues on their lobbying agendas, and the list was generally made up of large bio-pharmaceutical firms that spend a lot of money on Medicare policy lobbying.

It should be kept in mind that the time periods are not comparable between retirement and Medicare. The retirement data covered larger and longer time periods; the size of the Medicare data limited my time coverage. Additional data and analysis of Medicare policy may show an eventual filtering down of influence, but the big corporate players are playing a monitoring role within the domain in the early time periods.

Why would this be the significant driver of agenda change? Similar to the illustration in Figure 4.3 earlier in the chapter for retirement policy, the distribution of outdegrees among the lobbying organizations in Medicare policy shows a significant skew such that we can say that most lobbing pairs focus on a very limited number of bills with a relatively small minority generating the majority of outgoing ties to legislation. But what organizations are generating all these ties? In terms of the lobbying organizations that have at least six outgoing ties, which are more than two standard deviations above the mean, certain facts stand out. Pharmaceutical interests are highly represented in this group, and among the top dozen or so are trade associations like the American Hospital Association, the American Psychiatric Association, the Pharmaceutical Research and Manufacturing Association, and the National Committee to Preserve Social Security and Medicare. These are large organizations that have the staff to track legislation as it is introduced in Congress and that likely disseminate congressional developments out to their members. Most of the pharmaceutical firms and hospitals that are actively lobbying on Medicare issues belong to PhRMA and the American Hospital Association, respectively. For the corporations with limited staff coverage or smaller lobbying firms that are on tight budget, it may not be possible to monitor the developments in the Medicare and Medicaid area, and so they belong to membership associations in order to augment their advocacy efforts. In addition, organizations are also connected via overlapping hiring of lobbyists when a client hires two or more lobbying firms and when a lobbying firm has more than one client. For example, 38 percent of hospitals, hospital associations and their external lobbying firms are connected to each other in such hiring relationships.

Although it is difficult to capture these relationships in the dynamic network model, the monitoring effect is much more prominent in the Medicare data, and the underlying relationships suggest that social processes are likely occurring.

CHAPTER SUMMARY

This chapter of the volume focused on interest groups' relations with other groups and the outcomes, if any, associated with such relationships. Given a network of lobbying organizations and legislative proposals, I argued that an organization's lobbying choices are, in part, conditional on the choices of other lobbying organizations. The longitudinal model of network change was used to explain the agenda choices of lobbying organizations over several time periods and, hence, the evolution of the agenda itself. The results provided support for both the influence and the bandwagon hypotheses.

The qualitative evidence from Chapter 2 of this volume provides an understanding of the results. Although information and influence can come from different sources, lobbyists in a policy domain, particularly long-term players, tend to know each other, share information, and exchange interpretations about developments. This flow of information evokes the information subsidy that is borrowed from Hall and Deardorff (2006). In such an environment lobbyists learn about the choices of other lobbyists, which likely conditions their choices as a result. In short, networks imbued with repeated interaction and with transfers of fine-grained knowledge affect policy agenda development.

These findings fit with other work on interest groups like Holyoke's (2009) competition model and the *Hollow Core* structure of influence of Heinz et al. (1993). If they are on opposing sides on an issue, they nonetheless can influence each other on what is the issue on which to disagree. In the Heinz et al. (1993) study, which had a more macro-level focus, the authors suggest not a central coordinating set of actors but a network organized as a sphere around a hollow core. There, the structure of representation was paired with a high degree of uncertainty in the policy making process as private interests increasingly developed representation in Washington over the late 1970s and early 1980s. My results suggest that policy actors deal with this uncertain and unmediated environment by looking to others in the policy domain, particularly those who provide reliable information about policy developments.

Are these results limited to a particular policy domain? Clearly, my very brief discussion about Medicare & Medicaid data suggests that these network proxies for social processes may not work everywhere. Medicare is a large and complex area so it may not have the social community that the retirement policy area appears to have. More generally, Lowi's (1964) argument about types of policies having specific implications for political behavior may be useful. The retirement policy domain may encourage embedded relations in that the technical complexity of pension tax law puts a premium on expertise and provides a benefit to long-term players who invest in the details of policy. Thus, these findings may be limited to similar domains with a regulatory or technical emphasis, such as intellectual property, and may not extend to more particularistic/distributive areas such as budget politics like Medicare. Moreover, size and composition of the policy domain may matter (Olson, 1965; Ostrom, 1990).

However, I expect to see quantitative and qualitative evidence of these social processes across a range of policy domains and even across levels of government for at least two reasons. First, politics and policy work are specialized according to experience and expertise such that we should see institutionally created communities within which are dense ties but between which are weakly connected to each other. Such communities reduce the distance between actors with the result that actors tend to know and interact with each other. Second, actors face complex and information-rich environments with limited resources. Social relationships augment one's resources and leverage one's knowledge and expertise into effective advocacy. The real pleasure we feel from positive social interactions in work situations also reinforces the strategic benefits of these social processes (Homans, 1961). For these reasons, policy agendas likely develop neither through elite consensus nor through aggregation of independent choices but rather through social processes like bandwagon and influence that are supported by trust-based relations in close-knit communities. Such close-knit communities may not be the elite-driven models of policy making, but they do suggest a different kind of elite hierarchy, one consisting of expertise and experience.

The next chapter takes a different perspective on lobbyist influence. Instead of lobbyists influencing each regarding coalitions or agendas, Chapter 5 of this volume examines the relationship between networked relations and reputations for policy influence.

NOTES

1. For example, S. 741 was listed ninety-eight times by the lobbyists in the first half of 1999.
2. Social network analysis uses the term 'degree' for a tie, and in the case of directional relationships 'indegree' means ties coming into a node and 'outdegree' means outgoing ties.
3. As opposed to the legislative bill-lobbying organization two-mode or bipartite network, the coalition network is a one-mode network.
4. I used RSiena version 4.0 (Ripley, Snijders, and Preciado, 2012). A free copy of the latest version and documentation are available at http://www.stats.ox.ac.uk/~snijders/siena/.
5. A key assumption of the dynamic model is that observations are made of a gradually changing network. Because the data collection is based on time periods of fixed length for lobbyist reporting, the six-month time periods do not match the actual rates of change in the networks. In order to see if the data collection points are not too far apart, Table 4.2 shows the 'Jaccard Index,' which is a function of the number of ties present at both observation points as well as the number of ties added and dropped between the two observation points. In general, Jaccard values should be above 0.3 (Snijders et al., 2010), and for each Congress the values meet this criterion except for the middle time period in the 107th Congress. However, Snijders et al. (2010) note that when the network is

in a period of growth and the second network has many more ties than in the prior network, one "may look instead at the proportion, among the ties present at a given observation, of ties that have remained in existence at the next observation" (49). Such a period of growth in the middle of each Congress is present in Table 4.1 as 704 new ties were added from the end of 2001 to the beginning of 2002, which is significantly higher than other time periods. Most likely, this growth spurts makes sense if it reflects, at least in part, the continuing introduction of legislation over the course of the first year of a Congress as well as information gathering by lobbying organizations on newly introduced legislation. Using the alternative index calculation proposed by Snijders et al. (2010), the value is 0.563 from the end of 2001 to the beginning of 2002.

6. As Ripley, Snijders, and Preciado (2012: 92) note, the rate parameter "refers to unobserved changes, and that some opportunities for change lead to the decision 'no change,' and moreover some of these changes may cancel (make a new choice and then withdraw it again), so the average observed number of differences per actor will be smaller than this estimated number of unobserved changes."

5   Reputations for Influence

1. If you agree with the aims of the group, it is a "crusader in the public interest," a "voice of the people," or a "force for good." 2. If you're indifferent to its cause, it is a "special interest group." 3. If you disagree with its position, it's a "lobby."

—Kiplinger and Kiplinger (1975: 203)

In the early 2000s, the sluggish economy induced a period of very low interest rates, which, while good for spurring lending and overall growth, was bad for funding employer-sponsored pension plans. Low interest rates inflated future pension liabilities and forced firms to increase contributions to pension funds. Corporate sponsors of pensions were looking for at least some short-term legislative or regulatory relief from what was viewed as an artificial burden. A coalition of lobbying organizations had been formed over the issue, and an important congressional hearing had just been announced. One trade association in the coalition received advanced notice of the hearing and was able to secure a coveted spot at the witness table. Because there were very limited opportunities to testify, the prestige of the trade association would have been boosted by having a witness appear before the congressional committee. But when one member of the coalition found out, they angrily told the representative from the trade association that the witness needed to appear on behalf of the whole coalition rather than on behalf of just the trade association. A prolonged and loud argument ("You can't do this!") ensued.

How do certain lobbyists come to be known as influential? Is a reputation for influence a cumulative process, or do hot issues make hot lobbyists? In the prior two chapters, I discussed the connection between social relations within a policy domain and coalition participation and the development of lobbyist agendas. In this chapter, we extend the discussion to consider some of the reputational outcomes of relationships within a policy domain. These outcomes I call 'reputational influence.' Does embeddedness enhance a reputation for influence? This chapter of the volume examines whether superior network position helps to enhance an organization's reputation for influence.

The chapter starts with a discussion of the concept of 'reputational influence' and why I adopt a particular perspective on that term. I next discuss how the relevant influence concepts are used in this chapter and review the applicable methodology. As in prior chapters, I use longitudinal quantitative and network data, but for reasons explained further on, I use data from the federal and state levels and a different method of analyzing the data. At the federal level, there are two influence outcomes: congressional hearing appearances and news media mentions. At the state level, the outcome measure is based on a biennial poll that rates the most influential lobbyists. The chapter concludes with a summary of the findings in the context of the prior chapter's empirical findings.

INFLUENCE

The issues of political power, access, and influence have been theoretical and empirical puzzles for quite some time (Hunter, 1953; Dahl, 1961; Bachrach and Baratz, 1962). The explosion in interest group activity beginning in the 1960s convinced many scholars in sociology and political science that interest groups do, in fact, have influence over the political process (see, for example, Salisbury, 1992; Arnold, 1990; Wilson, 1974; Berry, 1999; Smith, 2000). But despite the plethora of studies on lobbying, a critical problem has been disagreement or confusion about the nature and processes of influence. "The literature on influence is an interesting example of avoidance based on a recognition that previous studies had mostly generated more smoke than fire, more debate than progress, more confusion than advance" (Baumgartner and Leech, 1998: 13).

A second problem that is likely related to the first is that there is little or no agreement on exactly what is 'influence.' "Influence occurs when one actor intentionally transmits information to another that alters the latter's actions from what would have occurred without that information" (Knoke, 1990). But translating general ideas of influence into concrete research applications creates problems. Each study produces its own definition of influence, which in turn means that each definition has its own measure. Is influence the ability to change the contents of a bill? Is influence the power to change a legislator's vote? Is it getting your pet issue on the decision maker's agenda? Because of data availability, roll call votes are a popular method of studying influence, but findings of studies have not produced agreement on what interest group activities generate changes in roll call voting (Smith, 1995). Most scholars agree that if legislators are influenced by interest groups at all, they are least likely to be influenced when votes are cast (Baumgartner and Leech, 1998). A second area of focus for prior studies has on been on campaign contributions from political action committees (PACs). But here again, the large number of studies have produced contradictory findings most likely because there are a wide variety of resources available to politicians other than PAC money (Cigler, 1991) and probably because the causal mechanisms are not very clear.

I do not intend to reconcile these divergent approaches to influence. The difficulty associated with studying influence is that the underlying quality of influence is one of multidimensionality. Influence is a form of capital—another term for influence might be political capital. Much like money in the financial system, influence circulates through the political system, crossing boundaries (Parsons, 1963). And like other forms of capital such as financial, human, and social, political capital or influence can be created from a variety of sources, stored, and then expended or used for a variety of other purposes. Influence can be created from financial sources, expertise over an issue, credibility, or persuasiveness through interpersonal relations, to name a few. Influence can then be applied to enhance the public visibility of a group, gain access to important meetings, engage in gossip, and help shape the content of policy products. I argue that social capital that is a product of close-knit ties is readily convertible into political capital or influence.

Robert Salisbury (1994) criticizes influence studies because they treat politics as a game with clear winners and losers when in fact the political process often continues without either a discernible endpoint or winner, with even the rules of the game evolving over time. With this admonition in mind, it might be better to view influence at least in some political contexts as not so much an input that creates a political output but rather as a signal (Spence, 1976) or mark of status (Podolny, 1993) within a political domain characterized by a set of relations. A signal is usually defined as an indicator of quality that has two criteria: One must be able to manipulate, at least partly, the signal, and the difficulty of obtaining the indicator must be inversely related to the level of quality (Spence, 1976). Lobbying organizations have some control over their reputations, and a reputation for influence is more difficult to obtain if you are not a 'player.' Status in turn can be translated to the political context as the perceived quality or importance of that actor's *previous* contributions to the development of policy (Podolny and Stuart, 1995).

In this case, then, influence is more a perception and can be contrasted rather than conflated with power. For example, Weber (1978) defines power as the probability that one actor in a social relationship will be able to carry out his or her own will despite resistance. Few lobbying organizations have actual power in this sense of the word. On the other hand, influence can be direct and/or indirect. One can observe another's influence even when the other does not act, and if actors perceive influence as real, then influence will be real in its consequences (Thomas and Thomas, 1928). For example, when the lobbying organization AARP claims to represent over thirty-five million Americans on some issue, few actually believe that all thirty-five million support the AARP's position. But, the clout of the AARP is undeniable.

Because of the role of perceptions, influence might be thought of as a concatenation of mechanisms (Gambetta, 1998) that creates and reinforces a hierarchy (Podolny, 1993). High status actors can become focal points that other actors naturally gravitate towards (Schelling. 1960) for the allocation of resources within or around the policy domain (Podolny and Stuart, 1995). Those lobbying organizations with great influence may become the leaders of coalitions or be quoted more often by journalists, and prior leadership and media mentions beget additional status or influence. A Mathew Effect may take hold in part because influence-as-status engenders a 'self-fulfilling prophecy' ('Call Sarah—She's plugged in') with respect to the contribution of the lobbying organization (Merton, 1968; Podolny and Stuart, 1995).

Embeddedness should have an effect on organizational outcomes; in the business context it might be survival or profitability, but organizational outcomes in politics should include perceived influence (Uzzi, 1997). If embeddedness facilitates joint activity and affects policy agendas, it should also contribute to one's reputation for influence. To be clear, however, influence is often a function of resources, which can include financial campaign contributions, expertise, or the ability to generate a grassroots campaign in favor of a particular issue.

In any event, superior network positions created through embedded ties create those focal points of influence. Laumann and Knoke (1987) showed that interest groups base their reputations for influence over health policy on structural positions in communication networks. Lobbying organizations that are more central in the network have greater access to better information, and as noted previously, these positions are reinforced by participation in coalitions of lobbyists. In turn, such central lobbying organizations are able to transmit that superior information to policy makers. This makes the lobbyists more valuable and more influential. Thus, those who have the superior network positions via their embedded ties are more likely to be called for their opinion and feedback. In short, embeddedness should translate into more influence.

As I discussed in the prior chapter of this volume, Dür (2008) distinguishes three broad approaches to measuring interest influence: process-tracing, assessing attributed influence, and gauging the degree of preference attainment. In this chapter, I focus on attributed or reputational influence, which usually involves a survey of groups as to their own influence and/or the influence of other groups, in effect, a poll of reputed influence. For example, Heinz, Laumann, Nelson, and Salisbury (1993) rely on a large survey of interest group representatives and their perceptions of their own success on their preferred issues.

How might influence operate in practice? In the case of a congressional hearing, a member of Congress (in practice, the staffer to the member of Congress) invites the lobbying organization to testify before a committee; for media stories, the decision is in the hands of the journalists who are writing a story; the state-level data uses, in effect, a popularity poll of peer lobbyists and other political actors. Lobbying organizations increase the likelihood of their influencing policy when linked to a group network formed around embedded ties. The following argument flows from the ideas discussed previously: *The more superior the network position of an organization within its policy network, the more influence that organization will possess.*

Because the data for federal retirement policy and state-level policy are fairly different, I present the data, methods, and results separately.

FEDERAL POLICY INFLUENCE

Congressional Hearings

Members of Congress believe that committee hearings are an important vehicle for efficiently gathering information and for exerting influence over pending issues (Kingdon, 1981). The final shape of a bill is often affected by conflicts among witnesses about how issues should be framed (Baumgartner and Jones, 1993), and simply holding a hearing broadcasts the judgment of the committee that the issue under discussion is important (Diermeier and Fedderson, 2000). But why should lobbying organizations participate in hearings? Hearings are often scripted affairs in which questions (and sometimes answers) are crafted in advance. In some cases hearings might be thought of as propaganda channels. However, the fact that organizations with private information usually testify is crucial. Legislators considering whether to support a bill may find testimony from experts informative (Burstein and Hirsh, 2007), and experts may care about establishing a reputation for correctly predicting policy outcomes (Diermeier and Fedderson, 2000). Testimony may be the first time that an organization's private information or claims on an issue become public and so may be especially influential (Baumgartner and Leech, 1998). Interest groups may also see the news media and external publics as the real audience rather than the committee members (Milbrath, 1963). In short, the lobbyists themselves see committee testimony as a measure of influence and status (Laumann and Knoke, 1987).

In the interest group and policy-making literature, linking interest group preferences to committee preferences has been done in the case of congressional testimony (Baumgartner and Jones, 1993; Jenkins-Smith, St. Clair, and Woods, 1991). These studies conclude that hearing testimony tends to target sympathetic lawmakers. Lobbyists tend to specialize and interact with similar types of people, be they lobbyists, legislators, congressional staff, or administration officials (Leyden and Borelli, 1994).

Moreover, congressional committees exert considerable gatekeeping and agenda-setting powers. Theoretical work on interest groups often begin with the assumption that members of Congress seek to promote their conceptions of good policy, to be reelected, and to gain the recognition of their legislative peers (Fenno, 1973). In order to promote these goals, members seek information of three types: agenda information about the importance of problems they are asked to address (Kingdon, 1981; Baumgartner and Leech, 1998), political information on the electoral consequences of their decisions (Amenta et al., 1992), and policy information regarding the consequences of a policy change (Arnold, 1990; Hansen, 1991). Thus, interest groups likely influence legislators through the information that they provide, and the concept of information is a broad one that encompasses not only facts but the interpretation that gives meaning to those facts, including causal arguments or claims (Burstein and Hirsh, 2007).

In specifying what leads to access or influence, whether through congressional testimony or other avenues, researchers tend to focus on organizational resources or policy preferences. Interpersonal relations, however, are also important. Lobbying organizations spend considerable time establishing ties with committee staffers or members in order to convince them that the information they wish to convey is relevant or important to the hearing proceedings. The importance of prior and repeated contact, in terms of months or years in advance, cannot be stressed enough (Leyden and Borelli, 1994).

News Media Stories

Interest group scholars often distinguish between inside and outside lobbying strategies, with inside strategies being those actions that target government insiders such as personal lobbying and outside strategies focused on external audiences such as the general public (Baumgartner and Leech, 1998). Working with the news media has been considered, however, as both an insider and an outsider tactic (Gais and Walker, 1991). Lobbyists are a frequent source of comment on policy proposals for journalists because they often are conveniently located near the halls of power and they are attuned to what the press needs and wants (Berry, 1977). Usually, lobbying organizations have spokespersons who are articulate and have some expertise on an issue.

Speaking with journalists is a fairly common tactic among lobbyists: Studies have found that between 72 percent and 86 percent of lobbyists who were surveyed report using the mass media (Schlozman and Tierney, 1986; Walker, 1991; Nownes and Freeman, 1999).[1] Kollman (1998) notes that press conferences by lobbying organizations are an important tactic, but that the targets of press conferences are not necessarily the general public: "It seems that group leaders tend to use press conferences to explain technical material to the press or to communicate to people within the policymaking community" (95–6). When asked about media publicity campaigns, 51 percent of interest groups in the Kollman study responded that their primary targets were the president or Congress as opposed to the general public.

It is not very clear how lobbying organizations get quoted in the news media. What research exists suggests that an organization's media strategy matters, but that organizational structure and organizational identity color these strategies (Rohlinger, 2002).

Analyzing Reputations for Influence

As noted previously, the federal level data had two outcomes. The first measures the number of times that an organization testifies before a congressional committee of jurisdiction during a six-month time period. In retirement policy, there are four committees that have broad jurisdiction over retirement policy issues. In the House of Representatives, the committees are the Ways and Means Committee and the Education and the Labor Force Committee, and in the Senate there are the Finance Committee and Health, Education, Labor, and Pensions Committee. I looked at every full committee or a subcommittee hearing on a retirement-related issue over 1998 through 2004, the time period of this study, and collected data for each instance that one of the organizations included in this study testified before a committee. These counts were aggregated into six month time periods in order to correspond with the six month reporting periods for lobbyist disclosure filings.

A similar method was used to collect every instance that a lobbying organization was mentioned in the news media. I used the Lexis-Nexis database to search mentions of lobbying organizations in the major U.S. newspaper and wire service sub-database in connection with some aspect of pensions or retirement. I made, however, an important distinction in collecting news data relative to congressional committee. For the news media variable, I only used those organizations that were membership-based such as trade associations, professional associations, broad-based public interest groups, and labor unions. Membership organizations are inherently representative of some group and are likely to be quoted or mentioned for that reason. The Appendix provides more detail on the data collection and sample.

Network Position and Coalitions

In testing the effects of network positions on reputational influence, I focus on three measures. First, I expect that organizations that are more centrally located in their issue network have better access to information. Therefore, their superior network position would be appealing to congressional staffers who are looking for witnesses. The greater the centrality of an organization within its policy network, the more likely that organization will be asked to testify before a congressional committee.

Moreover, an organization that has a high degree of agenda overlap with other organizations in the policy domain may be a useful witness for a couple of reasons. Recall from prior chapters that agenda overlap is simply a measure of the number of issues two organizations have in common divided by their total set of issues.[2] An organization that has a high agenda overlap number averaged over all organizations therefore is representative of all the issue-based interests of active lobbying organizations. In addition, a high agenda overlap measure may indicate an organization's expertise in the policy domain. In either case, the higher the organization's agenda overlap with other groups, the more likely that organization will be asked to testify before a congressional committee.

A third network measure is structural constraint, and this measure may also be important for predicting a group's tendency to testify. As discussed in Chapter 2 of this volume, constraint measures the extent the other organizations to which an organization is tied are themselves tied to each other. In other words, if organization A has ties to B, C, and D, and if B, C, and D are in turn tied to each other, then the sheer group density of the ties may inhibit A from acting in a way that is contrary to the wishes of B, C, and D. In the lobbying and congressional testimony context, a lobbying organization that is highly constrained may have little latitude in presenting information that elevates it above the other lobbying organizations. Moreover, a committee looking for witnesses may want only those organizations that stand out from the group and that can reliably deliver testimony that suits the purposes of the committee chair and members. The greater the constraint on a lobbying organization in terms of its membership relations, therefore, the less likely is that organization to testify before a congressional committee.

For the retirement policy data, Chapter 3 of this volume established the importance of networked relations in participating in lobbying coalitions, and I would expect in turn that coalition participation would have an effect on reputational influence. The very purpose of participating in coalitions is to elevate the issues of common interest as well as to raise the profile of participating organizations. Prominence within a coalition or across coalitions may signify an organization's expertise on an issue as well as the gravity of the issue itself. If an organization participates in more coalitions, it seems reasonable that its prominence would be higher both among other lobbying organizations and to congressional committees. The more coalitions in which an organization participates, the more likely that organization will be asked to testify before a congressional committee or will appear in the news media.

In order to isolate the structural effects on influence stemming from network position and coalition participation, I control for group interest like professionals, financial services, labor, and private employers, with public interest groups being the reference category. I also include variables for organizational resources (number of staff and amount of expense or income averaged on a per policy domain basis), activity (in terms of total policy domains in which an organization is active), and longevity (a dummy variable indicating a long-term presence—six or more years in the retirement policy domain).[3] I also add two period-specific variables in order to capture exogenous events. There is a dummy for the 2001–2002 period in which George W. Bush was president and during which the country was in recession (Bush recession) as well as the post-recession period of 2003–2004 (Bush recovery)—the Clinton years of 1998–2000 are the reference period.

STATE-LEVEL POLICY INFLUENCE

In addition to the federal policy outcomes, I look at reputations for influence at the state-level by using data from North Carolina. In terms of numbers, the data includes 1,129 lobbying organizations. Of the 1,129 North Carolina lobbying organizations, 339 entities also lobbied at the federal level from 1999 through 2008. The number of North Carolina organizations that lobby at the federal level is relatively consistent on a year-to-year basis. In 1999, the number was 277, but by 2007 the number of North Carolina organizations lobbying in Washington, D.C., reached 299.

Poll of Reputational Influence

Since the 1980s, the North Carolina Center for Public Policy Research (NCCPPR) has polled members of the legislature, the news media, and the lobbying community as to the most influential individual lobbyists. I use this data source from 1993 to 2008 to construct a measure of a lobbying organization's reputation for influence during each two-year legislative session. Each individual lobbyist's ranking is attributed to the organization that employs him and if an organization has more than one influential lobbyist, the scores are added together. The state-level lobbying data come from mandatory lobbyist registration information collected and maintained by the Office of the North Carolina Secretary of State. Lobbyists—individuals and organizations—are required to register with the Secretary of State and file periodic reports. Reports were downloaded for each two-year period beginning for 1993–1994 through 2007–2008.

Variables

As with the federal policy data, I use centrality and constraint for the state-level data. In addition, I control for organizations that may be trying to influence the political process by hiring lots of other organizations, we use a measure called 'outdegrees.' This measure is the number of ties going 'out' from an organization to hire others.

I also coded state-level lobbying firms according to lobbying activity at the federal level. To determine this, I used some rules. Trade or membership organizations that are state-wide chapters but that have a national-level body count as lobbying at the federal level if the national body is registered at the federal level. For example, AARP and the North Carolina Medical Society lobby in North Carolina, but their national-level counterparts (AARP and the American Medical Association, respectively) have a presence in Washington, D.C. Therefore, AARP-NC and the North Carolina Medical Society are coded as being active at the federal level. A sub-state affiliate (e.g., the City of Charlotte Chamber of Commerce) is not being coded as lobbying at the federal level despite the existence of a national level entity (e.g., the U.S. Chamber of Commerce).

Using an organization's status as a law firm or as a non-law firm, we interact federal-level lobbying with law firm status to create three dummy variables. Organizations that are neither law firms nor lobby at the federal level are the reference group such that we have:

- Federal-level lobbying by law firms (D.C.*law firm)
- No federal-level lobbying by law firms (Non-D.C.*law firm)
- Federal-level lobbying by non-law firms (D.C.*non-law firm)

I also included attributes of the organization. For-hire status is indicated for any time period when a lobbying organization is representing another organization. Self-representing status is indicated by organizations that use their own on-staff lobbyists to represent themselves. I also controlled for the number of lobbyists at an organization, if any. As there is a large number of organizations that move in and out of the network over time, I used a dummy variable called 'New Entrant,' which is coded as 1 if the organization is a first time lobbying organization. Finally, I controlled for organizational type, which has three values: a stand-alone entity (like a corporation or non-profit group), an individual membership organization (like the AARP), and an organizational membership organization (like most trade associations).

METHOD OF ANALYSIS

For *federal retirement policy*, I divide the independent variables into two models. The baseline model includes the control and coalition variables. The Full Model incorporates the control variables, the social network variables, and the coalition variable.

Unlike prior chapters, this chapter of the volume uses the negative binomial regression to model the relationship between network position and reputational influence. The longitudinal network analysis of the prior chapters simply does not fit the kind of outcome data that I use here.

These dependent variables exhibit three qualities that dictate the modeling choice: They are over-dispersed, they are longitudinal, and they are count data. Approaches based on the Poisson distribution are appropriate for analyzing count data, but because the variances for both the hearing (1.29) and news media (91.38) variables exceed their means (0.35 and 35.84 respectively), the negative binomial regression model is favored. The longitudinal format of the data further complicates the methodology by violating the assumption of independence in conventional models (Long, 1997). Problems of autocorrelation and heteroskedasticity can occur, producing spuriously low standard error estimates. However, random effects models for cross-sectional time series data have been developed to account for the non-independence of events. I use a random effects design rather than a fixed effects because those organizations with 0 outcomes—organizations that do not testify and/or do not get mentioned in the news media—are dropped from the fixed effects analyses, resulting in substantial attrition. The models are estimated using the 'xtnbreg' function in STATA 12 with standard error estimates adjusted for clustering within organizations in terms of multiple observations over time.[4]

Similarly, the *state-level* outcome, which is the number of times an organization is rated as influential, has a mean of 0.302 and a variance of 1.519. Therefore, a negative binomial regression model may be appropriate. But whereas the negative binomial model takes over-dispersion into account, it may not deal adequately with a high number of zeroes in the count data. In our data, 90 percent of the lobbying organizations are never perceived as influential and therefore carry a value of 0 for both total influence and the number of periods influential. When the dependent variable has a large number of zeroes, an important consideration is whether different processes are producing the excess number of zeroes. For example, an organization may not be seen as influential because it lacks the resources or network position to be perceived as influential. Alternatively, the organization may not be influential because although it maintains a registered lobbyist, there is simply nothing on the policy agenda during a given time period on which it wishes to deploy its influence. Thus, two states are present, the former being a normal count-process state while the latter is a zero-count state in which we have an organization that is referred to as a 'certain zero.' Thus, the number of zeroes may be inflated and the number of organizations with zero influence cannot be explained in the same manner as those with influence.

The standard negative binomial model as is used for the retirement policy data does not distinguish between these two processes, but a zero-inflated negative binomial (ZINB) model allows for the different processes and permits testing between the standard negative binomial model and the zero-inflated negative binomial. ZINB regression generates two separate models and then combines them. First, a logit model is used to determine whether selected independent variables predict whether or not an organization would be a 'certain zero.' Then, a negative binomial model is generated predicting the counts for those organizations that are not certain zeroes.

RESULTS

Congressional Hearing Testimony

Table 5.1 provides the results for congressional committee hearing appearances with four models. In terms of the baseline model, the result for the coalition variable is a positive and strongly significant association with hearing appearances. Each additional number of coalitions an organization participates in is associated with a 29-percent increase (exponent $(0.251) = 1.285$) in the level of appearances before congressional committees. Thus, joint activity may heighten visibility and attractiveness

Table 5.1   Results of Negative Binomial Regression of Testimony at Congressional Hearings, 1998–2004 ($n = 392$)

	Base	Full
Professionals	0.156	0.198
	(0.600)	(0.560)
Financial Services	–0.130	–0.028
	(0.480)	(0.490)
Labor	0.366	0.487
	(0.530)	(0.560)
Private Employers	–0.930*	–0.862
	(0.550)	(0.560)
Expense/Domain	0.003	0.002
	(0.006)	(0.006)
Staff	0.096*	0.108**
	(0.051)	(0.051)
Policy Domains	–0.022	–0.019
	(0.023)	(0.024)
Long-Term	0.449	0.448
	(0.370)	(0.370)
Bush Recession	0.060	0.062
	(0.220)	(0.230)
Bush Recovery	–0.589**	–0.531*
	(0.270)	(0.290)
Issue Centrality		–0.498
Agenda Overlap		–2.059
Membership Constraint		–0.289
Membership Centrality		0.002
Coalitions	0.251***	0.255***
	(0.046)	(0.048)
Constant	0.451	11.620
	(3.190)	(464.000)
Log Likelihood	–334.824	–332.460

Note: Standard errors are in parentheses. There were 2,107 total observations over time.

***$p < 0.01$; **$p < 0.05$; *$p < 0.1$.

for congressional committees. However, the addition of the coalitions variable results in the long-term variable losing both the strength and significance of its effect, which reflects the relationship between long-term participation in policy and the level of participation in coalitions. In addition, an organization that is or represents a private employer shows a weakly negative relationship with hearing appearances. Membership in multiple coalitions may be bringing out a negative effect in being a private employer.

The Full Model confirms the main effects discussed previously. The more coalitions in which an organization participates, the more it will be involved in congressional committee hearings. The effect of coalitional participation is also shown by the model fit statistic of Log Likelihood. The model fit is significantly improved in the two models in which the coalition is included. Prominence within a coalition or across coalitions (which the number of coalitions in which a group participates acts as a proxy) may signify an organization's expertise on an issue as well as the gravity of the issue itself. These results show, in addition to organizational resources such as the number of staff working on retirement policy issues, the importance of joint activity and the social relations that underpin that activity.

In terms of congressional hearing appearances, the social network measures showed no significant effects. Coalition participation clearly trumps network position, and this may occur in this context for a couple of reasons. First, because congressional committees have (somewhat) clear boundaries in terms of jurisdiction over policy issues, those organizations with a long history of working on those issues may have a clear advantage in being invited to testify over organizations that just dabble in a policy domain. Second, because congressional staffers running hearings typically have more requests to testify than actual slots, inviting those organizations that are part of broad coalitions may be easier to justify both to committee members and to disappointed applicants. Third, a latent effect may also be significant. As mentioned previously, relationships with congressional staffers may matter a great deal more in terms of getting an invitation to testify than inter-organizational relations in a policy field, but I do not have a direct measure for the congressional staffer relationship.

News Media Appearances

We see similar results for news media analysis, which is presented in Table 5.2. As in the prior table, being a long-term player in retirement policy boosts the level of news media visibility, but this effect is insignificant with the coalition variable in the mix. The coalition variable is strongly significant at the $p < 0.01$ level. We also see a consistently negative, strong, and significant effect of representing a private employer.[5]

A striking difference from the results for congressional testimony in Table 5.1 is the effect of private employers' interests. Relative to other types

Table 5.2 Results of Negative Binomial Regression of Number of News Media Stories, 1998–2004 (n = 120).

	Base	Full
Professionals	–0.750	–0.743
	(0.500)	(0.490)
Financial Services	–0.633	–0.694
	(0.510)	(0.500)
Labor	–0.231	0.041
	(0.460)	(0.460)
Private Employers	–2.034***	–1.882***
	(0.630)	(0.630)
Expense/Domain	0.003	0.002
	(0.002)	(0.003)
Staff	0.036	0.049
	(0.043)	(0.043)
Policy Domains	0.002	–0.006
	(0.012)	(0.013)
Long-term	0.324	0.343
	(0.290)	(0.290)
Bush Recession	0.423***	0.348***
	(0.086)	(0.088)
Bush Recovery	0.347***	0.220**
	(0.086)	(0.096)
Issue Centrality		0.018
		(0.060)
Agenda Overlap		0.320
		(0.490)
Membership Constraint		–0.266*
		(0.140)
Membership Centrality		0.004**
		(0.002)
Coalitions	0.111***	0.102**
	(0.040)	(0.042)
Constant	0.568	0.602
	(0.530)	(0.520)
Log Likelihood	–1342.588	–1337.683

Note: Standard errors are in parentheses. There were 835 total observations over time.

***$p < 0.01$; **$p < 0.05$; *$p < 0.1$.

of interests, groups and trade associations that represent private employers are not likely to receive as much media. Why might this be so? Recall that this sample only covers membership groups like trade associations and unions. One answer may be that a news story that focuses on employer or corporate interests may be more likely to quote the corporation or employer directly rather than its representative trade association. Larger corporate employers certainly have their own public relations staff.

We do see some significant effects for two network variables. Membership-level constraint is negatively and robustly associated with media attention, although its statistical significance is weak at the 0.10 level. Thus, being more constrained by redundant ties to others in the network of trade association and for-hire relationships is likely to dampen an organization's ability to attain media visibility, which makes sense in that redundant ties probably indicate a lack of distinguishing characteristics or limited information that would be of use to the news media. In addition, higher centrality at the membership level boosts, albeit weakly, an organization's visibility in the news media. In general, an organization that can belong to other organizations in way that makes it the center of relationships with diverse ties to other membership organizations is likely to receive more mentions in national news media coverage. Journalists may have a sense through repeated interaction that organizations with such central network positions are able to provide more insights on policy questions.

In terms of our arguments, then, we see some weak support for the idea that superior network position boosts influence in the form of news media visibility. However, we see consistent and strong support for the argument that greater participation in coalitions would be associated with greater influence, although this effect is not as strong as was the case with congressional committee testimony.

State Poll of Influence

Table 5.3 provides the results of the ZINB regression. For this analysis, the dependent variable is the number of times an organization is selected as influential and is therefore a count variable. As discussed previously, the ZINB regression first determines whether or not an organization will be chosen as influential. The second part of the analysis then estimates the effects that are associated with the level of influence.

For the zero-inflation portion of the regression, the total amount of time that an organization spends lobbying in North Carolina is associated with any mention of influence. I suspect that the prevalence of zeroes in the dependent measure reflects the fact that many organizations do not lobby consistently over time—it is difficult to be viewed as influential when an organization is not actually lobbying. The average betweenness of an organization, the total amount of time spent lobbying in North Carolina, and the number of lobbyists employed by an organization are significantly

Table 5.3   North Carolina Data: Zero-Inflated Negative Binomial Regression of Total Number of Times Ranked as Influential, 1998–2008 (n = 1,119)

	Any Influence		Level of Influence	
	coeff.	SE	coeff.	SE
Betweenness Centrality	24.077***	5.721	0.824	0.512
Outdegrees	−126.336*	53.970	2.850	15.820
Total Time Lobbying	0.263**	0.085	0.260***	0.061
For-Hire Status	0.644	0.431	0.382	0.255
Self-Representing	−0.404	0.562	−0.047	0.220
Number of Lobbyists	0.544***	0.155	0.085	0.058
Organization Type	0.202	0.226	0.045	0.128
D.C.*Law Firm	−1.304	1.173	0.062	0.337
Non-D.C.*Law Firm	−0.850	0.568	0.438	0.259
D.C.*Non-Law Firm	−0.425	0.428	0.148	0.253
Constant	−4.614***	0.794	−1.908**	0.589
LN alpha	1.524**	0.498		
alpha	0.218			
Vuong Test	z = 4.45***			
(influence > 0)	8.8%			
Mean Times Influential	3.45			
LR chi-square (10)	47.53			

*p < .05; **p < .01; ***p < .001.

and positively associated with being chosen as influential. The outdegrees variable is negatively associated with being chosen as influential: Hiring additional outside lobbyists for representation significantly decreases the chance that an organization will be viewed as influential. The Vuong test at the bottom of the table indicates that the zero-inflated negative binomial model is a better fit than just a negative binomial model.

The second part of the results models the level of influence for an organization. Time spent lobbying is positively and significantly associated with being perceived multiple times as influential, but no other variable is statistically significant. Organizations that are more central in the overall network of lobbying organizations, that are consistent players, and that employ more individual lobbyists on staff are more likely to be viewed as influential at any given point of time. However, it seems that time alone explains why an organization is consistently influential over the total time period.

CHAPTER SUMMARY

The purpose of this chapter was to move the discussion from the focus on the organizations and their relations with other groups to an analysis of the outcomes, if any, associated with such relationships. The major finding is that joint activity in the form of participation in coalitions is likely to boost an organization's influence in retirement policy in the form of congressional committee appearances and news media visibility, which is a striking result given that the outcomes are distinctly different. Underlying network positions such as centrality, constraint, and agenda overlap show some significant connection to influence but are not as important as coalitional activity.

At the state level, our regression results show that influence—at least in the eyes of peer lobbyists, journalists, and legislators—is a function of network position and ties to national-level lobbying activity. The reason that betweenness centrality exhibits such significance is that resources and information (the keys to the political realm) flow over these networks; those organizations best positioned to access these flows should be more influential.

Unlike prior studies of influence, this chapter has not tried to measure influence as an input, such as with campaign contributions. Rather influence is treated as an output, a reflection of position in the network of relationships. Status in the form of influence and network position reinforce each other as a continuous process. Those organizations with superior network position or that participate in more coalitions tend to get mentioned more in the news media. Others read those stories and seek out the representatives of those organizations, thereby contributing to their enhanced network position. As noted previously, a 'Mathew Effect' takes hold as a result.

So we have some basis to conclude that social relations among lobbying organizations matter in terms of cooperation and influence. But how do they matter? What is it about these relations that lead to these outcomes and others not studied here?

Next, Chapter 6 of the volume engages the qualitative evidence of networked relations among lobbyists and policy makers. In that chapter, we will hear these actors discuss what they think trust is and how it operates in everyday lobbying. This discussion provides some mechanisms that operate within the structure we have examined so far.

NOTES

1. But see Knoke (1990) who reports only 15 percent of lobbyists surveyed report using the mass media. Baumgartner and Leech (1998) suggest that the low percentage may be due to the large number of apolitical groups in Knoke's sample.
2. More technically, the agenda overlap index is equal to the total number of common issues between organizations i and j divided by the square root of the

product of the total number of issues each for *i* and *j*. This measure provides an index ranging from 0 to 1.

3. The analyses drops three variables due to collinearity: dummies for being a membership organization or for being a self-representing organization and a variable for the amount of time spent in the retirement policy domain in terms of six-month increments.

4. I also conducted a logistic regression analysis by recoding the dependent variables as binary. For example, rather than the number of times that an organization testified before Congress within a six-month period, the dependent measure was coded as 1 if the group testified one or more times during the same time period and 0 if not at all. The results of the logistic regressions were similar to the main effects reported here and are therefore not presented.

5. Recall that in this portion of the analysis, I am only looking at organizations that represent other organizations on a membership basis. Thus, private employers are excluded.

6 Trust

> So, those relationships of trust, you know, are, if not the most impor-
> tant, certainly the ones that come up most frequently because you
> interact with these people on a daily basis ... I would say that there
> are a lot of really positive issues of trust that really make the whole
> system work.
>
> —From an interview with the author

How do these interactions and relationships that are described in the prior
chapters work? Why do lobbyists cooperate in the absence of a central,
organizing authority? A primary answer is that they trust each other, and
this chapter explores what trust is, why it is important in the lobbying context, and how it comes about. Trust in social situations has been theorized
and discussed in a rich literature, and I provide a brief summary here of the
key elements. It should be noted at the outset that trust is not always necessary for people to cooperate with each other in many political contexts ('the
enemy of my enemy is my friend'). But what is striking when one reads the
literature as well as the field interviews I conducted is how much value is
placed on trust in these policy relationships.

This chapter of the volume engages lobbyists themselves as they describe
how trust operates, and I draw from my own interviews with lobbyists as
well as other works in which lobbyists are interviewed. When actors are
self-organized, trust is a foundation that makes enhanced policy interactions possible over a long period of time and across a diverse and dynamic
policy area. Lobbyists in a close-knit community realize that they can pursue
their interests when they take relationships into account. The everyday work
of lobbying and policy making is made possible by trust because it facilitates exchange and interaction by reducing risk and enabling joint problem
solving.

In this chapter I first summarize the theoretical work around trust. I then
review prior works on lobbying and policy making to look for how trust
works in everyday lobby work. Reports of trust arise in contexts of interactions among lobbyists and policy makers, most often expressed as the
necessity of the policy maker to have trust in the lobbyist. However, trust

is more multidimensional in application because lobbyists often have or seek some level of trust in the people around them whether they are other lobbyists or policy makers. I discuss this multidimensional aspect to the importance of trust to those who work in the policy domain through the words of the lobbyists themselves. The chapter concludes by summarizing the role of trust in policy making and provides a preview of the next chapter's discussion on norms.

WHY TRUST?

Trust is cited as important factor in generating collective action, and it is often expressed in the literature as social capital. Coleman (1990) defined social capital as not one entity but a variety of entities that consist of some aspect of social structure and facilitate certain actions within that structure.[1] But studies that incorporate trust are vague or inconsistent in terms of the mechanisms by which trust generates collective action such that theory development and empirical work on trust has lagged behind work on collective action (Raymond, 2006; Agrawal, 2002). Moreover, theory and research make the important point that trust or social capital is not always necessary for actors to act collectively (Cook, Hardin, and Levi, 2005), which suggests that political institutions could be designed to enhance mutual trust without actually achieving collective action.

But some trust-based processes have been identified. As individuals repeatedly interact with one another in a positive and collaborative way, such interactions tend to be reinforcing; individuals learn to trust one another and to become trustworthy themselves by not indulging in selfish behavior (Ahn et al., 2001; Lubell and Scholz, 2001; Ostrom, 2000). Greater familiarity with one another and a history of cooperation tend to increase future cooperation (Futemma et al., 2002; Schneider et al., 2003; Weber, 1998).

This last point seems particularly apt in the policy advocacy world for different reasons. First, lobbyists work in a space that is constrained both by issue specialization and geography. These boundaries guarantee to at least a sizable minority of lobbyists that they will meet repeatedly. The opportunities for developing a deep history of interactions with other lobbyists seem limitless. Second, the interactions could be multilayered: Lobbyists can interact with one another in coalitions, by belonging to the same associations—a more formal version of coalitions, by simply working on similar issues, by sharing the same clients or members or for-hire lobbyists. In total, therefore, the interactions have the potential for not just being frequent but deep as well.

Establishing trust and developing a sense of community are mechanisms for producing new institutions that solve collective action problems (Ostrom, 1990). The problem faced by lobbyists is a collective action problem but not in the sense usually meant by social scientists. Many scholars think about this in mobilization terms: Can an association get members to contribute to a lobbying effort? How can the group avoid members free-riding off the efforts of others? But I consider the collective action problem to be one of coordination and sharing. Why help another lobbyist? Why share information? Why divulge strategy? Why work in coalition when others will not help?

Trust forms the basis for repeated interaction and group contributions among actors, and it does this through enhancing reliability and credibility and by invoking emotions that are the basis for sanctions. In Chapter 2 of this volume I discussed relational embeddedness, which typically has direct effects on individual action and leads to trust. Information from a trusted source is cheaper, richer, more detailed, and known to be accurate precisely because continuing relations often become overlaid with social content that carries strong expectations of trust and abstention from opportunism (Granovetter, 1985). Embedded exchanges make expectations more predictable and reduce monitoring costs. They also carry 'thick' information in the sense that the information exchanged incorporates tacit and proprietary know-how and involves joint problem-solving arrangements that stress flexibility and feedback (Uzzi, 1997).

A critical component to trust and the thick relations that can generate trust is time, as noted in the discussion on communities, which consists of both a history of interactions and a view that such interactions will continue into the future. History gives us a basis for judging how a person will act in the future, and the future perspective provides some probability that we will interact again with that person. As discussed before, community is both a repository of relational histories and quasi-guarantor of future interaction.

These ideas mesh with Russell Hardin's conception of trust as encapsulated interest, in which one trusts another because the former knows the latter values the continuation of their relationship, and hence the latter follows her own interests in taking my interests into account (Hardin, 2002).[2] Mary knows what Steve needs to get the bill into shape so Steve's boss can introduce it. Mary helps Steve because she wants the relationship to continue. Steve trusts Mary because of past interactions, and he knows that she will want their relationship to continue.

When combining the interest group research with network analysis and communities as discussed in prior chapters, trust becomes important but is seldom discussed. Policy networks incorporate different types of relations including ties based on affection (Knoke, 2001). Kenis and Schneider (1991) define a policy network in terms of the constituent actors, the ties between actors, and the boundary around these actors and ties. "The linkages between the actors serve as communication channels and for the exchange of information, expertise, trust, and other policy resources" (41–2). But the continuing challenge in interest group network research is in trying to "understand what goes on within policy networks" (Raab, 1992: 78).

Nonetheless, research is incorporating trust in policy relationships. For example, Berardo and Scholz (2010) examines how trust provides a solution to collective action problems in emerging policy arenas such as estuary watersheds in which there are multiple independent authorities who work together because they lack the resources necessary to achieve positive outcomes on their own. These authors collected data on various stakeholders—governmental, nonprofit, and private—across several, interconnected estuary areas with a particular emphasis on networked relations and expressions of trust in network partners. Following Putnam, the authors tested the effects for bridging ties (such as open two paths and ties to popular alters) that provide assurance in low risk collective action dilemmas as well as bonding ties (such as reciprocal and transitive ties) that generate credible commitments in the presence of high-risk cooperation dilemmas. They found a strong presence of trust that was significantly associated with both bridging ties for efficient information transfer as well as reciprocal bonding relationships that facilitate projects and provide intelligence about partner trustworthiness.

Anecdotal Evidence from Other Sources on Trust

Trust is not usually an object of study in the interest group research literature. Trust is, however, frequently mentioned in various works on lobbying and interest groups. Often, these sources are descriptive and focus on what qualities make for successful lobbying but do not focus on trust, its sources, or its impact. But the references to trust are numerous. For example, former Member of Congress Tony Coelho explains:

> I trusted lobbyists because I believed they knew the particulars of their problems. If a lobbyist lied to me, if he caused me to do something that was not only wrong for me but also wrong for the public, even once, I had no further relationship with him. I didn't answer his phone calls or mail, or receive him in my office. Lobbyists are an extension of a congressional office . . . It's not the issue that makes lobbyists, but the trust and confidence they generate.
>
> (Zorack, 1990: 676)

Trust in these situations is exhibited through credibility. Lobbyists by definition are in the business of persuasion and advocacy, and the strength of their arguments is weighted according to the credibility of the advocate. The following quotes from three different policy actors demonstrate this point:

> The most effective lobbyists build credible relationships with the key players in a Member's office in order to get the cooperation they need from them.
>
> (Zorack, 1990: 795)

> A good lobbyist must possess a number of qualifications—experience, an understanding of industry problems, knowledge of the political system and policy matters, and credibility. To persuade policy makers in the Senate, the House and the Executive branch of the merits of a case, a lobbyist must possess credibility, the single most important qualification, in addition to the obvious need for contracts, experience, and understanding of the trends of policy making on a given issue over the years. A chief executive officer should always ask, "Will this individual (or firm) add credibility to my case?"
>
> (Zorack, 1990: 810)

> Personality differences make selecting good lobbyists difficult. Most people look for extroversion, but that characteristic doesn't guarantee success. Whether extrovert or introvert, the true measure of a successful lobbyist is effectiveness, which is linked to credibility.
>
> (Zorack, 1990: 824)

Much of this discourse indicates a trust that is one-way in nature: Members of Congress and their staff need to have trust in the lobbyists because they are reliant on lobbyists for information and services. But it is not clear if trust flows in both directions.

The sources of trust are time and repeated interaction, which is difficult to find a short cut around. One former Member of Congress put it this way, "Lobbyists arriving in Washington must either compete with those who already have access and proven track records or tie themselves to experienced lobbyists who are known and trusted and have probably been involved with political activities and fund-raising" (Zorack, 1990: 644)

These sources, which are anecdotal in nature, make clear that trust is a key part of the lobbyist-policy maker relationship and essential to influence. However, these quotes are limited in couple of ways. They say nothing about trust between lobbyists, which is particularly striking given the level of coalition or joint activity that occurs among interest groups. In addition, the quotes suggest that trust is unidirectional, flowing from the lobbyist to the policy maker. One might infer that the lobbyist has no need to trust the policy maker. The next section's discussion of the lobbyist interviews conducted by this author not only reinforce the importance of trust but show that trust flows in both directions between lobbyist and policy maker and between lobbyists.

The Importance of Trust in Lobbying

Nearly to a person, lobbyists stated that trust was important for their work and that most of their peers could be trusted. To be sure, relying on others carries risks, and these risks come in different guises. Certainly there is a risk that you could be a sucker in the proverbial Prisoner's Dilemma—you cooperate, but your partner does not reciprocate, which is more likely when there is a power imbalance, such as between a decision maker like a member of Congress and a lobbyist. In introducing bills or staking out a position on an issue, for example, members of Congress are particularly eager to show that they have support of different communities. The fear from the lobbying community is that communications could be misinterpreted. A lobbyist cites the risk that comes from providing feedback on legislation with a member of Congress:

> Do you 'commend' or do you 'applaud?' Or do you ever use the magical 'E' word of endorse or support, or do you just commend their efforts and not the final product? Whatever letter you may send that may be positive, even if it also lists a whole number of different concerns that you may have, that those letters get held up in a committee markup or on the floor of Congress, and the person says, "I am holding in my hands letters of support from trade association ABC and trade association XYZ." And we may not have meant it that way, but you take a certain calculated risk.

In some cases, merely engaging in dialogue or meeting together can be misconstrued. In the following passage, a pro-business lobbyist considered the downsides of attending a meeting convened by a liberal Democratic Senator in order to resolve a contentious employee benefits issue. The Senator took positions on the issue contrary to the lobbyist's trade association but had wanted different viewpoints represented at the meeting. For the lobbyist, the comfort level of such a meeting with broad participation was not high enough: "Since we didn't have a great deal, really, any confidence that we would like the final product, we were concerned, whether intentionally or not, that our ability to oppose it later on would be compromised."

Potential cooptation or even the perception of cooptation within these dense linkages is a critical risk for lobbyists in this situation. A lawyer representing financial interests makes a related point about the perceptions of allies and clients: "You've got to be careful that you are not seen by your clients or your stakeholders as compromising too much, being insufficiently strong in defense of the business perspective." Moreover, he notes that in the case of sharing information and services with congressional offices, one needs to be concerned about how that information is shared after it is sent. "But, nonetheless it wouldn't even just be with the [Senator's] staff, how the staff would characterize it. It is, how would other allies of the [Senator's] staff characterize it?" This issue of different audiences or publics was mentioned by another lobbyist: "I am less apt to call someone and pick someone's brain on a particular issue or tell them my strategy if . . . I think that telling them that is going to leak to the wrong person or they will perhaps ever use that against me in a conversation with somebody else."

Risk comes up in interactions between lobbyists, such as in coalition work. A lobbyist could be concerned that colleagues may take advantage of a coalition in order to further their own agenda. A different lobbyist stated, "You may not want them to, if you are in a meeting, you may not want them to take control and drive the bus, so to speak." Working together, I was told, requires knowledge of how your allies will act and trusting that they will play their part. One lobbyist spoke of situations in which his organization may be in a coalition with 'allies of convenience' such that all have the same goal, but there might be some distrust or distance. In these cases, coalition members have similar concerns that untrustworthy allies might take advantage of cooperation for their own gain:

> So, if you portray yourself as the leader of the coalition because you want to impress the media or your members or your prospective members, well, you know, why should this other organization that's working equally hard, is just as much a leader, you know, cooperate with you because you're trying to hog all the credit?

In such a close-knit environment, a lot of information is flowing in both directions through the policy domain, as noted by a lawyer who represented a group of organizations who have their own lobbyists. He said that the vast majority of his time is spent talking with other lobbyists:

> It's not just from me to them but from them to me as well when I have those conversations. But I am probably talking to non-client lobbyists everyday about something. I am probably on the horn with someone at one of the [trade associations] that I don't represent or somebody at one of the financial institutions that I don't represent almost every day because there's some significant nexus of interests and we're trying to coordinate, trying to get on the same page, trying to share information, trying to plan, so those relationships are important.

As many lobbyists pointed out, however, sharing information has risks and possible repercussions. In the anecdote that opened Chapter 2 of this volume, a lobbyist noted that the close-knit nature of the pension community made it easy to tell who said what to a journalist. Such noticeability makes it difficult to mischaracterize another's position because information flowed so easily, quickly, and transparently. In the typical situation in which the lobbyist has valuable and nonpublic information, withholding such information has an opportunity cost in terms of potentially boosting one's own prestige or influence but also carries certain risks.

> You know, you want to share it to be helpful in the common objective that you all want to achieve, but you may want to keep it quiet because you do want to be the first one to reveal it to the different audiences

so there may be some competitiveness on your part to do that. Or sometimes because you are afraid that if you share it with so-and-so, it could deliberately or inadvertently end up in the wrong hands and that would undermine your objectives, and that of course relates to the trust between and amongst allies because you may be withholding information for all the right reasons but you are still withholding information.

The Benefits of Trust

When present, trust not only reduces these risks but also confers benefits such as greater access to information. A corporate lobbyist noted, "When you've developed a relationship and you know the person, you are willing to share." Trust can come up in the context of working in alliance with other organizations. This lobbyist is discussing how trust relates to the use of information that is proprietary in nature, and the issues crop up in terms of the relationship with the information source as well as with possible allies and audiences.

> And [trust] can come up in innumerable ways in terms of somebody in your respective membership or someone on Capitol Hill shared some information with you on the one hand, you have to make a judgment call between sharing the information because it would be helpful for the other person to know; not sharing the information because maybe the person who shared the information specifically does not want it to be shared with this other group who is your ally for whatever reason that relates to their own relationship or their own distrust that it remain confidential or whatever it might be. You know, you want to share it to be helpful in the common objective that you all want to achieve, but you may want to keep it quiet because you do want to be the first one to reveal it to the different audiences so there may be some competitiveness on your part to do that. Or sometimes because you are afraid that if you share it with so-and-so, it could deliberately or inadvertently end up in the wrong hands and that would undermine your objectives, and that of course relates to the trust between and amongst allies because you may be withholding information for all the right reasons but you are still withholding information.

A relationship based on trust enables more fine-grained information to be transferred because the credibility of the information is a function of the relationship that transmits the information. Thus the quality and usefulness of the information that is being shared is higher.

> Now, there's information like the bill was introduced three days ago, which you can find out on Thomas.[3] Versus "my boss is going to introduce this bill in ten days and it is going to have these elements," and

that's nowhere to be found in the public domain. But it's not interpretative, it's more general, but it's still valuable because it's not out in the public domain. So, things that are purely informational can be valuable.

An attorney for a respected law firm remarked that when he is asked to review draft legislative proposals by congressional staffers, trust alleviates the usual worries about her input being mischaracterized as an endorsement. The relationship creates tacit expectations: "There are some staffers, some offices where you wouldn't have to ever think about that. It would just be understood." Similar to a quote previously provided, she also describes how information sharing generally works:

And you know it's a lot of what we do is sort of informational exchange. I often feel that I am a broker. Like I am gathering information from various sources and disseminating it out to various sources. It's a big part of what I do. And when you feel that you've clicked with someone, whether you're relatively early in that relationship or you've got a very significant relationship, it's easier to pick up the phone, it's easier to shoot the email than if you don't feel that connection with someone because you are less worried about putting somebody out, you're less worried about somebody taking it out of context, you're less worried about confidentiality, all the things that facilitate trust and information flow are easier when there's that sense of connection . . . And probably the degree to which you're careful and a degree to which you're explicit [in terms of explaining your position] rises as the commonality perspective decreases or the trust level decreases.

And trust is important for the congressional staffers, too. One person who represents an association of professionals explained this in terms of whether being a powerful lobbyist versus being technically smart and useful matters more.

Certainly with the committee staff the relationships, probably on the technical staff, that's where the relationships matter more because, like as we said, the stuff's complicated, and they want to know that the person I am talking to, one, knows what they're talking about and, two, is not going to give them bum advice or bum information.

A long-time lobbyist who works for a business trade association noted that close-knit relationships gave her access to views and information from policy makers relative to less experienced lobbyists:

Again I have noticed this in the last 4 or 5 years that we were having a meeting with other pension types downtown, and people would be worried about this or that or the other thing on, wondering where labor is, or wondering where AARP is, or wondering where [a pro-labor Democratic staffer] is, and I just would go and pick up the phone and call.

Whereas these quotes demonstrate that trust-based relations provide real benefits in terms of better information, trust and cooperative norms also support ongoing relationships through what Uzzi (1996) calls joint problem-solving arrangements. Relationships that are characterized by durable ties that have a history and are predicated on trust provide more rapid and explicit feedback than in arms-length relations (Hirschman, 1970): "They enable firms to work through problems and to accelerate learning and problem correction" (Uzzi, 1996: 679). This process fosters new solutions and combinations of ideas. Some of the quotes referred to a competitive environment among lobbying organizations, and many organizations in the retirement policy domain do compete for members or clients. In this context, one lobbyist described coalition mechanics in which his trade association and another association were competitors in terms of membership.

> There wasn't a conflict between us and [the other trade association]; there were just problems that just arose in the course of this effort, and the existence of mutual trust helped us kind of end up in as good a place as we collectively wanted to be, you know. So that was an example of problems that arose that weren't necessarily either organization's fault but because there was this reservoir of trust and good faith we were able to work it through and get a resolution. Whereas if things had been more negative, it very much would have fallen apart.

Another person characterized problem solving in terms of the ability to talk through it: "We will have a call, and we will see if there is a way to resolve the dispute, and there may not be, I mean, there is maybe an impasse and a difference of opinion. Mostly it's communication."

For lobbyists without large resources, qualities related to trust might be critically important for their work. A lobbyist who works at a smaller trade association, is acutely aware of this fact:

> I think that trust is the single most valuable asset that a good lobbyist has, particularly if you a lobbyist for an organization that is not intrinsically powerful. Because, you know, if you work for one of the behemoths that is influential by virtue of political money that you can distribute, the amount of grassroots that you can muster, you can get away more readily with cutting corners and not being trustworthy and not dealing as professionally with all sorts of people that you interact with . . . But if you are like most of the advocacy community, you can't rely on that; then your word is your bond. And it's the old story, you know: Fool me once, shame on you. Fool me twice, shame on me.

I do not mean to suggest that lobbying is impossible without trust. As one informant noted, "I can work with a lot of people that I don't trust as well because we have a lot of commonality of issue agenda." Yet the same person noted how trust can affect what lobbyists do: "I can trust extensively someone with whom I don't have much of an issue agenda in common." Trust is an important concept to lobbyists, and they recognize that it is a critical element to doing their jobs. In situations in which lobbyists often must work together, trust makes working arrangements more efficient and less costly. But from where does trust originate?

Sources of Trust

The conversations with lobbyists indicate that a combination of factors tend to produce interpersonal and in-group trust. These factors include time and history in a relationship, personality and common interests, and the roles or positions of the lobbyists and/or their respective organizations. These factors come up in a variety of ways, but the most fundamental source is direct, interpersonal contact. "It is individual, it's not organizational." Another puts it this way: "You just spend time. You do issues with people and you just spend years on it . . . The only way to get them ultimately to rely on you is to help them do their jobs and that's true of associations, it's true of outside consultants. I mean you have to add value the same way in anything in the world."

But trust can be more meaningful to some lobbyists than to others. As one lobbyist noted, "But I do think that so much of lobbying relationships, the trust issues, is also likeability . . . People like to be among people that make them feel good about themselves. Washington's all about that." Certainly personal qualities and beliefs play a role in this, as one acknowledged:

> You go in, you have a meeting, and you'll sort of hit it off with the staffer or the member [of Congress]. The sense of humor is the same, the conversation is particularly stimulating, the back-and-forth across the issue is particularly interesting. So you go, 'Hmm. That was fun. That was a good engagement.' Therefore I'm more likely to take the volunteer assignment when a coalition has to go lobby that office.

But the personal qualities that feed trust go beyond mere likeability. By constant observation, lobbyists form opinions of each other, which feed into monitoring, which is discussed in the next chapter:

> Do you like the way they lobby? Do you like their style? Do you like their approach? Do they lay things out like you would lay things out? Do they not lay things out as much as you think they should? So that sort of observation of their lobbying approach has a lot to do with trust. Style is part of that. Do they lobby in a style that you are comfortable with or do

they lobby in a different style? And some of this, too, is, what is the culture of their individual company or trade? How above-board are they? How underhanded are they? Are they making side deals and backroom deals? Are they more Machiavellian in their approach? Are they more straight-forward? Are they more data-based in their approach? You get to know that about particular institutions and particular lobbyists.

Personal qualities, interests, and attributes can deepen existing professional relations as explained by a different lobbyist who works for a consulting group:

> But, I think you could probably talk to any of the lobbyists around town, there is an intersection between their personal circle and their professional circle, and when somebody is inside both of those circles in the Venn diagram, that's a unique relationship.

As an example, some informants remarked on what they called 'the tax coalition,' which is an informal group of women tax professionals consisting of current and former Ways and Finance staffers and lobbyists who are just doing tax policy. The group is exclusively for women, no male members. "That's a very connected group, and those women feel very, I mean, very loyal to one another." And all agreed that the ongoing interactions within this group of women influence working relationships and not just personal relationships.

From initial personal qualities, time and history of the relationship are important at solidifying trust among lobbyists and policy makers.

> And [another reason for trust] is the ongoing relationship; that these are the same people who, you know, may be our adversary on this issue but they may be our allies on another issue. And we have many issues in which the same member of Congress, in the same staff person, at the same time, is our champion on retirement policy and our adversary on health policy, and vice-versa. I mean, right now we're working very closely with a Senator on some healthcare issues even though we are largely at loggerheads on this retirement policy issues.

In a similar way, opportunities for developing relations can come through organizational contexts. The very fact that an organization is a long-term player is just as important as personal involvement, as a lawyer remarked: "To some extent, if you are hired into a role, the institution into which you are coming may have preexisting relationships." For example, narrowly focused groups that specialize in a policy domain or two may talk to each other more because they see each other more.

Thus, trust is produced in a variety of contexts and from a diverse set of sources. But how is trust made concrete in the everyday work lives of lobbyists? Cooperative norms that facilitate everyday lobbying are made possible in the trust generated by close-knit groups, as discussed in the next chapter.

CHAPTER SUMMARY

Trust among lobbyists is a product of a constellation of factors, such as personal chemistry, mutual interests, comfort with observed patterns of work-related behavior, and the organizational context into which a lobbyist is hired. The lobbyist community is a close-knit community in that information about what others say or do easily circulates within the community. Trust among lobbyists was important on many levels. Trust reduces risk for all parties and makes possible many positive outcomes, such as unity, division of labor, and joint problem solving.

Trust encourages these positive outcomes by enhancing reliability and credibility and by invoking emotions that are the basis for both loyalty and social norms. Trust, then, underwrites the social norms that generate cooperative behavior. We should expect to see group-oriented norms that support relationships[4] by incorporating information about interactions and expectations. Trust also ensures that these norms will be enforced: Emotions make credible commitments for us; shame, guilt, anger lead to trust because one would feel shame or guilt if they let others down. The next chapter develops this framework of trust-based social norms and provides evidence of its application to lobbying.

A question that remains is the relationship between trust and social norms. Trust might a necessary condition for social norms to operate. "Here, institutional arrangements encourage cooperation and solve the collective action problem by building more trust and social capital among actors, which then leads to greater cooperation" (Raymond, 2006: 40). Alternatively, trust may play a relatively minor rule relative to social norms or other institutional arrangements

NOTES

1. Putnam (1995: 66) is another commonly cited source for a definition of social capital: "By analogy with notions of physical capital and human capital—tools and training that enhance individual productivity—'social capital' refers to features of social organization such as networks, norms, and social trust that facilitate coordination and cooperation for mutual benefit."
2. Similarly, trust also enables political participation and interaction.
   Trust, which is so important for entry into the public space (either through conventional action or through protest), is a key concept in the explanation of why certain types of social ties are more important than others for individual participation. Social ties provide individuals with specific meaning

structures that significantly affect their perceptions of participation in social movement organizations. In this respect, close friends (especially in the case of organizations without salient public visibility), and participants already involved in the organization at the highest levels of participation, are better able to provide prospective members with trust than other types of ties. (Passy, 2003: 41)

3. Thomas refers to the Library of Congress website for legislative information—www.thomas.loc.gov.

4. Whereas I would expect that social norms would develop in smaller groups rather than larger groups, I do not think group size is the important criterion. As Olson (1965) notes, keeping the group small is one path to overcoming the collective action problem so we would expect that community-oriented norms are more likely to develop in smaller communities than in larger communities. This is so because we have a limit on the number of relationships that we can maintain. Therefore, embedded relations, and associated social norms, are more likely to be found in smaller networks of embedded relations. The focus here, however, is on a network of embedded relations and not a particular group size.

7   Norms as an Institution of Lobbying

Present-day legislative complexities are such that individual members
of Congress cannot be expected to explore the myriad pressures to
which they are regularly subjected. Yet full realization of the American
ideal of government by elected representatives depends to no small
extent on their ability to properly evaluate such pressures. Otherwise,
the voice of the people may all too easily be drowned out by the voice
of special interest groups seeking favored treatment while masquerad-
ing as proponents of the public weal.

—Earl Warren

How does trust translate into those interactions and relationships, described
in the prior chapters? Why do lobbyists cooperate in the absence of a central, organizing authority? This chapter of the volume returns to the words
of the lobbyists themselves as they describe how social norms operate. Lobbyists whose relations are characterized by close-knit ties are more likely to
maintain social norms that provide concrete, everyday benefits. Such norms
include general calls for cooperation, and they also include more particular
expectations such as 'provide both sides to an argument,' or 'don't speak
for others without permission,' and others. The everyday work of lobbying
and policy making is made possible by these norms because they facilitate
exchange and interaction by reducing risk and enabling joint problem solving. And despite the temptation to take advantage of others, people continue
to cooperate with each other because cooperative norms ensure that violators of the norms will be punished through a variety of means such as future
non-cooperation or reputation loss.

In this chapter, I first summarize the basic ideas of norms and informal
institutions. Social norms arise in contexts of interactions among lobbyists
and policy makers, and I will be focusing on typical interactions that involve
joint activity, including the congressional office visit, coalitional work, and
sharing of information. I next discuss the composition and operation of
norms and their enforcement. The chapter concludes by summarizing the
role of social norms in policy making.

NORMS AND INSTITUTIONS

Trust, as the prior chapter discussed, underwrites the social norms that generate cooperative behavior among lobbyists. As mentioned in the Introduction, social norms can be an informal institution or set of rules that are socially shared, that are usually unwritten, and are created, communicated, and enforced by members of the community outside of formal institutional processes (Helmke and Levitsky, 2004). An informal institution as comprised of social norms, which govern interactions across the set of relationships, must be shared by other people and partly sustained by their approval and disapproval (Homans, 1961; Blau, 1964; Elster, 1989).[1] Helmke and Levitsky (2004) make an important distinction by noting that such informal institutions are neither weak formal institutions—laws that are ignored may give rise to informal norms but the two should not be conflated—nor are they merely behavioral regularities. "Not all patterned behavior is rule-bound or rooted in shared expectations about others' behavior" (Helmke and Levitsky, 2004: 727).

Yet the informal institutions studied in this book do not operate in a vacuum but rather operate in the shadow of formal institutions of government and public policy. Whereas I will speculate a bit more in the next chapter about how the informal institutions of lobbying interact with formal policy making and democratic participation, a brief discussion here about how informal and formal institutions work in conjunction with each other also helps develop the discussion around specific norms—the subject of this chapter. Informal institutions can either enhance or hinder the operation of formal institutions. As to the latter, informal institutions may help solve collective problems in a way that improves the performance of formal institutions. On the other hand, informal norms that support corruption may undermine formal market mechanisms.

The informal institutions that may be found among lobbyists are often complementary to the formal processes of government. Such complementary informal institutions fill in gaps left by formal institutions by helping individuals pursue goals within the formal process, by increasing efficiency, by easing decision making, by increasing coordination between different entities, or just facilitating the workflow (Lauth, 2004; Helmke and Levitsky, 2004). Such complementary informal institutions strengthen incentives to comply with the formal rules. In other words, such informal institutions do not exist alongside formal institutions but enable the smooth operation of the formal institutions. This complementary effect might occur because the formal rules are incomplete so actors need to develop a set of informal yet shared expectations. "[W]e may understand mechanisms of emergence in terms of focal points, repeated interaction, or bargaining" (Helmke and Levitsky, 2004: 731). Once these informal rules emerge, they are communicated through a process of social learning in which members of the community observe the trial and error of repeated interactions within social networks.

Informal institutions of lobbyists emerge because of need to guide behavior in an uncertain and fluid policy area and because of the space left by the formal rules of the political process. The norms of lobbyists are unwritten and are informally shared and upheld. Most importantly, they not only contribute to the efficient running of government—a topic covered in the next chapter—but as discussed further on, informal institutions continue to exist because they provide concrete benefits to the lobbyists.

For social norms to work, the group must have the capacity to enforce them, either by rewarding adherence or punishing deviation (Horne, 2001). Enforcement usually takes the form of informal sanctions, such as shaming, negative gossip, and social ostracism (Coleman, 1990). However, sanctioning can be costly, and this cost could be higher if solidarity in the group is high (Hechter and Opp, 2001; Heckathorn, 1990).[2] The costs of punishing violations of shared norms include the risk of retaliation or at least the potential loss of a relationship (Hirschman, 1970), the loss of time or money, or negative affections (Horne, 2001). But, if a group is inter-dependent, sanctions can have spillover effects for the broader group, and such externalities may affect how other members of the group react; that is, whether they will monitor for violations of norms or support sanctions (Heckathorn, 1990).

How can lobbyists be sure that other lobbyists will engage in cooperative behavior and maintain trust-based norms in the future? According to the Robert Frank (1988), people are often assessing each other. People know each other when they engage in repeated interaction with them. As interactions intensify, the opportunities for cooperation and generalized reciprocity increase. If people can recognize defectors, they can simply refuse to interact with them. In other words, non-cooperators should be selected out over time.

So the collective action problem is *not* one about what to do when your partner does not reciprocate; it's about choosing the right partner. As Ridley (1996: 147) states:

> Frank's theory of moral sentiments resolves this paradox and builds another, more modern bridge—between reciprocity and groupishness. By emphasizing that the challenge in the prisoner dilemma game is to attract the right partner, he shows how reciprocators precipitate out of society, leaving the selfish rationalists to their fate. The virtuous are virtuous for no other reason than that it enables them to join forces with others who are virtuous, to mutual benefit.

But what keeps someone from shrugging off sanctions like ostracism and breaking commitments to reciprocate? When there is no third party enforcer, emotion may provide an answer to the commitment problem (Ridley, 1996). Emotions like shame, guilt, or anger make credible commitments for us.

I would feel guilt if I let others down and anger if someone let me down. Emotions that are based on past dealings and future expectations bring forward long-term costs that do not arise in short-term rational calculations.

Whereas we might expect trust-based social norms of cooperation and others to develop within a close-knit community, this is not necessarily so. Recall from Chapter 2 of this volume that under structural—as opposed to relational—embeddedness, ties can be voluntary as well as involuntary. If the ties are voluntary, trust is a natural outgrowth of embeddedness and reinforces embedded relations. For involuntary ties, trust seems more problematic and more susceptible to opportunism because any threats for misbehavior are lessened by the fact that the parties have to work in the same space. Lobbyists might work together on issues more out of an intersection of interests rather than out of any set of concrete relations. And we saw in the policy communities lots of short-term players. Therefore, the trust we might find in these relationships is likely to be conditional or short-lived because the shared interests are short-term in nature. Of course, initially involuntary relationships can over time turn into voluntary ties marked by trust and affection.[3]

Finally, what norms should we expect to see? In addition to time, specificity is critical to the development of trust-related social norms.[4] Homans (1961) suggests that as norms are particular to a group, the development of such norms is a function of the past history of the group.[5] Game theory has advanced the claim that not only do norms help solve problems of non-cooperation but also that non-cooperative dilemmas help generate specific norms (Ullman-Margolit, 1977). Axelrod's (1984) computer tournaments of cooperative games, for example, showed that tit-for-tat strategies were particularly successful in repeated play but not in every game context. We should expect to find social norms that are specific to the interest group context. Group norms that support embedded relationships develop more fully within a network of embedded actors; that is, where lobbyists are generally inter-dependent.[6] These group-specific social norms incorporate information about the prior interactions, about the other's expectations.[7]

Specific social norms of embedded lobbyists will be directed towards enhancing the welfare of group members as a whole rather than one specific person or actor. If members of the community perceive that the benefits only flow to a select few, those members will have little incentive to follow such norms if they do not benefit and even less incentive to enforce such norms if the sanctions are costly. It may be relevant to note here that group welfare is concerned with the group of close-knit lobbyists and not the welfare of the general population of lobbyists.

Moreover, the maximization of networked relations means that the operation of norms should minimize both 'deadweight losses' and the costs of enforcing norms through sanctions and punishments. Deadweight losses refer to the opportunity cost of non-cooperative behavior; in other words, the gains not achieved when players failed to cooperate (Ellickson, 1991).

Enforcing such norms—through information gathering about norm violators and through punishing the violators—also incurs costs, and if the costs
are sufficiently high, the costs may negate any benefits from cooperation.
The people who have to enforce the norms may let some violations go or
tailor penalties to the seriousness of the infraction.

Following Ellickson (1991), the social norms proposed here not only
relate to substantive norms (e.g., one should cooperate) but also procedural
norms (With whom can I expect cooperation? When do I complain about
non-cooperative behavior? To whom do I complain? What do I get for non-
cooperative behavior that damages my interests?).[8]

In practice, we should expect to see that most lobbyists with a long-term
stake in a policy area tend to cooperate, that detected defections from norms
are regularly punished, and that the community is rife with aspirational
statements about the virtues of cooperation. When it is difficult to observe
actual cooperation and enforcement, aspirational statements are likely to
provide the best evidence of the operation of norms (Ellickson, 1991). In
summary, *organizational representatives who value or exhibit durable ties
to other organizations in the policy domain will also value trust, uphold
trust-based norms of cooperation and reciprocity, and choose the least costly
forms of sanctions.*

EVIDENCE OF NORMS

The evidence for norms in the retirement policy domain primarily comes
from the semi-structured interviews I conducted with individuals in the
retirement policy domain. The Appendix at the end of the book has more
information about the data collection and sources. It should also be noted
that many of the interviewees, who are long-term players, have experiences
in different organizations. A person might have worked over time as a congressional staffer, a lawyer, an executive branch official. I have provided
context when appropriate to clarify the passages, but much of the text
contains lengthy quotes as I believe the informants make the best case for
trust-based cooperative norms.

Cooperative norms arise in several situations, but I focus on certain
routine or typical interactions that characterize workaday lobbying. In the
interviews, informants often referred to typical situations that framed their
comments so some preliminary background is appropriate. The typical
interactions discussed here are coalitional work, the congressional office or
'Hill visit,' and information sharing.

Coalitional Work

If one were to sit in on a coalition meeting, one might observe the following
events. Usually, there is a steering committee of a few people who perform a
couple of coordinating functions such as agenda development and schedul-

ing. Outside of this inner group are organizational representatives who are of two types. One type is the organization that has a stake in the outcome of the relevant issue but whether because of time or other constraints cannot take a leading role. They likely will contribute something to the group, such as financial support, sign group letters, or help in setting up advocacy meetings with policy makers. They will have input but will not, however, drive coalition meetings or decisions. The other type is the organization that has an interest in the issue but is not deeply committed to it. They may be just monitoring developments or have an ancillary issue. This second type of organizational representative is not likely to contribute much in the way of time or other resources and may be present but not actively.

The typical meeting goes through the agenda, which involves reviewing the latest intelligence on the issues, bills, and regulations of interest. "I heard Senator Smith is introducing his bill next week." "The XYZ issue will not be added to the budget bill moving through the House." Much of this is gossip, but by sharing what they know, the group can get confirmation or disconfirmation by triangulation: "That's not what I heard." After taking stock of where things stand, strategy and tactics are updated or revised. Should we send a group letter to Capitol Hill? What about releasing it to the press? Can we schedule some visits with the key Republicans on the Ways and Means Committee? Ideas are thrown out and a consensus is reached. At that point, action items are agreed upon: "We need to set up meetings with key staffers on Capitol Hill—Who will take the lead?" The steering committee members (and others with a big interest) pull out their congressional directories and datebooks. "I know the staffer at Representative Smith's office; I'll call her to schedule a meeting." "I'll go with you—we have a client in her district." Others on the periphery hang back and do not volunteer.

The Hill Visit

The 'Hill visit' is a catch-all term used by lobbyists to describe meetings with congressional staff (hence the reference to Capitol Hill) in which lobbyists advocate for their position. At the appointed hour, the lobbyists gather at the congressional office, waiting until all have arrived before notifying the staffer that they are present. After being ushered into a room, introductions, if necessary, are made and business cards are given to the staffer. As the lobbyists make their presentations, sometimes the staffer will interrupt with questions or wait until the end. After discussion of questions or issues that come up in the course of the meeting, the meeting ends with the staffer giving her feedback and any request for follow-up. Follow-up may include more detailed analyses of the issue, relevance to the member of Congress in terms of local constituents affected by the issue, and/or simply filling in gaps in information. Very often, the lobbyists will have prepared written materials that present the arguments made during the meeting with perhaps background material. These 'leave-behinds' are then left with the staffer before the lobbyists exit. Whether in the hallway or in the cab ride back to the offices (many lobbyists are within walking distance of each other and hence share cabs), a brief post-mortem ensues. The lobbyists discuss additional steps need to be taken, new information to be digested or disseminated, and/or who will follow-up with the staffer.

Information Sharing

The act of information sharing occurs throughout the interactions that occur in the course of a lobbyists' day, including the events described in the preceding paragraphs. Here I focus on a specific kind of information sharing in which the information is proprietary in nature and when there are very good reasons not to share. For example, congressional staffers do call on lobbyists to provide input and technical assistance during the course of legislative drafting. This kind of information transfer between policy maker and lobbyist can occur in other contexts that can be more public or formal, such as a letter of endorsement for a legislator's proposal or the giving of testimony at a congressional hearing. And certainly the information transfer is two-way as the policy maker can supply a lot of intelligence about process and substantive policy. This sort of information sharing also can occur among lobbyists. Lobbyists are looking for information from each other about policy developments, strategy, and opportunities for policy advocacy.

Substantive Norms of Workaday Lobbying

In terms of specific norms, I divide norms among lobbyists into substantive and procedural norms. Substantive norms are the dos and don'ts of everyday interactions, and procedural norms are what you do when others do not follow the dos and don'ts. In summary, the following are substantive norms that were discussed by the informants:

- Do cooperate
- Do be a straight shooter (present both sides of an argument)
- Don't purport to speak for someone else without their permission
- Don't pursue your own agenda at the expense of the group
- Don't misrepresent or undermine another's position
- Do keep information confidential

Cooperation

The first substantive norm is of a general call for cooperation, which in turn is made concrete in a number of informal rules that govern certain ordinary interactions. Information sharing is one form of cooperation that has been noted many times in prior studies, such as when Hall (1969: 161) noted that in coalition meetings all participants contributed to the group about where things stood with legislative issues. Providing services is another form of cooperation. One of the lobbyists in this study spoke about occasions when her organization was asked to provide feedback on ideas or proposals, either from policy makers or other lobbyists. In terms of cooperation in this instance, time and history figure quite large, as she explained:

> But for the most part, we do agree [to cooperate] for many, many reasons. The first of it is that who is your friend and who is your opponent, adversary, in retirement policy is not by any means a clear cut issue. Right now on this pension funding issue, among some of our best allies are the Democrats who very often would be elsewhere because they share a lot of the same concerns about these pension funding bills that we do. They're not really our strongest allies necessarily on the issue of hybrid plans, for example. So it really can change very much on the basis of the dynamics of the particular issue.

Lobbyists who specialize on retirement policy are generally forward-looking, and their future discount rate is quite low. In this context, lobbyists discussed cooperation in terms of information sharing such as a situation in which a congressional staffer has requested a review of draft legislation even though his association is likely to oppose the bill when introduced:

> So back to your original question, why cooperate? ... there's always the possibility that even if we are going to oppose it, and they know we are going to oppose it, and we tell them that we are going to oppose it, that they could win, we could lose, therefore we want to make the bill as good as we possibly can. I mean, is it true that it's easy to oppose a really bad bill or a really bad regulation rather than one that through our efforts and the efforts of others has been made better? Sure. They do take away some of your arguments if they address your concerns. And, they may even somewhat take away your credibility—not credibility perhaps—but you've cooperated with them so you have to be careful that it doesn't look like bad faith that you were cooperative and now you're bashing them over it.

Cooperation also includes a generalized reciprocity as was illustrated by the Mary and Steve story at the beginning of the volume. This norm of reciprocity has been noted in anecdotes by political observers: Clift and Barzaitis (1996: 123) profiled Paul Equale of the Independent Insurance Agents of America, which would sponsor forty-five or fifty Hill staffers for opening day baseball in Baltimore. "How does the staffer repay Equale? 'When I have a document coming down, and I know it won't hurt my boss if I leak it, I call Equale. I say, "Check this shit out," and I send it over on a fax machine.'" But in these conditions, reciprocation does not always happen, as the National Organization for Women found out early in its history:

In the early years of the movement NOW felt taken advantage of, that people just wanted us in coalitions because of our numbers. When it came down to the meat of the matter, they would not come out for causes. There was a lot of lip service by many groups for the ERA, but were burned many times in many states when the groups suddenly switched around their priorities and their support for the ERA vanished after we had given them support for their issues. "Since then, NOW has developed strict guidelines for joining coalitions," Ferone said. "The groups that we are in are fairly feminist groups, and the issue is reproductive freedom"

(Mattison and Storey, 1992: 141)

Stay on Message

The idea of complementary strengths and the division of labor are forms of cooperation in the context of joint activity. The following quote frames this in the context of a group visit to the office of a member of Congress. In the case of the Hill visit, there are agreed-upon expectations of who will do what during the meeting. One person describes this arrangement:

I think also that there is an informal pecking order . . . If we are going into a meeting today, the first person who would talk would be the person who organized the meeting. If they want to turn it over, their choice to turn it over to someone more technically-oriented, whatever. And then if there are any companies that are constituents of that staff person, they definitely get top billing on that because at the end of the day, that's going to make a huge difference . . . But you almost got a script together after a while as to who was going to say what. There would be one person at the end who sort of cleans up and makes any point that people have just not made. And it's like a little routine that you get into that hopefully the staff person didn't realize it and say that. . . . You have people that really do have assignments throughout the group. And actually with the most recent effort, there was a stage at which we were doing visits and before the meetings we would say, "Okay, who wants to talk about [interest rate] smoothing?" And someone would say this. "And who wants to talk about, you know, whatever, premiums," or whatever the issue was. And someone would volunteer.

Following these group roles avoids problems in practice:

As noted above, the appearance of unity among the group (even if the reality is lacking) is critical in these situations. Staying within your role and on the group message prevents opponents and congressional staffers from driving wedges between group members. The lobbyist has to accept the part in the drama that is put on by the group even if their key issue might be somewhat different.

Don't Speak for Someone Else without Their Approval

Coalitional work involves group decision making, and there are norms related to that process. Probably the most important tool that any coalition has is the group letter because it states the position of the group as well as often indicates the strength and unity of the coalition ("we represent X million Americans"). Letters from broad coalitions are designed to impress policy makers with their long list of signatories so the temptation is there to pad the membership list. However, as an attorney noted, individual organizations will closely guard the use of their names:

> There are clearly dos and don'ts although people break the rules. There is a constant struggle I think and it's come up in the Pension Coalition to never put another association's name on something without their okay. And because of a few guys in association, you have lost, you can't let other people do that to you, it's just wrong, but I mean lot of people do it; inadvertently, maybe, but they do it. And the fact is, it's not like it makes that big a difference, not like anybody's studying this list of people who signed this letter and there are twenty-three names, they are on it. But it is very touchy subject and that can be tense.

This norm is designed to give all coalition members some control when, as is often the case, the coalition is being run by a small group of members.

Present Both Sides

A trust-related norm that applies to lobbyist-policy maker relations is 'present both sides of an argument.' Arguably, this might be related to the norms from McCaulay's classic study (1963) of Wisconsin businessmen: commitments must be honored; one should produce a good product and stand behind it. In a similar vein, the arguments made by lobbyists should not just be persuasive but also be accurate and acknowledge the opposing view.

> [O]ne of the most effective ways to be a credible lobbyist is to acknowledge to those you are trying to persuade the weakness of your own position . . . I also think that you earn yourself a great deal of trust with the people you are lobbying—and this is probably also true in your interactions with others, within the advocacy community; it most comes up between those who are lobbying and those who are being lobbied—I think that they are grateful that you are alerting them that, "Hey, there's another side to the story here." And because it saves them a lot of time, first of all. It saves them from being embarrassed, either themselves or

giving their boss only half the story. And it shows that you are an honest, honorable person.

And it never ceases to amaze me that you sometimes see advocates who are unwilling to portray that, the weak side of their own argument. Now, do you always try to put your own spin on it? Try to craft something in the most positive way? Of course you do. Do you always want to bring all the negative things, particularly if it's in a written document? Well, you want to be careful about that, you know, you want to make sure that you putting out stuff in written testimony or in written talking points for a meeting that leaves people with the impression that you want to leave them with. But, it's also just a very effective way to be an advocate, just to say you know, "Critics of this legislation would say X, but here is where their argument falters." And the other side. And I think that to the extent that people take those intellectual shortcuts, they undermine their own credibility.

A pro-worker activist notes, "I guess I would say to someone new doing this [job] is, do it on an issue you really believe in, but listen to the other side and make sure that you are advocating a position as fair and balanced." Congressional staffers, whether they work for a committee or for an individual member of Congress, are very smart and expect technical proficiency from lobbyists:

> They have got to believe that you are good at giving them the straight scoop whether it's both the good and the bad. I mean, they recognize that you have got an agenda and that you are trying to push something. But you need to tell them, right here is what people could criticize it about, here is what people could say positively about it and you need to be able to convey both sides of something otherwise they are not going to feel confident in relying on you because, like I said, the stuff is so technical that trust issue is critically important.

The norm of presenting both sides connects back to the core issue of trust:

> I think you [create trust] by showing up time after time with good, substantive information and not seeming like a sales person. And the way I try to do it is by making sure that when I am presenting information on the Hill that I try to present both sides. I know that when I worked on the Hill I always felt a little uneasy when someone would come in and give me a big sales picture and not acknowledge that there was another side to it.

One lobbyist who represents a group of professionals, noted that these qualities matter in developing trust with congressional staffers: "You have got to be right, and you have got to be able to give folks correct answers and be balanced in terms of the presentation. And you have got to do that consistently."

Don't Undermine Another's Position

In general, lobbyists should be upfront with each other, as one commented: "Another do and don't that is violated sometimes is never stab people in the back. It's just be upfront about what you are doing and that's violated all the time but at great risk." If you are a lobbyist, and you have represented your client's position in a certain way, you would care very much if others tried to undermine or misrepresent what your client wants ("they won't mind if you insert my provision into the bill" or "the bill failed because that other group refused to compromise"). Whereas the lobbyists I interviewed acknowledged that a certain amount of this goes on and can be tolerated, they did indicate that this was an issue that invited a response, as will be discussed further on.

Keep Information Confidential

As noted previously, lobbyists are mindful of the level of trust when they are conveying confidential information, which may be new developments, strategy, or simply asking what others are doing. Also, when deciding to give information to others, a lobbyist has to consider whether those others are allies who would need the information. Again, this is a calculation that considers the interests of others because he wants the relation to continue.

As a corporate lobbyist noted, information sharing provides a key example: "When you've developed a relationship and you know the person, you are willing to share." As another explained:

> When somebody in your respective membership or someone on Capitol Hill shared some information with you, on the one hand, you have to make a judgment call between sharing the information because it would be helpful for the other person to know; [or on the other hand] not sharing the information because maybe the person who shared the information specifically does not want it to be shared with this other group who is your ally for whatever reason that relates to their own relationship or their own distrust that it remain confidential or whatever it might be.

Norm Violations and Remedies

Substantive norms, either like a general call toward cooperation or more narrow norms like "don't send out anything with an organization's name without first getting permission" enable everyday transactions in the community of lobbyists. However, violations can and do occur, particularly in pressure-packed situations.

> And I mean, let's say somebody up in Congress, you know, one staff member will say, "Well, my Senator is really going to bat for you all, but the other ones are really the source of the trouble here." And that may be an exaggeration or misinterpretation or an outright bald-faced lie that they're doing for whatever reason to promote themselves.

What do you do? What happens when someone does not consult with you first or misrepresents your position to third parties? What are the remedial tools available to you? Sanctions and remedies fall into rough categories of what is the process of sanctioning violators, what is the appropriate remedy, who are members of the group subject to sanction, and who gets to enforce the rules.

What Is the Process?

The issue here is the process of identifying and correcting a violation. How do we obtain and weigh the information about violations of others? When can we apply sanctions? As noted in Chapter 2 of the volume, getting information about others in the policy domain is not difficult; the problem is acting on it. Lobbyists, particularly those that work in a particular area over long stretches of time, have densely overlapping ties and relations that are an important component of their work. As Lester Milbrath (1963: 141) finds, the "lobbyist is basically dependent on the actions of others, and as such he dare not offend. One respondent said, 'Lobbyists must be careful to hold their tempers; they dare not explode.'" The nature of the work and structure of the relations help define the process through which one seeks to correct violations of norms. Because of this context, lobbyists are initially reluctant to confront other lobbyists who violate expectations of certain behavior. "If it's a minor thing and you just suspect it, it's part of the rough and tumble and give-and-take, you know, you by and large let it go, and you don't make a stand over every specific instance."

Why let some infractions go? More broadly, sanctioning one person may affect the broad pattern of relations, say in a coalition: "If you are working with someone who is working for another trade association or lobby organization, and they have been assigned to this issue, you're not in a position to fire them . . . so you try to make the best of it."

However, at some point the cost of doing nothing outweighs the cost of ensuring expected behavior. Resembling almost a logistic function, the propensity to sanction another lobbyist is quite low at first and then accelerates after some threshold has been reached. One informant said, "Is the conflict or is the problem of significant size that it's worth the engagement that will be necessary to address it or correct it?" Another spoke to this:

But sometimes something gets bad enough that you have to make a stand. It's never pleasant, but if somebody did something that deliberately double-crossed you, you can't let them make you out for a chump because it will happen again and again and again. So you have to stand up and let them know that you are not pleased about it. It may come from a quarter where it is an organization that you deal with every day so you can't let it affect the ongoing relationship that serves both of you well. You just have to get it out there and clear the air. A lot of that depends on how much trust is there in the underlying relationship.

Therefore, in terms of process, among the close-knit community of lobbyists, one does not immediately seek a remedy for run-of-the mill infractions because of the high cost to sanctions in a close-knit community. Obviously, this entails some judgment and depends on context.

What's the Remedy?

Remedial norms deal with the nature and magnitude of the sanction. What is the type of remedy that is most appropriate to the violation? Ellickson's (1991) Shasta County ranchers used both gossip to third parties and direct action or 'self-help' such as 'borrowing' farm tools from offending neighbors. Depending on the context, lobbyists apply certain remedial norms that could be called 'direct and discrete.' In the context of the Hill visit, a lobbyist may be suspected of not toeing the coalition line in an upcoming meeting with a congressional staffer. Before the meeting, the lead lobbyist might approach a 'loose cannon' in this way:

Well, what I have said is, "Look this meeting is, say, on thirty-year Treasury [interest rates]. I know that you're supporting it even though you have a different number one issue. I can't prevent you from bringing it up in the meeting, but please let the staffer know that it is separate and distinct from this issue and that's an issue that you're pushing because you know, it's really not fair to us." And I have never had anyone who balked at that kind of thing.

Another lobbyist mentioned the importance of assigning roles prior to a Hill visit meeting as a technique to keep people in line. This role assignment is done as a group and helps enforce mutual expectations within the group.

You huddle pregame with the problem people and just make sure that this meeting is about XYZ, and here's our message points, remember here's what we want to drill into their heads. That type of thing. Sort of reinforce the message. Not that, you know, you want to do it, obviously you have to approach it delicately. You wouldn't want to be singling them out. A lot of times what we'll do, and I think it's a good thing, if you're starting up a new coalition and it's a new issue that a lot people haven't worked on. . . . And we would meet five or ten minutes beforehand just to sort of go over what we were going to talk about, just in the hallway, and, you know, make sure we reinforce the talking points in our minds, who was the leader, who was going to say what.

Or, a *little* more directly: "The other way of approaching the problem is, I guess, is to go about it more gently and to say, 'You know, well maybe in future meetings we should stick to the point,' as a suggestion and not, 'Let's not talk about something.'"

With the latter quote, the lobbyist is appealing to the other lobbyist's sense of process rather than trying to shut the second lobbyist's issue down. If it occurs during a meeting, you also approach it gently but firmly by speaking directly to the person involved: "But I have indicated or had someone else in my group indicate that, 'Hey, we are not really here on that issue.'"

Sometimes more direct methods have to be employed. One informant lobbyist provided an example of direct self-enforcement:

But I certainly had conversations where, somebody in a trade association was out giving speeches, asserting or hinting that one of my clients was doing X. And my client wasn't doing X. But this person wanted to be sure that my client didn't think about doing X. So I had to sort of engage with them directly with them and say my client is not doing X, we're not planning on doing X, stop giving the speech.

This author witnessed direct pressure to cooperate in a coalition context, a story that was summarized at the beginning of Chapter 5 of this volume. A coalition had been formed over an issue that was under active contention, and an important congressional hearing had just been announced. One trade association in the coalition received advanced notice of the hearing and was able to secure a spot at the witness table. Because there were very limited opportunities to testify, the prestige of the trade association was boosted by having a witness appear before the congressional committee. But when one member of the coalition found out, they applied very direct pressure on the trade association to have their witness appear on behalf of the coalition rather than on behalf of just the trade association. After some shouting ("You can't do this!"), the trade association yielded. In this instance, the parties involved knew each other very well from years of working together. This familiarity may have made the individuals feel that they could speak more freely because they needed to clear the air. Because of that, the anger felt by some was likely very effective in changing the association's decision.

As noted previously, norm enforcement is costly so lobbyists are reluctant not just in when they apply sanctions but also in the choice of remedial tools available to them. In what way are remedial tools costly? A lobbyist was asked why when another deliberately misrepresent his organization's position he does not spread gossip about the offender. He replied,

> I mean, I don't do that only because my mama and daddy didn't raise me that way! Does it go on? Sure. Do I vent my frustrations or concerns about that within the family of my own colleagues, within my own organization? Yes. But, do we also try very, very hard to make sure that that kind of disappointment or criticism just doesn't get out to the outside world and other member companies or other associations or the Hill? Yeah, I think we try very hard to make sure that that does not get outside because, you know, that's the type of thing that irreparably damages a relationship, to try to use some information to hurt others and . . . you just sort of have to hope that, in the final analysis, that it all comes out in the wash and that kind of having a reputation as being somebody who doesn't bad-mouth others inures to your benefit more than it may sometimes hurt you not to be able to tell people exactly what went on.

Part of the answer, then, lies in protecting one's own reputation and for a very practical reason: By spreading gossip to third parties, you are essentially signaling that you cannot be trusted or that you might violating the norm against "don't stab someone in the back" through malicious rumor. A lobbyist expressed the common concern that your gossip may get back to the party that is the object of the gossip: "Well, it's also a very small town, and like you said, if you are going to be working on a certain set of small issues, you're going to see these people again and again and again. And, you know, you really don't want to have any bad blood."

Aside from 'direct and discrete' remedial norms, there are long-term effects—reductions in cooperation—that reflect the culture of lobbying. When possible, a lobbyist who has offended another or violated one of the norms is not included in interactions (Compare with the following: "When everyone of importance has stopped listening, the offender has literally been ejected from the system" [Milbrath, 1963: 324]). As one lobbyist said, "If I am working with someone and I discover that that someone is dishonest then I don't want anything else to do with him."

The nuanced mechanics of such norms were explained at length in the context of a lobbyist working with congressional staff:

Respondent: It's not that the doors would be closed to them at all. I think it's just more of people behind closed doors would roll their eyes. And they wouldn't necessarily pick up the phone and call that person if they needed off-the-record advice . . . I think, lobbyists are people pleasers. And so with some exceptions it's not necessarily in our nature to say, "you lied to me or I heard you were on the Hill lobby against our proposal, can we talk about that?" and it's been going on for seven years. That's just my perception. And then to get to your question about this credibility issue, I think that there are consequences, but the consequences are not always obvious. There are definitely people that I feel like I have learned not to trust and yet I do work with them and I'm perfectly cordial to them and I would never say to them . . .

Interviewer: "I don't trust you"?

Respondent: "I don't trust you," yeah. And that has lot to do with my personality and maybe that's probably why I'm lobbyist, I am a people pleaser. But those people are also not people that I would ever voluntarily make contact with. I'm forced to, because of the work situations and that's fine; it's not like I hate them, I just don't trust them. So I think that those consequences are a lot harder to measure.

In some situations that do not involve trust or cooperative behavior, coalitions did erode or fall apart. In the situations I am about to discuss, there is a norm that says you do not send out anything in writing with an organization's signature or do anything in the coalition's name without getting prior approval from all members of the coalition. In those cases in which there were not very good or strong relations, exit was the only sanction option for violating this norm. The following quotation discusses a situation in which a coalition of some seventy organizations sent out a joint letter. A couple of months later, a new development on the issue inspired the coalition to re-send the letter with modest changes. Because it was basically the same letter, to save time coalitions were asked to opt-out of the letter rather than opt-in: A pro-business lobbyist discloses what happened next:

Well, you know, one person who was out on vacation didn't have a chance to respond. They were very angry. And they just exited the coalition just like that despite my *mea culpa*, and I should have got their opt-in ahead of time. . .I didn't know this person, there was not a lot of good will between us to begin with, I mean, they were just part of this coalition, more passive. And they were able to withdraw without any consequences because it wasn't like we could work it out because we knew each other over a period of time. If it was someone like [a similar trade association], they would say, "Hey, I didn't like the way you did that. Just make sure you contact me directly, etc."

I asked another about violations against the norms of not stabbing people in the back, which he said is violated all the time. Interviewer: "Yeah but is there a cost to that?" Respondent: "Over the long haul. If you bite somebody on their behind, you know you are going to have to work with them in the future so you better not. And that's kind of an unwritten rule, that is, you might meet someone going up, you might meet the same person going down, so you don't do it." As another informant mentioned in the context of congressional staff relationships, "people on the Hill remember who's been on the team and who's not been on the team."

Who's in the Group and Who Enforces the Rules?

Finally, I should offer a brief word about norms that define who is subject to group norms and who can apply those sanctions in the lobbying context. So-called constitutive norms identify who is part of the group through various ways, including dress, speech, etiquette, and/or rituals. These are the membership rules and rituals of solidarity. In some ways, the sources of trust mentioned previously make up some of these constitutive norms: Common interests and ways of doing your job are but one example, and the dress of lobbyists might be thought of as distinctive (the lobby outside the Senate Finance Committee hearing room has been referred to in the past as 'Gucci Gulch' due to the preponderance of expensive footwear loitering outside the hearing room).[9] It is telling that one of the outsider pension activist leaders remarked that the Congressional staffers enjoy hearing from him because he is not the typical lobbyist—he does not wear a tie on purpose.

As to who does the enforcing, again, this is a close-knit group that knows each other by how they are quoted by the news media, as a previous passage showed. Membership in this particular sub-community is measured in terms of doing the work, day in and day out, for years. In terms of who enforces the rules, in the case of lobbyists, it is pretty clear that first person enforcement is expected for reasons mentioned previously.

CHAPTER SUMMARY

Cooperative norms underpin everyday relations among lobbyists in a policy domain. Lobbyists in a policy domain are connected to each other through repeated and multiple relations. What this chapter shows is that these close-knit ties have content in the form of mutual and overlapping expectations. If you meet these expectations—if you play by the rules—you can gain some concrete advantages.

The trust generated through these sources translates into a general trust-based norm of cooperation, which also is expressed in concrete situations as norms of "present both sides to an argument," "be a straight-shooter," "stay within your assigned role in Hill visits," and "don't send out letters with organizational signatures without permission," among others.

It may be objected that these are not norms at all because they are not enforceable; that the sanctions mentioned previously are not really sanctions. And indeed the quotations indicate that violations occur and that lobbyists were reluctant to call out others when they stepped over a line. I argue that these specific expectations are enforceable, but lobbyists carefully choose enforcement strategies that are not damaging to their own reputations, to their direct relations, and to the fabric of the community at large. Therefore, most lobbyists will let some infractions go up to a point, after which they confront the offender directly, particularly if they know the other lobbyist. Lobbyists do not engage in gossip as a sanction tool because of reputation effects, but third parties who have power, such as congressional staffers, can enforce some norms by keeping parties 'out of the loop.' Moreover, lobbyists in a web of relations take the long view about everything including sanctions. The price, as a lobbyist told me, is paid "over the long haul," which is not to suggest that self-interest never comes into play. Trust matters, however, for maximizing group welfare because it is built on the desire to continue the relationships that constitute the group. Hence, norms that maximize group welfare come into play—not in every situation, but in many. The interests of the members of a close-knit group are part of the calculations of any member of the group.

NOTES

1. Sociology has not always been adept at developing coherent theories of social norms. Functionalist schools of thought (Durkheim [1893] 1984; Parsons 1951; Merton 1968) held that social norms serve to promote the survival of the group. Whereas the functionalist approach has many issues associated with its analysis—tautology and the difficulty of translating evolutionary biology to social systems among them—the idea persists that social norms develop and exist because they provide a benefit of some kind. Another approach has been Marxist and other interest group theories that hold that the most powerful groups in society exploit norms in order to further their own interests. Thus, the idea of false consciousness in Marxist thought would hold that social norms encourage proletarians to engage in behavior that does not question or challenge the pro-capitalist social order. The difficulties here are in proof: For example, how does a neutral social norm like reciprocity reflect the dominant capitalist order?
2. "However, punishing one's friends is costly. Because these costs are likely to be higher the more solidary the group is, certain norms might be less likely to emerge in highly solidary groups" (Hechter and Opp, 2001: 399).
3. "A player with a network rich in information benefits has: 1) contacts established in the places where useful bits of information are likely to air, and 2) a reliable flow of information to and from those places. The second criterion is as ambiguous as it is critical. It is a matter of trust, of confidence in the information passed and in the care with which contacts look out for your interests. . . . We use whatever cues can be found for a continuing evaluation of the trust in a relation, but really don't know it until the trusted person helps when you need it" (Burt, 2000: 288).
4. "In ongoing relations, human beings do not start fresh each day, but carry the baggage of previous interactions into each new one. . . . Structures of relations

also result from processes over time and can rarely be understood except as accretions of such processes" (Granovetter, 1992: 34).

5. "A norm is a statement made by a number of members of a group, not necessarily by all of them, that the members ought to behave in a certain way in certain circumstances. . . . Our example is an output norm in an industrial group: a statement that no member ought to turn out more than a certain number of pieces of work in an hour or a day. Whereas we call the value put on social approval or on money a generalized reward, a norm remains specific to a particular situation: a different industrial group might value conformity to a different norm. Why the group should find conformity valuable is a question whose answer, again, depends on the past history of the members in a particular factory or industrial community" (Homans, 1961: 46).

6. Although I expect that social norms develop in smaller groups rather than larger groups, I do not think group size is the important criterion. As Olson (1965) notes, keeping the group small is one path to overcoming the collective action problem so we expect that community-oriented norms are more likely to develop in smaller communities than in larger communities. This is so because we have a limit on the number of relationships that we can maintain. Therefore, embedded relations, and associated social norms, are more likely to be found in smaller networks of embedded relations. The focus here, however, is on a network of embedded relations and not a particular group size.

7. "To generalize the point, if researchers do not analyze the conditionality of a norm, it is unclear just what they are explaining" (Hechter and Opp, 2001: 406).

8. As to content, Ellickson makes the further requirement that group-oriented norms deal with what he calls 'workaday affairs' or interactions. Ellickson (1991: 174–6) makes this restriction in order to solve problems of potential indeterminacy stemming from foundational rules that enable voluntary exchange and purely distributive norms. While, I, too, restrict my hypothesis to routine interactions, the concerns raised by Ellickson have less weight in lobbyist relationships than in the market for beef cattle.

9. There is a well-known popular book on lobbying in the 1980s that incorporates this moniker: *Showdown at Gucci Gulch* (Birnbaum and Murray, 1988).

8 Lobbyists, Norms, and Public Policy

> Yeah, my neighbor occasionally calls out when I am leaving the house
> in the morning, "So, you taking your bags of cash with you to work?"
>
> —From an interview with the author

Are close-knit communities of lobbyists good for democracy? What are the policy implications of these workaday professional practices? The prior chapters showed how interest groups are connected to each other and how such connections affected policy outcomes and workaday interaction. The chapter preceding this one discussed in particular how underlying the common, everyday social interactions of lobbyists are norms that guide behavior and improve the workaday business of policy advocacy and the making of policy. Such norms operating across a network of lobbyists and policy actors help solve collective action problems in policy environments that are dense and information-rich. They provide efficiencies in finding and processing information.

But, networked lobbyists and their norms might reinforce the status quo and act as shibboleths for someone outside of the community. For the citizen or activist who is not part of such a community, such practices reduce the effectiveness of their message or block it altogether.

This final chapter summarizes the prior six chapters, poses possible implications of social norms in policy making, and provides new ideas about how we might study policy making. I first summarize the theoretical basis for this work and the associated findings of the prior chapters. I then consider how close-knit relations and associated social norms fit into ideas of policy stability and change, and how such norms both hinder and encourage good policy making. In concluding, I argue that scholars of policy making have to go beyond the key players and even the networks of actors and consider nature of interactions within policy domains in order to understand how policy endures or changes.

SUMMARY

To restate the questions asked in the Introduction, how does cooperation come about in lobbying work? How does cooperative lobbying affect policy making? I told the Mary and Steve case study for a reason: Like the use of circumstantial evidence in law, one piece of data is not much by itself, but multiple pieces can be put together to tell a rich narrative. The case study and other stories and quotes enabled different types of data, methods, and perspectives to get at what really happens inside policy making.

Whether it's sharing common policy interests and goals, being at the 'center of the action,' or belonging to 'webs of affiliations,' embeddedness enables faster and 'thicker' flows of information; it establishes trust and thereby the reliability of information, and it helps solve problems of collective action and cooperation among parties that are in some ways competitors. Formal political institutions foster deep and durable ties by creating conditions of repeated exchange, rewards for cooperation, and positive incentives for collective action. The political and policy processes encourage specialization in particular policy areas: The description and history of lobbying in Chapter 1 of this volume told a story of a shift from individualistic and particularistic lobbying—the man waiting for the legislator in the lobby—to one of clusters of interest groups that increasingly are specialized by subject matter expertise and within policy domains. In these policy domains, the lobbyist deals with uncertainty and complexity that comes from both the substance of issues and the dynamics of the interest groups, some of which are long-term players but others of which only have a fleeting presence.

Chapter 2 of this volume was concerned about the idea that embedded networks of organizations that replicate themselves over time develop community within these policy domains. Within the overall group of organizations, a smaller set of lobbying organizations consistently worked on retirement policy. Embedded relations formed over time among these long-term organizations made shared interests more likely and ties more durable. This idea of community was illustrated in the retirement policy area, as many of my informants told me that a community existed among a small group of organizations and individuals who recognized and knew each other.

Chapters 3, 4, and 5 of this volume took an empirical look at this idea of community by examining social network influences on lobbying activity. The argument in Chapter 3 was that embedded ties facilitated participation in coalitions. Coalition participation was a function of increased centrality in the network of association memberships and for-hire relationships as well as work in prior coalitions. In Chapter 4, the longitudinal network analysis indicated that influence processes between lobbyists as well as 'bandwagon' effects were significant sources of agenda change. In Chapter 5, the outcome was the reputation for influence, whether being called to testify; getting your organization's name in the news media; or, in the case of North Carolina, being judged influential over the course of a legislative session. Prominent network positions and joint activity were linked to heightened reputations for policy influence.

Whereas the prior chapters connected being embedded in a policy network and specific policy actions, Chapters 6 and 7 of this volume focused on the mechanisms that explain those relationships and outcomes. Lobbyists discussed the importance of trust in their daily dealings with each other and with politicians, and trust is not just unidirectional from the politician to the lobbyist, but is reciprocal between politicians and lobbyists and between lobbyists themselves. Lobbyists in embedded relationships are likely to uphold trust-related social norms that maximize group welfare, and cooperative norms figured very prominently in their descriptions of routine interactions. Sanctions for violations of cooperative norms, however, were carefully selected and cautiously applied, probably because of the highly dense relations within the policy domain.

POLICY STABILITY AND CHANGE

Norms and relationships matter for everyday lobbying, but do they matter for policy stability and change? In Chapter 2 of this volume, I reviewed some of the key theoretical approaches to understanding policy communities. Policy communities operate as shared knowledge groups that operate in information-rich environments. Instead of a market metaphor in which information-armed policy actors—lobbyists and policy makers and others—contribute to policy stability by holding each other in check, I see policy actors as boundedly rational: the problem in decision making is not information scarcity but attention scarcity and cognitive limitations. To overcome these limitations and environmental constraints, actors rely on bias and heuristics. Rather than a war of talking points, policy actors repeatedly interact with trusted people and organizations for information and interpretation. This idea forms the structure of policy communities and facilitates policy stability.

The concepts discussed in this book have application to how we understand the way policy development works. With regard to policy stability, for example, Paul Pierson applied the economics concept of path dependence to the study of politics (2004), noting that positive feedback effects make policy change difficult under certain conditions. Path dependence can occur when a new policy or institution has high set-up costs, when the benefits from a new policy or institution increase when one learns how to use it, when others learn how to use and innovate on the new institution, and when people adapt their behavior to the policy or institution that they expect to dominate in the future. A social perspective among policy actors partially fits within this framework as part of the benefits from a policy choice flowed to an actor when other actors coordinated their actions in line with the policy and when people adapted to the expectation that the policy would continue in place. The influence and bandwagon effects discussed in Chapters 3 and 4 are related to these mechanisms for path dependence.

The social process of lobbying also provides new insights into John Kingdon's (1995) 'garbage can' model of policy change. In Kingdon's conception, policy entrepreneurs, who can be a variety of actors from lobbyists to academics to decision makers, circulate in the policy domain, shopping their particular policy solution among other actors in that domain, using the feedback in the process of these interactions to revise or repackage their preferred policy idea. A relational perspective that incorporates information transfer and norms of cooperation and exchange works well in this context and suggests a way to study Kingdon's entrepreneurial framework in a more rigorous manner.

These results also speak to ideas of policy change as discussed by Baumgartner et al. (2009) as well as to the earlier work by Baumgartner and Jones (1993) on punctuated equilibrium. As these authors note, policy can be characterized by long periods of stability or equilibrium, but when change occurs, the magnitude of change is much more significant than a mere marginal adjustment in policy. For significant change to occur, context matters in that the social nature of Washington, D.C., lobbying ensures that policy actors will look to each other before investing resources into particular proposals. A key part of the punctuated equilibrium framework was the idea of the policy image in which actors in the policy domain adhered to a shared set of perspectives and language as applied to policy problems, issues, and solutions in their particular domain. When perspectives and actions are conditional on others, a social cascade can occur that punctuates a period of stability with a significant policy shift (Baumgartner et al., 2009: 251–3). The results in Chapter 4 lend support to this process: Lobbyists' choices for their agendas are conditional on the choices of others. By this we can understand a policy domain as social and dynamic space.

Social Ambivalence—Beyond application to existing ideas of policy stability and change, policy change mechanisms might incorporate the idea that lobbying plays a socially ambivalent role in society. In this framework lobbying creates situations when norms of workaday affairs can change when actors are under pressure, and these shifts can affect policy. With social ambivalence, as distinguished from psychological ambivalence, one needs to examine ambivalence "in terms of the dynamics of social structure to see how and to what extent ambivalence comes to be built into the very structure of social relations" (Merton, 1976: 4). People occupying a status can be exposed to ambivalence not because of personal history but because ambivalence is inherent in the social positions that they occupy (Merton, 1976). As applied to professionals, Merton (1976) writes:

> Yet the interests built into the professional role have a dual character: they require him to give the best possible service to his clients, to remove or ameliorate their troubles so far as he can, and at the same time the continuing problems of clients provide him with his livelihood. It is in this objective sense that professionals have an institutionalized stake in trouble, that they 'live off' the troubles of their clients.

(27)

Dependent situations breed social ambivalence (Smelser, 1998). These relationships often involve other kinds of dependence, such as friendships or alliances between those who are unequal in a political and status sense. Certain social structures can be seedbeds of ambivalence because their participants are 'locked in' by personal or institutional commitment or other situational constraints and can escape only at great cost. People have to live with one another, but this does not mean they have to love one another; it implies, rather, that they both love and hate one another (Smelser, 1998: 9).

For lobbyists ambivalence is multidimensional, flowing from various roles or positions or relationships of dependence. When roles combine or intersect, norms and counter-norms also intersect. It is the intersection of different or conflicting norms that produce ambivalence.[1] Some examples, but not an exhaustive list, of overlapping roles and conflicting norms include:

- Lobbyists should work together to achieve goals, *but* a lobbyist has to represent a client's interests against others. For example, a coalition of lobbyists trying to reach a common policy position may require compromises from lobbyists in terms of their clients' positions. Alternatively, a lobbyist might be constrained in the actions he or she could take on behalf of a client because of obligations to allied lobbyists. Perhaps this explains what lobbyists in the prior chapter meant when they stated the common observation that (a) trust matters, (b) people often violate trust-based expectations, and (c) members of the community are slow to punish these violations. Repeating a quote from Chapter 6: "You've got to be careful that you are not seen by your clients or your stakeholders as compromising too much, being insufficiently strong in defense of the [client's] perspective."
- Lobbyists should always present both sides of an argument, *but* a lobbyist should represent a client's interests against others. For example, when presenting an issue to a friendly politician, many note the importance of the lobbyist giving both sides of an argument so the politician is not caught off-guard by opposing interests. However, presenting both sides may not help in convincing the politician to take action on the lobbyist's behalf. The lobbyist spins the description of the other side's position in a way that makes his argument seem more attractive.
- A lobbyist should represent a client's interests against others, *but* a lobbyist needs to acquire clients. For example, lawyers who act as lobbyists may not be adhering to the American Bar Association Code of Ethics on conflicts of interest in representation. Thus, the lobbyist might be representing competing interests. Whereas there may be no initial conflict because the issues do not overlap, conflicts could arise over time.

Social ambivalence in lobbying may contribute to policy change. The embedded relationships and path dependencies usually provide 'negative feedback' such that policies change very little, but these negative feedback loops are vulnerable when external events apply pressure. Due to the alternating mechanism, the sudden swing to counter-norms allows positive feedback and the political system overreacts. Overreaction occurs from an underlying tension from interests that are pushing for particular proposals but previously were unable to achieve their goals.[2] As one of the informants in an interview noted, it's not that unusual for behavior to change in conditions of great pressure:

> [T]he closer you get to a bill coming to the floor for a vote or in a conference, the more this stuff happens because the more pressure things get in terms of time, the more misrepresentations are made or things are being done in haste and people are forgetting to cross all the t's and dot all the i's and a lot of stuff can get nasty just because people are not paying attention and doing it in haste and maybe have other, their own agendas to try portray somebody as being less helpful than they are or that they are being more helpful, you know.

GOOD OR BAD FOR POLICY MAKING?

> Power can turn anyone into a jerk. A large body of evidence (hundreds of peer-reviewed studies) shows that giving ordinary people power over others can make them selfish and insensitive. I wrote a detailed post about this research on my other blog. The upshot is that giving people power causes them to be more focused on satisfying their own needs and less focused on the needs and reactions of those around them, especially those with less power. They act as if social norms don't apply to them.[3]

I noted in Chapter 7 of this volume that informal institutions like social norms do not exist in a vacuum but interact with formal institutions. Prior theorizing about informal institutions has followed a split in that informal rules can strengthen formal institutions or they can undermine or hinder the operation of formal rules. The argument of the last chapter was that social norms provide real benefits to lobbyists, but do social norms among lobbyists help democracy or make policy better? The answer is mixed.

Ambivalence in another form can applied to lobbying in the sense that we can think of lobbying as both good and bad for democratic policy making. A seemingly endless list of anecdotes and quotes illustrate this dual view. "Winding in and out through the long, devious basement passage, crawling through the corridors, trailing its slimy length from gallery to committee room, at last it lies stretched at full length on the floor of Congress—this dazzling reptile, this huge, scaly serpent of the lobby" (Briggs, 1906).

Of course, lobbying has always been viewed with suspicion if not outright revulsion. "The name [lobby], therefore, does not necessarily impute any improper motive or conduct, though it is commonly used in what Bentham calls a dyslogistic sense" (Bryce, 1907: 691). The first large-scale lobbying effort, the anti-slavery campaign by the Quakers mentioned previously in Chapter 1, obviously was not well-received by southern congressmen who owned slaves. But Pasley (2002) notes that members of Congress as a whole resented being pressured so intensely by men who were not their constituents and questioned the constitutionality of the campaign.

The negative imagery of lobbying reflected its growth as the Gilded Age saw the most widespread and negative imagery of lobbyists. In fact, the term 'Gilded Age' comes from the novel of the same name, written by Mark Twain and Charles Dudley Warner, and which tells the story of Colonel Seller's tawdry efforts to lobby for a bill that would make him rich.

Negative portrayals of lobbyists in popular culture continue to the present day. In 1989, Dennis Quaid starred in *Suspect*, playing the lobbyist Eddie Sanger. Although he helps the public defender, played by Cher, in a murder case, he is not above seducing the chairwoman of the House Ways and Means Committee so he can get his issue approved. In *Thank You For Smoking*, a movie based on the Christopher Buckley novel of the same name, tobacco industry lobbyist Nick Naylor promotes cigarette smoking in a time when the health hazards of the activity have become too plain to ignore.

Lobbyists have been painfully aware of their image and the consequences of publicity. The term 'lobbying' was not popular with late nineteenth-century corporations or their Washington, D.C., representatives, who were referred to as 'attorneys' and their fees labeled as 'retainers' in order to provide a patina of respectability (Rothman, 1966). Another example is taken from Bryce (1907), who remarked on the contrast of lobbying for appropriate ends:

> It must, however, be remembered that although no man of good position would like to be called a lobbyist, still such men are often obliged to do the work of lobbying—i.e., they must dance attendance on a committee, and endeavor to influence its members for the sake of getting their measure through. They may have to do this in the interests of good government of a city, or the reform of a charity, no less than for some private end.
>
> (682)

Part of the reason for the many negative perspectives is that lobbying has been viewed as a barrier between the elected representative and the citizenry. In its holding on the 1946 lobbyist registration legislation, the Supreme Court stated,

> Present-day legislative complexities are such that individual members of Congress cannot be expected to explore the myriad pressures to which they are regularly subjected. Yet full realization of the American ideal of government by elected representatives depends to no small extent on their ability to properly evaluate such pressures. Otherwise the voice of the people may all too easily be drowned out by the voice of special interest groups seeking favorable treatment while masquerading as proponents of the public weal. This is the evil which the Lobbying Act was designed to help prevent.[4]

Despite the persistent negative imagery,[5] lobbying has been, and continues to be, seen as necessary or useful chiefly because of the representation service provided by lobbyists. For example, even in the Gilded Age people defended the institution: "It is of the utmost importance," avowed Nelson Aldrich [the powerful Senator who represented Rhode Island from 1881 to 1911], "to manufacturers and to members of Congress . . . to have in existence some representative organization whose officers or agents can speak with authority on the various complex questions constantly arising" (Rothman, 1966: 207). Similarly, the American League of Lobbyists, an association of professional lobbyists, takes the high road: "Public officials need to receive factual information from affected interests and to know such parties' views in order to make informed policy judgments."

In addition, Rice (1962) makes the functional argument for pressure groups: "When the views of the interested occupational and other groups are available to the legislators in a coherent and responsible form, the process of legislation is simplified and the end product is more likely to elicit the support of the majority of those affected" (110). Senator Robert Byrd of West Virginia, in his magisterial history of the United States Senate, remarked, "We listen to representatives from the broadest number of groups: large and small; single-issue and multi-purposed; citizens groups; corporate and labor representatives; the public-spirited and the privately-inspired. They all have a service to fulfill" (Byrd, 1991).

Community as Exclusive?

The kind of group norms that have been discussed here can cut both ways in that cooperation, sharing information, keeping confidential information secret, and not deviating from the group agenda can also lead to collusive outcomes. If a group of lobbyists are colluding to change the law in a way that is purely in their self-interest and to which most would object, at least most of these norms would assist them as well. Collusion involves a secret agreement to gain something illegally or fraudulently. Graham Crow (2004: 12–13) makes this connection, citing Robert Putnam's work:

> The type of social capital identified by Putnam as 'bonding' is, he recognizes, by its nature 'exclusive' and liable to reinforce social decisions; it therefore 'bolsters our narrower selves'. . . . Simmel's examples of secret societies include a conspiracy and a gang of swindlers and these serve to illustrate that highly integrated social networks pursuing their group interest do not always contribute to the wider social good.

A secret agreement would almost certainly require a high level of trust and may require norms of cooperation such as the kind discussed here. The lobbyists I have interviewed believe that they are not colluding for any illegal purpose, but for someone on the outside of a close-knit group looking in, these norms appear to operate on a knife's edge. If you are an outsider to the group, you have no time or history in terms of relationships. Thus, full participation in the information flows in a policy domain may be limited for those without close ties to insiders.

Several informants to this book noted differences between lobbyists and outsider-activists in the retirement policy domain. During the late 1990s through the 2000s, many pro-worker and pro-retiree activists were advocating on pension issues as large corporations cut back on benefits. Ad hoc lobbying groups, like the National Retiree Legislative Network (NRLN), sprang up to first pressure their former employers and then eventually Congress. More than one person remarked on the differences between insider and outsider.

One of the outside social movement activist leaders I spoke to was a retiree who spent his career with a manufacturing firm, and he became concerned that his pension benefits were being reduced to cut costs for the firm. He often flew in from his home out in the Western U.S. to meet with congressional staffers as a representative of the many retiree groups. He remarked that the congressional staffers enjoy hearing from him because he is not the typical lobbyist—he did not wear a tie on purpose, and he did a lot of walking.[6] This kind of outlook may have enabled these activists to engage in actions that would not be deemed acceptable to those on the inside of the community. When asked about some of the more aggressive assertions against corporate lobbyists made by these citizen activists, a lobbyist who was sympathetic to worker issues was quick to disassociate himself: "We didn't do that . . . At one point, you set these activists in motion, there is no controlling them after that." Both lobbyists and activists seemed aware of a social distance between the two groups.

But does this social distance affect policy making? As the activist noted previously, being an outsider might provide credibility in some circles. But on the other hand, a member active with the NRLN as well as his own company-based organization expressed frustration. "It's difficult to get the attention of members of Congress, particularly in the House. Access is often based on campaign contributions, which are made by major companies."

He gave the example, reported in The New York Times, of Senator Lautenberg (D-NJ) and the pension bill that was then pending before Congress. A lobbyist working on behalf of Prudential got Sen. Lautenberg to ask Sen. Baucus to insert a new provision in the Senate bill, making it easier for corporate employers to transfer money from their pension plans to fund other corporate benefits. This provision was inserted into the legislation after the Senate had already voted 98 to 2 for the bill prior to the change and without anyone seeing the new provision. The Prudential lobbyist just made a telephone call; the informant said he doesn't have that kind of access. He continued:

> Washington is unlike any other place in the world. You see it in the restaurants and other places: the credit card society. I have to work to get policymakers to put that attitude aside and get them to see our viewpoint, the real life experiences of our members. Translating that experience for Washington is a big challenge. Access is a very big problem. The insiders have the power, the contacts, and the access. Once we get in to see them and they hear us, they understand.

This view was inadvertently confirmed by an informant who represented a large corporation: "My contributions only buy me access."

Trust and Better Policy Making

Whereas exclusion and possible collusion are problems in policy making, close-knit relations may improve policy making especially if opposing views are brought together separate and apart from the necessary representation function mentioned previously and in Chapter 1 of this volume. Close-knit relations and group norms allow players on opposite sides to share ideas and feedback. I gave the example in the Introduction of Mary and Steve, which is a true story. One person spoke to this feedback process that formed the basis for the Mary and Steve story:

> So that's why there's this understanding upfront that you are not making any commitments to support something and you may even go further than that and say, "There's no way in the world that we are going to support you. But, you know, you've been good enough to ask for our help, or you haven't been good enough to ask for our help but we're going to give it to you anyway. So here's your bill and here are our comments and we're going to appeal to your sense that you will also want a bill that will be administrable at the end of the day." If you really mean what say, you are not really looking to wreak havoc; you are looking to make things better, and we can tell you based on our understanding

and our expertise and the reactions of our members that here are some helpful suggestions. So there's always the idea that at the end of the day that you want to do this.

More generally, a pro-worker activist who worked many years in retirement policy commented on the effect of personal relations and trust in terms of substantive public policy:

> I mean there is no way, first of all, you know I have a really good relationship with certain business lobbyists, I have got a really good relationship with [the president of a business trade association], . . . I think with [him] and I, when we're on TV shows together now, it's less adversarial in certain ways. I think we come off being more, looking at the same issue from different perspectives, we try to find common ground even we are doing TV shows and stuff like that together.

But a bigger example occurred in the retirement policy area in the mid-2000s during an event called the Conversation on Coverage. In 2001, the Pension Rights Center, a Washington, D.C., nonprofit organization, held a conference to discuss ways of increasing pension coverage in the U.S. Historically, approximately half of working Americans were participants in a retirement plan of any kind (Munnell and Bleckman, 2014). The Center invited a balanced group of seventy-five retirement-income experts representing businesses, financial institutions, unions, retiree, women's, minority, and consumer organizations, as well as experts from professional and academic communities, to participate. This first event aimed at building a sense of camaraderie among participants as an environment for generating promising policy proposals.

Two years later, the Center brought together a similar set of representatives to focus their expertise on developing concrete ways of increasing coverage. Participants were divided into three working groups: encouraging new forms of defined benefit plans and new types of hybrid plans, encouraging more individual private-sector workers to save for retirement, and creating new approaches to increase pension coverage among small businesses. In 2005, the working groups reconvened, with some new members, to refine the interim recommendations from the 2003 meetings. The final recommendations, released in 2007, produced concrete legislative proposals.

The development of these proposals highlights the feasibility of an institutional approach to developing policy. The process of discussing the relevant problems and wrestling with a wide variety of proposed solutions helped stakeholder representatives develop the requisite mutuality of interest as well as lengthened their future perspectives, the qualities necessary to induce cooperation discussed at the beginning of this book. The development of the recommendations was accomplished without formal institutional roles but through a voluntary process predicated on trust and continued interaction.

Perhaps we need to look at the stakeholders in a policy domain as (potentially) linked together such that any policy prescription should encourage and institutionalize these linkages. Such an institutionalization need not mean the kind of corporatist structure that one might see in the European Union in which bargaining takes place among peak associations but rather it strengthens the kind of trust-based interactions that we have seen in this book. William Riker (1986) argued long ago that political actors often had contradictory preferences that led to policy disequilibrium, which could be stopped by an active intervention. In the case of retirement policy, specific proposals need to generate a self-sustaining sense of mutuality and inter-dependence among stakeholders. Creating institutional venues or opportunities for interaction is one way.

LIMITATIONS AND CONCLUSIONS

As the discussion in this concluding chapter demonstrates, I think there are numerous benefits as well as pitfalls to the kind of social processes that we see in lobbying in the United States, and I hope I have been able to provide some evidence in support of my claims. At this point, it seems worthwhile to highlight some tasks that this study did not do or could have done better as a guide for future work.

First, although I did look at some different levels of relationships among lobbyists (e.g., issue-based, coalitions, membership, for-hire contracting), there are other levels of interaction that may be of interest to the interest group researcher. One type of connection or relationship might be that of ideas or policy framings. Whether through explicit coordination or subconscious adoption, interest groups make similar arguments and express similar ideas and values. Research might look at policy advocacy networks in terms of shared understandings as expressed, for example, in regulatory comment letters. Another such level is that of providing services, such as when an accounting firm provides financial or consulting services to an employer. These service-based relationships may also be conduits of information about policy developments and spurs to lobbying. An additional level is that of campaign contributions. Similarity in campaign contributions between any two organizations may be an outgrowth of other relationships, but it indicates a deepening of a relationship between two lobbying organizations. Moreover, it would connect our lobbyists to the members of Congress who receive such contributions.

Another area of interest is the source of an organization's network position. Whereas some of the variables used in this study would be relevant (particularly time spent in retirement policy), the personal biographies of the individuals working for the organization may also be a factor in an organization's network position. Does prior government service matter? What about turnover in personnel? These qualities and others seem to speak to trust and credibility and hence to organizational position in a policy network.

How broadly applicable are these arguments? It is hard to say; even the lobbyists interviewed felt that the retirement policy domain was unlike other areas of lobbying. Although this is likely to be an empirical question, the institutional framework that I described in the beginning of the book, with policy specialization and a linear process that incorporates both formal and informal interactions, makes it likely that such durable relations are seen in many other policy domains. The existing literature on interest groups and policy making, small portions of which were excerpted here, also suggest the presence of these processes. If there are differences between policy areas, what features of a policy domain make social processes more or less likely?

NOTES

1. There are other sources of social ambivalence towards lobbying that do not involve norms and counter-norms. For example, the public might feel that lobbyists make democracy less open (violating social norms relating to democracy), but they may also feel that lobbying is desirable and glamorous (the latter involving stereotypes of a highly paid profession and exciting entertainment activities like golf and expensive dinners).
2. 'Garbage can' models of policy making seem applicable at this point (Kingdon, 1995; March and Olsen, 1976).
3. The quote is taken from the blog post, "It Isn't Just a Myth, Power Turns People into Assholes," at Work Matters, by Bob Sutton, posted on January 30, 2007, and can be found at http://bobsutton.typepad.com/my_weblog/2007/01/it_isnt_just_a_.html. I accessed this quote on May 20, 2014.
4. United States v. Harriss, 347 U.S. 612 (1954) at 625.
5. Over a century ago, one commentator speculated on the public fascination with lobbyists and scandal:
   Scandal and corruption are interesting, and they always have been: The most that is known about the lobby and corrupt bills is derived from the principal newspapers, and one may live in Washington for years and never meet a live lobbyist. It is highly probable that the amount of legislative dishonesty is at least not greater in Washington than in London or Paris. The difference lies in the amount of publicity given to it in America, and to the public craving for that sort of news which stimulates the supply of it, to an extent far exceeding what is warranted by mere truth. ("The New Washington," 1884: 654–5)
6. Interview conducted by the author, March 22, 2006.

Appendix

Because the discussion of the research data and the different ways of analyzing the data are spread across more than one chapter, it made sense to me to discuss the details of data sources, network creation and methods of analysis in a single appendix. Moreover, for readers who are interested in the substance and not so much the technical details, I hope that the use of an appendix will make the chapters more accessible.

DATA

Quantitative and Network Data Sources

Federal Policy Data

Quantitative and network data on the lobbying organizations in the retirement policy and Medicare domains were found from publicly available sources. For the retirement policy domain, the population of lobbyists is derived from publicly available disclosure reports required by the Lobbying Disclosure Act (LDA) that were filed by lobbying organizations on a biannual basis with the U.S. Congress[1] over four years for a total of eight time periods. The Medicare policy data comes from the same source, but I used more recent data from 2009 when reporting was, as is now the case, quarterly. These reports indicate the issues and bills on which organizations lobbied, policy domains in which the organization was active, lobbying expenses/income, and basic organizational information.

The data source has limitations. The LDA does not cover all possible interest group activity or even all face-to-face lobbying. Lobbying for registration purposes only includes informal contacts between lobbyists and policy makers (Furlong, 1998) and as such does not cover other activities such as public relations campaigns. LDA expenditure minimums may exclude groups using volunteers or that are active only for a short time or on a single issue (Baumgartner and Leech, 2000). So in terms of sample selection I am not capturing every actor or group, but the LDA nonetheless is an appropriate source for this study. As a practical matter, it would be difficult to expand upon the richness of the LDA's longitudinal data by trying to survey over time all who work on retirement or Medicare policy issues, and a cursory inspection of the LDA report data indicates that all major groups are represented (business, labor, public interest, financial services, etc.). Moreover, as discussed further on, the LDA reports provide detailed organizational and legislative data, and I have a complete sample of lobbying organizations, which is important for social network analysis. As Baumgartner and Leech (2001) note, other methods of data collection in this area have their own limitations and sources of bias, and these are is the best available data for this study.

Another concern is the unit of analysis as this paper focuses on lobbying organizations that register with the Congress as opposed to their clients. Theoretically, I am interested in those organizations that directly lobby policy makers on specific issues in this domain over time. Clients that hire lobbyists are not always present in Washington, D.C., so the social processes discussed previously would not apply to them.

A third concern has to do with the construction of lobbying organization-by-legislation networks. The network only includes the specific legislation (e.g., "H.R. 3028") listed by the lobbyist on their LDA report but not general descriptions of issues (e.g., "savings"). This focus on specific legislation raises a couple of issues. Data from the LDA reports are self-reported, which poses the question of whether specific legislation is accurately reported. This book does not address these concerns, which requires a different study, but I argue that the data in this study is appropriate. I collected all listings of issues no matter how vague or specific and inputted them into the dataset. For each time period in retirement and Medicare & Medicaid policy data, for example, I created a sub-dataset containing only the specific legislative bills as identified by the use of, for example, "H.R." for House resolution or "S." for Senate bill and followed by the identification number. In the retirement policy data, from 1999 through 2002, the lobbying organization listed a cumulative amount[2] of 7,522 issues or bills, and 80 percent were identifiable legislation. Interestingly, the percentage of specific bill mentions to all issues showed a gradual increase within each Congress. For example, in the 106th Congress, the percentage of specific bill listings began at 81 percent in early 1999 and finished at 84 percent by the end of 2000. At the start of the 107th Congress, 69 percent of issues were identifiable pieces of legislation and by the end the percentage rose to 81 percent. This makes sense because the choices for listing legislation in the LDA reports is more limited at the beginning of a Congress than at the end because legislation is introduced over time.

Even if it were possible to use both identifiable bills and non-bill issue descriptions, I was interested in seeing how concrete agendas developed over time. Specific legislation seemed a better indicator of actionable agenda formation than descriptions of non-bill issues, which is not to say that a reference that does not identify a specific bill is vague as some descriptions are very specific. However, even within fairly narrow sub-issues there are different approaches that are possible, and these approaches are captured by concrete legislation. Therefore, I focus on identifiable bills.

Retirement Policy Coalition Data

I gathered the retirement policy coalition data from several sources: by researching various Web sites related to retirement policy, witness lists at congressional hearings, press releases produced by the coalitions themselves, qualitative information from my interviews with individual lobbyists, and going to organizational and coalition websites, including archived websites from the Internet Archives (www.archive.org). I was able to identify 31 coalitions that operated between 1999 and 2004 although not all coalitions operated continuously. The coalition data was converted into longitudinal network data in which the lobbying organizations are tied to each other if they share one or more coalitions in common.

Legislative Data

Not all proposed legislation was created equal, and scholars have made a point of distinguishing among legislation (see, e.g., Mayhew, 1991). As noted previously, the LDA reports allowed lobbyists to report specific issues on which they lobbied. However, I collected additional information on proposed legislation from the Library of Congress (www.thomas.loc.gov) using an algorithm written in the Python programming language by a former student, Om Patel. I included attributes about the sponsor, such as party identity and whether a member of a committee of jurisdiction or a member of the congressional leadership. I also included the number of cosponsors for the bill. Legislation associated with a powerful sponsor or that have many cosponsors may attract interest group attention. In addition, lobbyists often speculate on which bills move through Congress as relatively few might make it out of committee. Therefore, for legislative bills I control for the (a) number of cosponsors for that bill, (b) whether the bill sponsor is the member of the committee of jurisdiction for that bill, and (c) the bill's ultimate progress in terms of an ordinal scale ranging from 1 (not reported out of committee), 2 (reported out of committee), 3 (approved by one chamber), 4 (reported out of committee in the second chamber), 5 (approved by the second chamber), to 6 (passed into law).

State-Level Policy

The data for North Carolina lobbying organizations include 2,624 organizations that lobbied or were represented by lobbying organizations in North Carolina over the 1993 through 2008 time period. Of these, 2,292 were principals and 1,129 were lobbying organizations. The reason that the number of principals and the number of lobbying organizations collectively are larger than for the entire dataset is that many organizations have, at one time or another, been both principals and lobbying organizations. In total,

797 organizations have been in both categories (although not necessarily at the same time).

Of the 1,129 North Carolina lobbying organizations, 339 entities also lobbied at the federal level from 1999 through 2008. The number of North Carolina organizations that lobby at the federal is relatively consistent on a year-to-year basis. In 1999, the number was 277 but by 2007 the number of North Carolina organizations lobbying in Washington, D.C., reached 299.

In terms of other key state-level variables, I coded lobbying firms according to lobbying activity at the federal level. To determine this, I used some rules. Trade or membership organizations that are state-wide chapters but that have a national-level body were counted as lobbying at the federal level if the national body was registered at the federal level. For example, AARP and the North Carolina Medical Society lobby in North Carolina, but their national-level counterparts (AARP and the American Medical Association, respectively) have a presence in Washington, D.C. Therefore, AARP-NC and the North Carolina Medical Society were coded as being active at the federal level. A sub-state affiliate (e.g., the City of Charlotte Chamber of Commerce) was not being coded as lobbying at the federal level despite the existence of a national level entity (e.g., the U.S. Chamber of Commerce).

Using an organization's status as a law firm or as a non-law firm, I interacted federal-level lobbying with law firm status to create three dummy variables. Organizations that are neither law firms nor lobby at the federal level are the reference group such that we have:

- Federal-level lobbying by law firms (D.C.*law firm)
- No federal-level lobbying by law firms (Non-D.C.*law firm)
- Federal-level lobbying by non-law firms (D.C.*non-law firm)

I also included attributes of the organization. For-hire status is indicated for any time period when a lobbying organization is representing another organization. Self-representing status is indicated by organizations that use their own on-staff lobbyists to represent themselves. I controlled for the number of lobbyists at an organization, if any. As there is a large number of organizations that move in and out of the network over time, I used a dummy variable called, 'New Entrant,' which is coded as '1' if the organization is a first time lobbying organization. Finally, I controlled for organizational type, which has three values: a stand-alone entity (like a corporation or non-profit group), an individual membership organization (like the AARP), and an organizational membership organization (like most trade associations).

Table A1 provides some descriptive statistics for the North Carolina sample.

Table A1 Descriptive Statistics for North Carolina Sample, 1993–2008

	Obs	Mean	SD	Min	Max
Influence	17710	0.46318	4.17012	0	90
Betweenness Centrality	17710	0.00979	0.06257	0	1.723
Outdegree	17710	0.39289	0.95285	0	16
Constraint	5844	0.84828	0.27169	0.018	1.531
Organization Type	17710	1.62885	0.88969	1	3
For-Hire Status	17710	0.0681	0.25192	0	1
Self-Representing	17710	0.10102	0.30136	0	1
No. of Lobbyists	17710	0.25455	0.78016	0	13
D.C.*Law Firm	17647	0.00992	0.09909	0	1
Non-D.C.*Law Firm	17647	0.05672	0.23132	0	1
D.C.*Non-Law Firm	17710	0.12372	0.32927	0	1

Note: Unique observations equal 1,129 organizations.

Federal Reputation Data

Chapter 5 of this volume examines reputations for influence, and the data is taken from both the federal retirement policy data and the North Carolina data. As noted previously, the federal level data had two outcomes. The first measures the number of times that an organization testifies before a congressional committee of jurisdiction during a six-month time period. In retirement policy, there are four committees that have broad jurisdiction over retirement policy issues. In the House of Representatives, the committees are the Ways and Means Committee and the Education and the Labor Force Committee, and in the Senate there are the Finance and Health, Education, Labor, and Pensions Committees. I looked at every full committee or a subcommittee hearing on a retirement-related issue over 1998 through 2004, the time period of this study, and collected data for each instance that one of the organizations included in this study testified before a committee. These counts were aggregated into six month time periods in order to correspond with the six month reporting periods for lobbyist disclosure filings.

From 1998 through 2004, the four committees of jurisdiction held 64 hearings related to retirement policy. The lobbying organizations used in this study made a total of 119 hearing appearances over this time. In terms of the types of interests represented in these committee appearances, the following list shows the percentage of witnesses:

- Private employers—37 percent
- Financial services—23 percent

- Labor—15 percent
- Professionals—13 percent
- Public interest groups—12 percent
- Public employers and workers—0.8 percent

A similar method was used to collect every instance that a lobbying organization was mentioned in the news media. I used the Lexis-Nexis database to search mentions of lobbying organizations in the major U.S. newspaper and wire service sub-database in connection with some aspect of pensions or retirement. I checked the news stories to filter out irrelevant news stories (e.g., obituaries in which the deceased's affiliation with an organization was mentioned). I made, however, an important distinction in collecting news data relative to congressional committee. For the news media variable, I only used those organizations that were membership-based such as trade associations, professional associations, broad-based public interest groups, and labor unions. The reason for narrowing the sample is that a corporation will make the news for a variety of reasons completely unrelated to its activities on policy. In contrast, membership organizations are inherently representative of some group and are likely to be quoted or mentioned for that reason. By narrowing the category of organizations in this way, the sample was reduced from 392 to 120, but as we are looking at the same organizations over time, there are in fact 835 total observations.

The 120 lobbying organizations were mentioned in news media stories 4,323 times over the seven year timeframe. In terms of the types of interests represented in these news stories, the following list shows the percentage of mentions:

- Labor—51 percent
- Public interest groups—21 percent
- Private employers—14 percent
- Financial services—9 percent
- Professionals—5 percent
- Public employers and workers—0.4 percent

NC Poll of Reputational Influence

Since the 1980s, the North Carolina Center for Public Policy Research (NCCPPR) has polled members of the legislature and the lobbying community as to the most influential individual lobbyists. An example illuminates the process. For the 2004–2005 legislative session, NCCPPR conducted the survey during the first three months of 2006. All 50 state senators and 120 state representatives, 442 registered lobbyists (including the lead state agency legislative liaisons), and 16 state capital news correspondents were asked to choose the top ten most influential lobbyists during the prior two-year session from a list of all registered lobbyists. The overall response rate was 48 percent, though there was wide divergence in the response rate of different groups: 68 percent of representatives, 72 percent of senators, 39 percent of lobbyists, and 63 percent of news correspondents responded that year. There is no publicly available data on the distribution of the respondents compared to the overall sample. The rankings are calculated by aggregating the number of times each lobbyist is listed as amongst the top ten and then constructing a list of the top 50 individuals ranked in terms of perceived influence.

I use this data source from 1993 to 2008 to construct a measure of a lobbying organization's reputation for influence during each two-year legislative session. First, I construct a total influence variable by reversing the coding such that the scales are reversed—the number 1 lobbyist is coded as a 50 and the 50th ranked lobbyist is coded as a 1. In this way each lobbyist is rated on a point scale from 1 to 50 with 50 representing the most influential lobbyist. Each individual lobbyist's ranking is attributed to the organization that employs him and if an organization has more than one influential lobbyist, the scores are added together.

Our state-level data source is mandatory lobbyist registration information collected and maintained by the Office of the North Carolina Secretary of State. Lobbyists—individuals and organizations—are required to register with the Secretary of State and file periodic reports. Periodic reports must identify clients that hire lobbyists as well as the amount paid for lobbying services. These reports are publicly available,[3] but they do require data manipulation and recoding. Reports were downloaded for the following time periods: the two year periods of 1993–1994; 1995–1996; 1997–1998; 1999–2000; 2001–2002; 2003–2004; 2005–2006; and 2007–2008.

Social Network Variables

In a number of chapters, I use some measures of network position as variables. A key explanatory variable touches on an actor's centrality in the network. Although there are a number of measures that capture centrality, betweenness centrality is used here. Betweenness centrality captures the number of paths passing through a particular actor. Specifically, betweenness is a measure of the number of times an actor occupies a particular path that connects two other actors.[4] This measure captures a fundamental dynamic in politics, the flow of information and resources among actors. In theory, those actors that are positioned at the junction of multiple flows should be the most advantaged. Actors with greater betweenness centrality should have higher reputations for influence because they have greater access to information and resources.

However, network position may also act as a constraint on strategic behavior and information flows. If I have ties to a group of people, and those people only have ties to each other, I will be highly constrained in my network. Conversely, if I have ties to different groups who are not tied to each other, I will not be constrained in my actions and indeed have the flexibility to engage in a number of roles such as a broker or representative.

In order to control for this aspect of networks, another social network variable called 'Constraint' reflects the situation that organizations may be trapped in their own 'echo chamber' of being tied to other organizations that are themselves tied to each other. The constraint measure is based on Burt's (1992) notion of structural holes, and it represents the extent to which an actor is limited by his relationships with others. For example, if A is tied only to B and C in a large network, A is limited to the information that flows through those two nodes. If B and C also have few ties to actors other than A, we say that A is constrained by his relationships. Similarly, if B is connected to a lot of other actors and A is not, A will have to pass through B to access the information in the broader network. This has a limiting effect on A's potential influence because he has to rely on his relationship with B.

In order to control for organizations that may be trying to influence the political process by hiring lots of other organizations, I use a measure called 'outdegrees.' This measure is the number of ties going 'out' from an organization to hire others. This measure is normalized by dividing the number of outgoing ties by the number of possible outgoing ties in order to produce a measure that can be compared across networks of different sizes.

Qualitative Data Sources

The qualitative data for the retirement policy lobbyists primarily come from a series of semi-structured interviews I conducted with a range of individual lobbyists, but I also rely on survey data collected from a sample of organizations. For the individual interviews, I met with 25 people from January through September 2006. The interviews lasted anywhere between 45 minutes to nearly 2 hours. I used a set of standard questions, but I allowed interviewees considerable latitude in discussing topics. Moreover, as opportunities to probe and delve more deeply into specific topics presented themselves in the course of the discussion, I departed from the standard interview format.

In terms of the composition of the interview sample, the following provides a breakdown in terms of interests:

- Private employer/management/professional—44 percent
- Financial services—16 percent
- Public interest and labor—28 percent
- Governmental (legislative and executive branches)—12 percent

These do not match the representation of interests in a broad sample of groups in this policy area, but there is a reasonable approximation. The interview sample is under-weighted in terms of the financial services, public interest, labor, and public employer/civil service/military sectors and somewhat over-weighted in terms of the public interest sector. In terms of the organizational types represented, the interviewees were constituted as follows:

- Membership organizations—40 percent
- For-hire firms (law firms/lobbying firms)—20 percent
- Self-representing organizations (corporations/non-profit organizations)—28 percent
- Governmental organizations—12 percent

It should also be noted that many of the interviewees have experiences in different organizations. A person might have worked over time as a congressional staffer, a lawyer, or an executive branch official. I do not account for such overlapping experiences here, but for some these long periods of different experiences in policy making no doubt color their remarks.

Interview Schedule
Following are the questions that I used:

Introduction
- Major focus: Why people cooperate in policy areas, how that cooperation is sustained over time, and the role of trust and norms. [cite business studies?]
- Why I chose you
- Confidentiality—masking, erasing, and review
- Consent form

Background and Warm-up Questions
- How long have you worked in Washington?
- Why advocacy work? Why pensions?
- What do you like about lobbying?
- What, in your view, are the downsides to lobbying?

Retirement Policy Domain
- Describe the level of cooperation among retirement policy advocates and policy makers.
- Has that level of cooperation and goodwill changed over time? Why or why not? Can you give more details about that? What issues are driving any change?

Lobbying Generally
- What makes for effective lobbying in this area?
- Is trust important? How important is a reputation for trustworthiness? How does trust compare with size, resources, etc.?
- If norms are expectations of behavior, the violations for which are punished in some way, are there norms among lobbyists? Examples?

- What is the basis of a good relationship with other lobbying organizations? With policy makers?
- House versus Senate: Do you lobby the chambers differently? Offices versus committees?

Social Activities
- Do you socialize (lunches, dinner, cocktails) with other retirement policy lobbyists?
- How important are social connections in establishing trust?
- Role of 'clicking' with a lobbyist/staffer/policy maker?

Information Gathering and Sharing
- How important is past interactions in getting different types of information?
- If you hear about new and nonpublic information (e.g., a draft bill or regulation), do you share that information with others?
  - Under what conditions?
  - When you learn of new information from someone, do you feel obligated to reciprocate in any way?
  - If someone were to leak that information in an inappropriate way, what would you do?
  - Do other lobbyists contact you looking for information?

Services
- It's not uncommon for organizations to supply services to policy makers, such as draft legislative and regulatory language, questions for committee hearings, and review and feedback of draft bills and other proposals, for example.
  - How does that work—Who initiates that? Do you do that or do others in your organization do that? Does it matter whom it is for?
  - Have you ever declined to provide such services?

Coalitional Activity
- Who initiates a coalition?
  - (Is it the larger organizations, organizations with expertise, those with a particularly large stake in the issue, or does it depend?)?
  - If you have been involved in many coalitions, are the same groups the initiators or do different groups start coalitions? Why is that, do you think?
- If you can generalize, what types of groups tend to be more active?
  - About groups that are passive participants: Do the more active organizations express frustration over their lack of activity?
  - Are more active participants less willing to share information with less active participants?

Group Visits with Congressional Staffers

- Who typically arranges the visit?
  - Do large organizations take the lead in setting up meetings, do different reps volunteer to schedule meetings, does it depend on contacts with a particular office, or what?
- At the meeting, who initiates the conversation?
  - How do different representatives participate in the meeting (i.e., do you take turns, follow a 'script,' etc.)?
- Now about written materials or 'leave behinds.' Who prepares them and brings them?
  - Do you each leave your own materials?
  - How long should they be?
  - What do staffers look for in written materials that accompany a meeting?
- Has it ever happened that lobbyists have not worked with the group on a visit, such as not following the script or common message?
  - What happened?
  - What did you do, if anything?
  - What about other lobbyists—what did they do?
  - Did you talk about it with others?

Interview Transcription and Coding

After the interviews were transcribed and checked for consistency and modified to remove personal references, draft transcripts were sent to the informants for their review. The interview texts were then coded using Max-QDA, a software for qualitative data analysis. All interviews were conducted with promises of confidentiality. Therefore, I do not cite the identity of the interviewees and in the text recode their names to protect their identity.

METHODS

Quadratic Assignment Procedures (QAP)

The QAP analysis (Hubert and Baker, 1978; Baker and Hubert, 1981) provides Pearson correlations of network structures such that we can identify in a statistically significant way whether one network structure is similar to another. In general, QAP indexes the probability that the similarity between two matrices can be explained as a random permutation of the rows and columns of either matrix—the lower that probability, the more likely it is that the two matrices are in fact similar (Walsh, 1994). In the permutation process, QAP entails first computing the Pearson correlation between two matrices, then holding one matrix constant and randomly altering the rows and columns of the second matrix. By altering rows and columns rather than the individual cells, the dependence within rows and columns is built into the significance test. An empirical distribution of correlations over some number of random permutation trials is thereby generated and the observed correlation prior to any permutations is compared to the values in this distribution. The p value is the proportion of correlations in the permutation trials that are equal to or greater than the observed correlation. The minimum p value that can be attained is equal to $1/k$, where k is the number of trials (Walsh, 1994).

Negative Binomial Regression

Chapter 5 of this volume analyzes reputation outcomes in the form of count data. The analysis of continuous outcome data using linear regression models assumes that the errors are independent and identically distributed with a mean of 0. Because discrete data often do not follow this underlying assumption of normality, other analytic methods should be considered, particularly when the distribution is highly skewed as when there are many counts of 0. Absent the ability to transform the variable, such as through a logarithmic transformation, other modeling approaches for discrete outcomes should be used such as the Poisson regression. In this study, the variable for the total time an organization is influential is a count variable, and it resembles a Poisson distribution.

However, a classic Poisson distribution is characterized by a mean that is equal to its variance (Kennedy, 1998). In many studies of discrete outcomes, the sampling distribution often results in a higher variance or over-dispersion than would be expected from a Poisson distribution. In this study, the variable for the number of times an organization is influential has a mean of 0.302 and a variance of 1.519. Therefore, a different model that accommodates over-dispersion usually is used. An alternative strategy for analyzing discrete data is to fit a negative binomial regression model (Allison, 1999). This model is a generalization of the Poisson regression model that accounts for over-dispersion by including a disturbance or error term. The usual functional form of the negative binomial model is given by

$$\text{Log } \lambda_i = \beta_0 + \beta_1 x_{i1} + \beta_2 x_{i2} + \beta_k x_{ik} + \sigma \varepsilon_i$$

Where λ_i is the expected value of the outcome variable y_i for subject i, x_i are the independent variables with corresponding regression coefficients β_n, and $\sigma \varepsilon_i$ is the disturbance term. One important benefit of this methodology is that it accounts for the dependence among observations that arises from clustering or from repeated samples or observations being taken from the same respondent over time (Byers, Allore, Gill, and Peduzzi, 2003).

Whereas the negative binomial model takes over-dispersion into account, it may not deal adequately with a high number of 0s in the count data. In our North Carolina data, 1026 lobbying organizations out of a total of 1129 (or 91 percent) are never perceived as influential and therefore carry a value of 0 for both total influence and the number of periods influential. When the dependent variable has a large number of zeroes, an important consideration is whether different processes are producing the excess number of zeroes. Zero-inflated probability models assume that a dual-state process is responsible for generating the data. For example, an organization may not be influential because it lacks the resources or network position to be perceived as influential. Alternatively, the organization may not be influential because although it maintains a registered lobbyist, there is simply nothing on the policy agenda during a given time period on which it wishes to deploy its influence. Thus, two states are present, the former being a normal count-process state while the latter is a zero-count state in which we have an organization that is referred to as a 'certain zero.' Thus, the number of zeroes may be inflated and the number of organizations with zero influence cannot be explained in the same manner as those with influence. A standard negative binomial model does not distinguish between these two processes, but a zero-inflated negative binomial (ZINB) model allows for the different processes and permits testing between the standard negative binomial model and the zero-inflated negative binomial.

ZINB regression generates two separate models and then combines them. First, a logit model is used to determine whether selected independent variables predict whether or not an organization would be a "certain zero." Then, a negative binomial model is generated predicting the counts for those organizations that are not certain zeroes.[5]

Longitudinal Network Modeling

To model changes in the networks as was done in Chapters 3 and 4, I use the stochastic actor-oriented model that represents network dynamics on the basis of observed panel network data and evaluates that data through statistical inference (Snijders, van de Bunt, and Steglich, 2010).[6] In this model, each actor in the network maximizes a utility function that represents the costs and rewards for an actor to be in a specific state (e.g., choosing, dropping, never choosing, or keeping a piece of legislation on their agenda) at one moment in time given the network structure, the changes made by other actors, and random influences. In general, the choice of action for an actor at time t is based on the endogenous and explanatory effects. If an action can be described as a function of one or more substantive utility arguments, the model assumes that the actor is able to determine the immediate effects of currently contemplated actions. Therefore, each decision about an actor's network ties is associated with a change in utility. The choice of action can also be based on utility arguments that are not explicitly modeled in the utility function and for which measurement or specification errors exist; that is, the random utility model assumes that the actor would choose the action that would maximize utility combined with a random error term. When the expected change in utility is approximately the same for all actions, the actor's choice will be more or less entirely determined by pure chance. However, if compared to other actions one action is associated with a relatively large increase of expected utility, the probability of choosing this specific action is also relatively large.

In order to test the hypotheses, I estimate the different network structural effects on the probability of network change controlling for organizational and legislation-related effects using the following function:

$$f(x_{ij}) = \sum_{k} \beta_k s_{ijk}(x_{ij}) + \sum_{l} \beta_l e_{il}(x_{ij}) + \sum_{m} \beta_m d_{jm}(x_{ij}) + \varepsilon$$

Where k, l, and m are the number of parameters β to be estimated, s are the structural effects (e.g., in the case of the legislative lobbying agenda, the in-degree-popularity, outdegree activity, 4-cycle, and coalition degree), e represents the effects associated with the attributes of an organization, d represents the effects associated with the attributes of legislation, and ε is a stochastic error term. The model requires that the network structural effects include an 'outdegree' or density effect as intercept, which is the number of out-going ties from an organization and this effect controls for the density of the network. A negative outdegree coefficient indicates that choosing legislative bills for lobbying is costly.

As noted previously, organizations move in and out of the policy domain, coalitions rise and disband, and legislators introduce legislation throughout a Congress. The dynamic model can control for such changes that are not available or that do not exist at a particular observation point. In this way, I can distinguish between, for example, bills that have been introduced but not chosen from bills that have not yet been introduced.

In general, the model simulates what happens between observations using the random utility model. The organizational actions that make the network develop are the core of the simulation procedure. The SIENA software program estimates the model based on a maximum likelihood estimator using the method of moments, implemented as a continuous-time Markov Chain Monte Carlo simulation. The model (a) calculates likely starting values for the parameters, (b) simulates the choice process according to the starting values, (c) compares the resultant simulated network with the observed networks, and (d) adjusts values to reduce differences between the observed and the simulated data. The model then uses a number of simulations to determine the frequency distribution of predictions, which then are used to calculate standard errors for the final parameter values.

Explanatory Network Effects

I used some common explanatory network effects in Chapters 3 and 4. The main explanatory network effects included in-coming (popularity), out-going (activity), and 4-cycle (influence) effects. The popularity or indegree effect is simply the number of lobbying organizations that selected a particular bill or coalition. If a bill or coalition has a lot of ties coming from lobbying organizations, its popularity or indegree measure will be high, and the effect predicts that an organization will select a bill or coalition on the basis of its current popularity with other organizations. The following equation represents this effect:

$$s_i^{net}(x) = \sum_j x_{ij} x_{+j} = \sum_j x_{ij} \sum_h x_{hj}$$

The popularity or indegree effect for a lobbying organization (i) is defined by the sum of the indegrees of the bills/coalitions (j), to which a lobbying organization i may be tied, from other lobbying organizations (h) (Ripley, Snijders and Preciado, 2012).

The 4-cycle effect looks at the effect of similar choices made by any two organizations. If organization 1 is lobbying on, for example, bills 1 and 2 and if organization 2 is lobbying on bill 1, the 4-cycle effect predicts that organization 2 will then select bill 2 for lobbying because 1 and 2 have both selected 1. The equation following shows this effect:

$$s_i^{net}(x) = \sum_{i_2, j_1, j_2} x_{i_1 j_1} x_{i_1 j_2} x_{i_2 j_1} x_{i_2 j_2}$$

In the two-mode network of organizations (i) and bills (j), the 4-cycle effect counts and controls for the number of 4-path structures that consist of each pair of organizations (i_1 and i_2) completely connected to each pair of bills (j_1 and j_2) (Ripley, Snijders and Preciado, 2012).

The final network effect of interest is the outdegree activity effect, which represents the monitoring mechanism. The predicted activity of a lobbying organization (i) is a function of the squared out-going ties or outdegrees of that organization. The equation for the outdegree activity effect is,

$$s_i^{net}(x) = x_{i+}^2$$

I am also able to incorporate an effect for how, if at all, changes in one network affect changes in the network of interest. For example, alliances and coalitions are visible social processes within policy domains, and being connected to others in a coalition likely influences lobbying agendas. The coalition data allowed me to include a coalition activity effect, which is the effect of the number of an actor's coalition ties on that actor adding a tie to legislation in the legislative network. In the modeling literature (Ripley, Snijders, and Preciado, 2012: 133), this coalition activity effect is represented by the following equation:

$$s_i^{net}(x) = \sum_j x_{ij}(w_i - \bar{w}) = x_{i+}(w_i - \bar{w})$$

In this equation, w is the tie in the coalition network and x_{ij} is the outgoing tie from lobbying organization i to bill j. When looking at changes in coalitions back in Chapter 3, I did the reverse: I included an effect for legislative activity on coalition network change.

Explanatory Attributes

Agenda choices may be associated with organizational attributes such as time and resources. The dynamic model can control for such attributes. The chapters detail specific attributes used in the analyses.

Model Selection

Modeling network dynamics presents some challenges, particularly in this case when I had a lot of background data on the lobbying organizations and the bills. However, incorporating too many effects can cause a failure in convergence, and not all possible effects and variables add value to the model. Ripley, Snijders, and Preciado (2012) recommend a basic forward-selection process that chooses effects based on theory and research question, testing for goodness of fit and statistical significance, and then assessing the model for time heterogeneity. In the chapters, the key effects of interest included the 4-cycle and the in-degree/popularity effects so these were automatically included although both exhibited excellent goodness of fit scores. I then added different effects to the model and tested each for goodness of fit according to the score-type tests (Schweinberger, 2012; Ripley, Snijders and Preciado, 2012).

After a basic model was determined, I then tested the model for time heterogeneity. The basic model assumes that the effects do not vary over time, which is often not the case. When time heterogeneity is indicated, time dummy variables can be added to control for variance over time (Lospinoso, Schweinberger, Snijders, and Ripley, 2011). A number of the effects in this model indicated time heterogeneity, and time dummies were added only for time periods for which heterogeneity was indicated by the test.

Medicare Results

Chapter 4 discussed longitudinal network modeling results for Medicare policy, but tables were not provided in order to save space in the chapter. Below are the tables of descriptive statistics and results from the analysis of Medicare policy data. Table A2 provides descriptive statistics for the Medicare policy data. Table A3 provides a summary of observed changes in the Medicare lobbyist-legislation network over time. Finally, Table A4 provides the results of the longitudinal modeling, which were qualitatively discussed in Chapter 4.

Table A2 Descriptive Statistics for Medicare Organizational, Legislative, and Network Variables, 2009

	Mean (%)	
Pairs (*n* = 1,449):		
Device manufacturers (%)	8.8	
Health Professionals (%)	11.0	
Hospitals (%)	23.9	
Insurers (%)	8.9	
Other (%)	17.3	
Pharmaceutical (%)	15.8	
Public interest groups (%)	9.3	
Self-represented (%)	25.4	
Mean years in policy domain	7.95	3.9 *(SD)*
Number of unique clients	969	
Number of unique registrants	655	
Legislation (*n* = 434):		
Mean number of bill cosponsors	19.3	34.3 *(SD)*
Tax committee member (%)	65.9	
Mean bill progress	1.2	0.78 *(SD)*
Legislative Network		
Number of ties	2,559	
Number of 4-cycles	8,824	
Sum of squared indegrees	167,591	
Sum of squared outdegrees	21,385	

Note: Network statistics are generated as part of the output by the RSiena package.

Table A3 Changes in Medicare Lobbying Organizations' Ties to Bills, 1st through 3rd Quarters, 2009 (1,449 lobbyist-client pairs, 434 legislative bills)

Periods	No Bill (0 → 0)	New Bill (0 → 1)	Drop Bill (1 → 0)	Keep Bill (1 → 1)	Jaccard Index
1st Qtr → 2nd Qtr	1,043,514	1,374	1,025	3,163	0.569
2nd Qtr → 3rd Qtr	1,044,027	512	989	3,548	0.703

Note: Author's calculations of the data using the RSiena program.

Table A4   Longitudinal Model of Lobbyist-Bill Network Changes, Medicare, 2009

	Est.	SE
Rate Parameters:		
1st Qtr → 2nd Qtr	1.833	0.158
2nd half 1999 → 1st half 2000	1.099	0.183
Out-degree (density)	−8.483***	0.308
4-cycles	0.046***	0.015
Indegree: Popularity of bill	0.061***	0.003
Outdegree activity	0.534***	0.050
Time dummy	−0.263***	0.064
Self-represented	0.390	0.219
Time dummy	−0.804	0.440
Total years in Medicare policy domain	0.145***	0.018
Time dummy	−0.334***	0.065
Hospital	−0.832**	0.298
Time dummy	−1.784	0.564
Insurance	−6.923	1.347
Time dummy	−13.733	2.839
Other interests	0.404	0.242
Number of bill cosponsors	0.013**	0.010
Time dummy 2	−0.048	0.020
Committee member	0.496***	0.151
Bill progress	−1.475	0.148

NOTES

1. The U.S. Senate website for the federal lobbyist registration reports is http://sopr.senate.gov/.
2. For example, S. 741 was listed 98 times by the lobbyists in the first half of 1999.
3. The website can be found here: http://www.secretary.state.nc.us/lobbyists/thepage.aspx.
4. "The normalized betweenness centrality is the betweenness divided by the maximum possible betweenness expressed as a percentage" (Borgatti, Everrett, and Freeman, 2002).
5. The regression results were produced by the zinb routine in STATA version 12.
6. I used RSiena version 4.0 (Ripley, Snijders, and Preciado, 2012). A free copy of the latest version and documentation are available at http://www.stats.ox.ac.uk/~snijders/siena/.

References

Agrawal, Arun. 2002. "Common Resources and Institutional Sustainability." In E. Ostrom, T. Dietz, N. Dolask, P. Stern, S. Stonich, and E. Weber (eds.), *Drama of the Commons*. Washington, DC: National Academies Press.

Ahn, T. K., Elinor Ostrom, David Schmidt, Robert Shupp, and James Walker. 2001. "Cooperation in PD Games: Fear, Greed, and History of Play." *Public Choice* 106: 137–55.

Ainsworth, Scott H. 1997. "The Role of Legislators in the Determination of Interest Group Influence." *Legislative Studies Quarterly* 22(4): 517–33.

Ainsworth, Scott H., and Itai Sened. 1993. "The Role of Lobbyists: Entrepreneurs with Two Audiences." *American Journal of Political Science* 37(3): 834–66.

Allison, Paul. 1999. *Logistic Regression Using the SAS System: Theory and Application*. Cary, NC: SAS Institute.

Amenta, Edwin, Bruce G. Carruthers, and Yvonne Zylan. 1992. "A Hero for the Aged? The Townsend Movement, the Political Mediation Model, and U.S. Old-Age Policy, 1934–1950." *American Journal of Sociology* 98(2): 308–39.

Andrews, Kenneth T., and Bob Edwards. 2004. "Advocacy Organizations in the U.S. Political Process." *Annual Review of Sociology* 30: 479–506.

Annals of Congress, 10th Congress, 1st Session. 1852. *The Debates and Proceedings in the Congress of the United States: With an Appendix Containing Important State Papers and Public Documents, and All the Laws of a Public Nature; with a Copious Index; Compiled from Authentic Materials*. Washington, DC: Gales and Seaton. http://lcweb2.loc.gov/cgi-bin/ampage. Accessed May 19, 2008.

Arnold, R. Douglas. 1990. *The Logic of Congressional Action*. New Haven, CT: Yale University Press.

Axelrod, Robert. 1984. *The Evolution of Cooperation*. New York: Basic Books.

Bachrach, Peter, and Morton S. Baratz. 1962. "The Two Faces of Power." *American Political Science Review* 56(4): 947–52.

Baker, Frank B., and Lawrence J. Hubert. 1981. "The Analysis of Social Interaction Data: A Nonparametric Technique." *Sociological Methods and Research* 9: 339–61.

Barabási, Albert-László. 2003. *Linked: How Everything Is Connected to Everything Else and What it Means for Business, Science, and Everyday Life*. New York: Plume.

Baumgartner, Frank R., and Bryon D. Jones. 1993. *Agendas and Instability in American Politics*. Chicago, IL: University of Chicago Press.

Baumgartner, Frank R., and Beth L. Leech. 1998. *Basic Interests*. Princeton, NJ: Princeton University Press.

Baumgartner, Frank R., and Beth L. Leech. 2000. *Codebook for the Lobbying Disclosure Data Set*. Project on Lobbying Disclosure Reports. State College: Pennsylvania

State University. http://lobby.la.psu.edu/_Related_Projects/codebook_0900.pdf. Accessed August 20, 2007.

Baumgartner, Frank R., and Beth L. Leech. 2001. "Interest Niches and Policy Bandwagons: Patterns of Interest Group Involvement in National Politics." *The Journal of Politics* 63(4): 1191–213.

Baumgartner, Frank R., Jeffrey M. Berry, Marjorie Hojnacki, David Kimball, and Beth L. Leech. 2009. *Lobbying and Policy Change: Who Wins, Who Loses, and Why*. Chicago, IL: University of Chicago Press.

Becker, Gary S. 1983. "A Theory of Competition among Pressure Groups for Political Influence." *Quarterly Journal of Economics* 98: 371–400.

Bentley, Arthur. [1905] 1949. *The Process of Government*. Evanston, IL: Principia Press of Illinois.

Berardo, Ramiro, and John T. Scholz. 2010. "Self-Organizing Policy Networks: Risk, Partner Selection, and Cooperation in Estuaries." *American Journal of Political Science* 54(3): 632–49.

Berry, Jeffrey M. 1977. *Lobbying for the People: The Political Behavior of Public Interest Groups*. Princeton, NJ: Princeton University Press.

Berry, Jeffrey M. 1999. *The New Liberalism: The Rising Power of Citizen Groups*. Washington, DC: The Brookings Institution Press.

Berry, Jeffrey M. 2001. "Lobbying." In N. Smelser and P. B. Baltes (eds.), *International Encyclopedia of the Social and Behavioral Sciences*. Oxford, UK: Elsevier.

Besley, Timothy, and Stephen Coate. 2001. "Lobbying and Welfare in a Representative Democracy." *Review of Economic Studies* 68: 67–82.

Birnbaum, Jeffrey, and Alan Murray. 1988. *Showdown at Gucci Gulch*. New York: Vintage.

Blau, Peter M. 1964. *Exchange and Power in Social Life*. New York: J. Wiley.

Borgatti, Steven P., Martin G. Everett, and Linton C. Freeman. 2002. *UCINET 6*. Natick: Analytic Technologies

Bourdieu, Pierre. 1985. "The Forms of Capital." In J. Robinson (ed.), *Handbook of Theory and Research for the Sociology of Education*. New York: Glenwood.

Bowling, Kenneth R., William Charles diGiacomantonio, Charlene Bangs Bickford (eds.). 1998. *Documentary History of the First Federal Congress, 1789–1791, Volume VIII: Petition Histories and Nonlegislative Official Documents*. Baltimore, MD: Johns Hopkins University Press.

Bridgman, Raymond L. 1897. "The Lobby." *The Atlantic Monthly* 22(April 2): 151–61.

Briggs, Emily Edison. 1906. *The Olivia Letters: Being Some History of Washington City for Forty Years as Told by the Letters of a Newspaper Correspondent*. New York: Neale.

Brooks, Chad. 2012. "The Most Expensive Office Space in the World." *Business News Daily*, July 17. http://www.businessnewsdaily.com/2855-most-expensive-commercial-real-estate.html. Accessed September 23, 2014.

Browne, William P. 1989. "Access and Influence in Agriculture and Rural Affairs: Congressional Staff and Lobbyist Perceptions of Organized Interests." *Rural Sociology* 54(3): 365–81.

Browne, William P. 1990. "Organized Interests and Their Issue Niches: A Search for Pluralism in a Policy Domain." *The Journal of Politics* 52(2): 477–509.

Bryce, James. 1910. *The American Commonwealth,* 3rd ed. New York: MacMillan.

Burstein, Paul. 1991. "Policy Domains: Organization, Culture, and Policy Outcomes." *Annual Review of Sociology* 17: 327–50.

Burstein, Paul, and C. Elizabeth Hirsh. 2007. "Interest Organizations, Information, and Policy Innovation in the U.S. Congress." *Sociological Forum* 22(2): 174–99.

Burt, Ronald. 1992. *Structural Holes*. Cambridge, MA: Harvard University Press.

Burt, Ronald. 2000. "The Network Entrepreneur." In R. Swedberg (ed.), *Entrepreneurship: The Social Science View*. New York: Oxford University Press.

Byers, Amy L., Heather Allore, Thomas M. Gill, and Peter N. Peduzzi. 2003. "Application of Negative Binomial Modeling for Discrete Outcomes." *Journal of Clinical Epidemiology* 56: 559–64.

Byrd, Robert C. 1991. *The Senate, 1789–1989*. Washington, DC: Government Printing Office.

Carpenter, Daniel P., Kevin M. Esterling, and David Lazer. 2004. "Friends, Brokers, and Transitivity: Who Informs Whom in Washington Politics?" *The Journal of Politics* 66(1): 224–46.

Cater, Douglas. 1964. *Power in Washington: A Critical Look at Todays' Struggle to Govern in the Nation's Capital*. New York: Random House.

Center for Responsive Politics. 2012. *Lobbying Spending Data on Ranked Sectors and Other Data*. http://www.opensecrets.org/lobby/top.php?indexType=c. Accessed November 10, 2012.

Cho, Wendy K. T., and James H. Fowler. 2010. "Legislative Success in a Small World: Social Network Analysis and the Dynamics of Congressional Legislation." *Journal of Politics* 72: 124–35.

Chubb, John E. 1983. *Interest Groups and the Bureaucracy: The Politics of Energy*. Stanford, CA: Stanford University Press.

Cigler, Allan J., and Burdette A. Loomis (eds.). 1991. *Interest Group Politics*, 3rd ed. Washington, DC: Congressional Quarterly Press.

Clemens, Elisabeth. 1997. *The People's Lobby: Organizational Innovation and the Rise of Interest Group Politics in the United States, 1890–1925*. Chicago, IL: University of Chicago Press.

Clift, Eleanor, and Tom Brazaitis. 1996. *War without Bloodshed: The Art of Politics*. New York: Simon & Schuster.

Coleman, James S. 1988. "Social Capital in the Creation of Human Capital." *American Journal of Sociology* 94: 95–120.

Coleman, James. 1990. *Foundations of Social Theory*. Cambridge, MA: Harvard University Press.

Congressional Research Service. 1986. *Congress and Pressure Groups: Lobbying in a Modern Democracy: A Report Prepared for the Subcommittee on Intergovernmental Relations of the Committee on Governmental Affairs, United States Senate by the Congressional Research Service, Library of Congress*. Washington, DC: Government Printing Office.

Cook, Karen S., Russell Hardin, and Margaret Levi. 2005. *Cooperation without Trust?* New York: Russell Sage.

Costain, Anne N. 1978. "Eliminating Sex Discrimination in Education: Lobbying for Implementation of Title IX." *Policy Studies Journal* 7(2): 189–95.

Crews, Clyde W. 2002. *Ten Thousand Commandants: An Annual Snapshot of the Federal Regulatory State*. Washington, DC: Cato Institute.

Crow, Graham. 2004. "Social Networks and Social Exclusion: An Overview of the Debate." In C. Phillipson, G. Allan, and D. Morgan (eds.), *Social Networks and Social Exclusion: Sociological and Policy Perspectives*. Aldershot, UK: Ashgate.

Dahl, Robert A. 1961. *Who Governs? Democracy and Power in an American City*. New Haven, CT: Yale University Press.

Diermeier, Daniel, and Timothy J. Fedderson. 2000. "Information and Congressional Hearings." *American Journal of Political Science* 44: 51–65.

Dür, Andreas. 2008. "Measuring Interest Group Influence in the EU: A Note on Methodology." *European Union Politics* 9(4): 559–76.

Durkheim, Emile. [1893] 1984. *The Division of Labor in Society*. New York: The Free Press.

Ellickson, Robert C. 1991. *Order without Law: How Neighbors Settle Disputes.* Cambridge, MA: Harvard University Press.

Elster, Jon. 1989. *Nuts and Bolts for the Social Sciences.* Cambridge, UK: Cambridge University Press.

Emirbayer, Mustafa. 1997. "Manifesto for a Relational Sociology." *American Journal of Sociology* 103(2): 281–317.

Fang, Hanming. 2002. "Lottery versus All-Pay Auction Models of Lobbying." *Public Choice* 112(3–4): 351–71.

Fatka, Stacie, and Jason Miles Levien. 1998. "Protecting the Right to Petition: Why a Lobbying Contingency Fee Prohibition Violates the Constitution." *Harvard Journal on Legislation* 35: 559–88.

Feld, Scott L. 1997. "Structural Embeddedness and Instability of Interpersonal Relations." *Social Networks* 19(1): 91–5.

Fenno, Richard F., Jr. 1973. *Congress in Committees.* Boston, MA: Little, Brown.

Fowler, J.H. (2006). "Connecting the Congress: A Study of Cosponsorship Networks." *Political Analysis* 14: 456–87.

Frank, Robert H. 1988. *Passions within Reasons: The Strategic Role of the Emotions.* New York: Norton.

Freeman, J. Leiper. 1965. *The Political Process: Executive Bureau-Legislative Committee Relations.* New York: Random House.

Furlong, Scott. 1998. "The Lobbying Disclosure Act and Interest Group Lobbying Data: Two Steps Forward and One Step Back." *VOXPOP* 17(3): 4–6.

Futemma, Celia, Fabio De Castro, Maria Clara Silva-Forsberg, and Elinor Ostrom. 2002. "The Emergence and Outcomes of Collective Action: An Institutional and Ecosystem Approach." *Society and Natural Resources* 15: 503–22.

Gais, Thomas L., and Jack L. Walker. 1991. "Pathways to Influence in American Politics." In J.L. Walker (ed.), *Mobilizing Interest Groups in America.* Ann Arbor: University of Michigan Press.

Galambos, Louis. 1966. *Competition and Cooperation: The Emergence of a National Trade Association.* Baltimore, MD: Johns Hopkins University Press.

Galambos, Louis (ed.). 1970. *The New American State.* Baltimore, MD: Johns Hopkins University Press.

Gambetta, Diego. 1998. "Concatenations of Mechanisms." In P. Hedstrom and R. Swedberg (eds.), *Social Mechanisms: An Analytical Approach to Social Theory.* Cambridge, UK: Cambridge University Press.

General Accounting Office. 1991. *Federal Lobbying: Federal Regulation of Lobbying Act of 1946 Is Ineffective.* Washington, DC: Government Printing Office.

Giddens, Anthony. 1979. *Central Problems in Social Theory: Action, Structure, and Contradiction in Social Analysis.* Vol. 241. Berkeley: University of California Press.

Glanville, Jennifer L., and Elisa J. Bienenstock. 2009. "A Typology for Understanding the Connections Among Different Forms of Social Capital." *American Behavioral Scientist* 52(11): 1507–30.

Gould, Roger V. 1993. "Collective Action and Network Structure." *American Sociological Review* 58(2): 182–96.

Granovetter, Mark. 1973. "The Strength of Weak Ties." *American Journal of Sociology* 78(6): 1360–80.

Granovetter, Mark. 1985. "Economic Action and Social Structure: The Problem of Embeddedness." *American Journal of Sociology* 91(3): 481–510.

Granovetter, M. 1992. "Economic Institutions as Social Constructions: A Framework for Analysis." *Acta Sociologica* 35: 3–11.

Grossman, Matt, and Dominguez, Casey B.K. 2009. "Party Coalitions and Interest Group Networks." *American Politics Research* 37(5): 767–800.

Gulati, Ranjay. 1998. "Alliances and Networks." *Strategic Management Journal* 19: 293–317.

Gulati, Ranjay, and Harbir Singh. 1998. "The Architecture of Cooperation: Managing Coordination Costs and Appropriation Concerns in Strategic Alliances." *Administrative Science Quarterly* 100(1): 781–814.

Hall, Donald R. 1969. *Cooperative Lobbying: The Power of Pressure.* Tucson: University of Arizona Press.

Hall, Richard L., and Alan V. Deardorff. 2006. "Lobbying as Legislative Subsidy." *American Political Science Review* 100(1): 69–84.

Hansen, John Mark. 1991. *Gaining Access: Congress and the Farm Lobby, 1919–1981.* Chicago, IL: University of Chicago Press.

Hardin, Russell. 2002. *Trust and Trustworthiness.* New York: Russell Sage Foundation.

Heaney, Michael T. 2004. "Issue Networks, Information, and Interest Group Alliances: The Case of Wisconsin Welfare Politics." *State Politics and Policy Quarterly* 4(3): 237–70.

Heaney, Michael T., and Scott D. McClurg. 2009. "Social Networks and American Politics." *American Politics Research* 37(5): 721–44.

Heaney, Michael T., and Fabio Rojas. 2007. "Partisans, Nonpartisans, and the Antiwar Movement in the United States." *American Politics Research* 35(4): 431–64.

Heaney, Michael T., and Fabio Rojas. 2008. "Coalition Dissolution, Mobilization, and Network Dynamics in the U.S. Antiwar Movement." *Research in Social Movements, Conflict, and Change* 28: 39–82.

Hechter, Michael, and Karl-Dieter Opp. 2001. "What Have We Learned About the Emergence of Social Norms?" In M. Hechter and D. Opp (eds.), *Social Norms.* New York: Russell Sage Foundation.

Heckathorn, Douglas D. 1990. "Collective Sanctions and Compliance Norms: A Formal Theory of Group-Mediated Control." *American Sociological Review* 55(3): 366–84.

Heckathorn, Douglas D., and Steven M. Maser. 1987. "The Contractual Architecture of Public Policy: A Critical Reconstruction of Lowi's Typology." *The Journal of Politics* 52(4): 1101–23.

Heclo, Hugh. 1978. "Issue Networks and the Executive Establishment." In A. King (ed.), *The New American Political System.* Washington, DC: American Enterprise Institute.

Heinz, John P., Edward O. Laumann, Robert L. Nelson, and Robert H. Salisbury. 1993. *The Hollow Core: Private Interests in National Policy Making.* Cambridge, MA: Harvard University Press.

Helmke, Gretchen, and Steven Levitsky. 2004. "Informal Institutions and Comparative Politics: A Research Agenda." *Perspective on Politics* 2(4): 725–40.

Herring, Pendleton. 1929. *Group Representation Before Congress.* Baltimore, MD: John Hopkins University Press.

Hirschman, Albert O. 1970. *Exit, Voice and Loyalty.* Cambridge, MA: Harvard University Press.

Hojnacki, Marjorie. 1997. "Interest Groups' Decisions to Join Alliances or Work Alone." *American Journal of Political Science* 41: 61–87.

Holyoke, Thomas T. 2009. "Interest Group Competition and Coalition Formation." *American Journal of Political Science* 53: 360–75.

Homans, George C. 1961. *Social Behavior: Its Elementary Forms.* New York: Harcourt Brace Jovanovich, Inc.

Horne, Christine. 2001. "Sociological Perspectives on the Emergence of Social Norms." In M. Hechter and D. Opp (eds.), *Social Norms.* New York: Russell Sage Foundation.

Hubert, Lawrence J., and Frank B. Baker. 1978. "Evaluating the Conformity of Sociometric Measurements." *Psychometrika* 43: 31–41.

Hula, Kevin W. 1999. *Lobbying Together: Interest Group Coalitions in Legislative Politics.* Washington, DC: Georgetown University Press.

Hunter, Floyd. 1953. *Community Power Structure: A Study of Decision Makers.* Chapel Hill: University of North Carolina Press.

Investment Company Institute. 2006. "Appendix: Additional Data on the U.S. Retirement Market." In *Research Fundamentals,* 15(5A). Washington, DC: ICI.

James, William. 1981. *The Principles of Psychology,* Vol. 1. Cambridge, MA: Harvard University Press.

Jenkins-Smith, Hank C., Gilbert K. St. Clair, and Brian Woods. 1991. "Explaining Change in Policy Subsystems: Analysis of Coalition Stability and Defection over Time." *American Journal of Political Science* 35: 851–80.

Jones, Bryan D., and Frank R. Baumgartner. 2005. *The Politics of Attention: How Government Prioritizes Problems.* Chicago, IL: University of Chicago Press.

Jordan, Tim, and Paul Taylor. 2008. "A Sociology of Hackers." *The Sociological Review* 46(4): 757–80.

Kaiser Family Foundation. 2011. "Medicare Spending and Financing." *Medicare Fact Sheet,* September. http://www.kff.org/medicare/7305.cfm. Accessed November 3, 2012.

Kenis, P.N., and V. Schneider. 1991. "Policy Networks and Policy Analysis: Scrutinizing a New Analytical Toolbox." In B. Marin and R. Mayntz (eds.), *Policy Networks: Empirical Evidence and Theoretical Considerations.* Boulder, CO: Westview Press.

Kennedy, Peter. 1998. *A Guide to Econometrics,* 4th ed. Malden, MA: Blackwell.

Kimball, David C., Frank R. Baumgartner, Jeffrey M. Berry, Marie Hojnacki, Beth L. Leech, and Bryce Summary. 2012. "Who Cares About the Lobbying Agenda?" *Interest Groups and Advocacy* 1: 5–25.

Kingdon, John W. 1981. *Congressmen's Voting Decisions.* New York: Harper & Row.

Kingdon, John W. 1995. *Agendas, Alternatives, and Public Policies.* Boston, MA: Little, Brown.

Kiplinger, Austin H., and Knight A. Kiplinger. 1975. *Washington Now.* New York: Harper & Row.

Klijn, Erik H., and Geert Teisman. 1997. "Strategies and Games in Networks." In Walter J. M. Kickert, Erik-Hans Klijn, and Joop F. M. Koppenjan (eds.), *Managing Complex Networks: Strategies For the Public Sector.*

Knoke, David. 1990. *Political Networks: The Structural Perspective.* New York: Cambridge University Press.

Knoke, David. 2001. *Changing Organizations: Business Networks in the New Political Economy.* Boulder, CO: Westview.

Knoke, David, Franz Pappi, Jeffrey Broadbent, and Yutaka Tsujinaka. 1996. *Comparing Policy Networks: Labor Politics in the U.S., Germany, and Japan.* New York: Cambridge University Press.

Koger, G., S. Masket, and H. Noel. 2010. "Partisan Webs: Information Exchange and Party Networks." *British Journal of Political Science.*

Kollman, Kenneth. 1998. *Outside Lobbying: Public Opinion and Interest Group Strategies.* Princeton, NJ: Princeton University Press.

Laumann, Edward O., and David Knoke. 1987. *The Organizational State: Social Choice in National Policy Domains.* Madison: University of Wisconsin Press.

Lauth, Hans-Joachim. 2004. "Formal and Informal Institutions: On Structuring Their Mutual Co-Existence." *Romanian Journal of Political Sciences* 1: 67–89.

Lawler, Edward J., and Jeongkoo Yoon. 1996. "Commitment in Exchange Relations: Test of a Theory of Relational Cohesion." *American Sociological Review* 61: 89–108.

Levi, Margaret, and Gillian H. Murphy. 2006. "Coalitions of Contention: The Case of the WTO Protests in Seattle." *Political Studies* 54(4): 651–70.

Leyden, Kevin M., and Stephen A. Borelli. 1994. "An Investment in Goodwill: Party Contributions and Party Unity Among U.S. House Members in the 1980s." *American Politics Research* 22(4): 421–52.

Lieberman, Trudy. 2000. *Slanting the Story: The Forces that Shape the News*. New York: New Press.

Long, J. Scott. 1997. *Regression Models for Categorical and Limited Dependent Variables*. Thousand Oaks, CA: Sage.

Loomis, Burdett A. 1986. "Coalitions of Interests: Building Bridges in the Balkanized State." In A. Cigler and B. Loomis (eds.), *Interest Group Politics*, 2nd ed. Washington, DC: Congressional Quarterly.

Lospinoso, Joshua A., Michael Schweinberger, Tom A. B. Snijders, and Ruth M. Ripley. 2011. "Assessing and Accounting for Time Heterogeneity in Stochastic Actor Oriented Models." *Advances in Data Analysis and Classification* 5(2): 147–76.

Lowi, Theodore J. 1964. "American Business, Public Policy, Case-Studies, and Political Theory." *World Politics* 16(4): 677–715.

Lowi, Theodore. 1969. *The End of Liberalism*. New York: Norton.

Lubell, Mark, and John T. Scholz. 2001. "Cooperation, Reciprocity, and the Collective Action Heuristic." *American Journal of Political Science* 45: 160–78.

Lyell, Charles. 1855. *A Second Visit to North America*, 3rd ed. London: John Murray.

MacPherson, J. Miller, and Lynn Smith-Lovin. 1987. "Homophily in Voluntary Organizations: Status Distance and the Composition of Face-to-Face Groups." *American Sociological Review* 52: 370–79.

Mahoney, Christine. 2007. "Lobbying Success in the United States and the European Union." *Journal of Public Policy* 27(1): 35–56.

Mahoney, Christine, and Frank Baumgartner. 2004. "The Determinants and Effects of Interest Group Coalitions." A paper presented at the Annual Meeting of the American Political Science Association, Chicago, IL, September 2–5.

March, James G., and Johan P. Olsen. 1976. *Ambiguity and Choice in Organizations*. Bergen, Norway: Universitetsforlaget.

Markovsky, Barry, and Edward J. Lawler. 1994. "A New Theory of Group Solidarity." In B. Markovsky, J. O'Brien, and K. Heimer (eds.), *Advances in Group Processes*, Vol. 11. Greenwich, CT: JAI Press.

Mattison, Georgia, and Sandra Storey. 1992. *Women in Citizen Advocacy: Stories of 28 Shapers of Public Policy*. Jefferson, NC: McFarland.

May, Peter J., Joshua Sapotichne, and Samuel Workman. 2006. "Policy Coherence and Policy Domains." *Policy Studies Journal* 34(3): 381–403.

Mayhew, David R. 1991. *Divided We Govern*. New Haven, CT: Yale University Press.

McAdam, Doug, Charles Tilly, and Sidney Tarrow. 2001. *Dynamics of Contention*. New York: Cambridge University Press.

McCabe, James Dabney. 1873. *Behind the Scenes in Washington*. Philadelphia, PA: National Publishing.

McCaulay, Stewart. 1963. "Non-Contractual Relations in Business: A Preliminary Study." *American Sociological Review* 28(1): 55–67.

McCubbins, Mathew D., Ramamohan Paturi, and Nicholas Weller. 2009. "Connected Coordination: Network Structure and Group Coordination." *American Politics Research* 37(5): 899–920.

Mehra, Ajay, Josh Marineau, Alexander B. Lopes, and Ted K. Dass, 2009. "The Coevolution of Friendship and Leadership Networks in Small Groups." In G. Graen and J. Graen (eds.), *Predator's Game-Changing Designs: Research-based Tools 7*. Charlotte, NC: IAP.

Mencken, H. L. 1931. *The American Language: A Preliminary Inquiry into the Development of English in the United States*, 3rd ed. New York: Knopf.

Merton, Robert K. 1968. *Social Theory and Social Structure.* New York: The Free Press.

Merton, Robert K. 1976. *Sociological Ambivalence and Other Essays.* New York: The Free Press.

Milbrath, Lester W. 1963. *The Washington Lobbyists.* Chicago, IL: Rand McNally.

Mills, C. Wright. 1956. *The Power Elite.* New York: Oxford University Press.

Mizruchi, Mark S. 1992. *The Structure of Corporate Political Action: Interfirm Relations and Their Consequence.* Cambridge, MA: Harvard University Press.

Moody, James, and Douglas R. White. 2003. "Structural Cohesion and Embeddedness: A Hierarchical Concept of Social Groups." *American Sociological Review* 68: 103–27.

Morgan, Kimberly J., and Andrew L. Campbell. 2011. *The Delegated Welfare State: Medicare, Markets, and the Governance of Social Policy.* New York: Oxford University Press.

Munnell, Alicia, and Dina Bleckman. 2014. "Is Pension Coverage a Problem in the Private Sector?" *Issue in Brief* 14–7 (April). Boston, MA: Center for Retirement Research at Boston College.

"The New Washington." 1884. *The Century Magazine* 27(5): 643–49. http://cdl.library.cornell.edu/gifcache/moa/cent/cent0027/00653.TIF6.gif. Accessed February 10, 2008.

Nownes, Anthony J. 2006. *Total Lobbying: What Lobbyists Want (And How They Try to Get Tt).* New York: Cambridge University Press.

Nownes, Anthony J., and Patricia Freeman. 1999. "Interest Group Activity in the States." *Journal of Politics* 60: 86–112.

Office of Management and Budget. 2006. *Historical Tables, Budget of the United States Government.* Washington, DC: Government Printing Office.

Office of Management and Budget. 2010. *Budget of the United States Government, Analytical Perspectives.* Table 19–1. Washington, DC: Government Printing Office.

Oliver, Thomas R., and Paul Shaheen. 1997. "Translating Ideas into Actions: Entrepreneurial Leadership in State Health Care Reforms." *Journal of Health Politics, Policy and Law* 22(3): 740.

Olson, Mancur. 1965. *The Logic of Collective Action.* Cambridge, MA: Harvard University Press.

Olson, Mancur. 1982. *The Rise and Decline of Nations.* New Haven, CT: Yale University Press.

Ostrom, Elinor. 1990. *Governing the Commons: The Evolution of Institutions for Collective Action.* New York: Cambridge University Press.

Ostrom, Elinor. 2000. "Collective Action and the Evolution of Social Norms." *Journal of Economic Perspectives* 14(3): 137–58.

Ostrom, Elinor, Roy Gardner, and James Walker. 1994. *Rules, Games, and Common-Pool Resources.* Ann Arbor: University of Michigan Press.

O'Sullivan, Jennifer. 2008. *Medicare: A Primer.* CRS Report for Congress. Washington, DC: Health Care Financing Domestic Social Policy Division.

Oxford English Dictionary. 2013. New York: Oxford University Press.

Parker, Glenn. 2008. *Capitol Investments: The Marketability of Political Skills.* Ann Arbor: University of Michigan Press.

Parsons, Talcott. 1951. *The Social System.* New York: The Free Press.

Parsons, Talcott. 1963. "On the Concept of Political Power." *Proceedings of the American Philosophical Society* 107(3): 232–62.

Pasley, Jeffrey L. 2002. "Private Access and Public Power." In K. R. Bowling and D. R. Kennon (eds.), *The House and Senate in the 1790s.* Athens: Ohio University Press.

Passy, Florence. 2003. "Social Networks Matter. But How?" In M. Diani and D. McAdam (eds.), *Social Movements and Networks: Relational Approaches to Collective Action*. New York: Oxford University Press.

Peltzman, Sam. 1976. "Toward a More General Theory of Regulation." *Journal of Law and*

Podolny, Joel M. 1993. "A Status-Based Model of Market Competition." *American Journal of Sociology* 98: 829–72.

Podolny, Joel M., and Toby E. Stuart. 1995. "A Role-Based Ecology of Technological Change." *American Journal of Sociology* 100(5): 1224–60.

Porter, Glenn. 1973. *The Rise of Big Business, 1860–1910*. New York: Thomas Y. Crowell.

Powell, Walter W., Douglas R. White, Kenneth W. Koput, and Jason Owen-Smith. 2005. "Network Dynamics and Field Evolution: The Growth of Interorganizational Collaboration in the Life Sciences." *American Journal of Sociology* 110(4): 1132–205.

Putnam, Robert D. 1995. "Bowling Alone: America's Declining Social Capital." *Journal of Democracy* 6(1): 65–78.

Putnam, Robert D. 2000. *Bowling Alone: The Collapse and Revival of American Community*. New York: Simon & Schuster.

Raab, Charles D. 1992. "Taking Networks Seriously: Education Policy in Britain." *European Journal of Political Research* 21: 61–90.

Raymond, Leigh. 2006. "Cooperation without Trust: Overcoming Collective Action Barriers to Endangered Species Protection." *The Policies Studies Journal* 34(1): 37–57.

Rice, Charles E. 1962. *Freedom of Association*. New York: New York University Press.

Ridley, Matt. 1996. *The Origins of Virtue: Human Instincts and the Evolution of Cooperation*. New York: Penguin.

Riker, William. 1986. *The Art of Political Manipulation*. New Haven, CT: Yale University Press.

Ripley, Ruth, Tom A. B. Snijders, and Paulina Preciado. 2012. *Manual for SIENA* (June 9). Oxford, UK: University of Oxford, Department of Statistics.

Robbins, Suzanne M. 2010. "Play Nice or Pick a Fight? Cooperation as an Interest Group Strategy at Implementation." *Policy Studies Journal* 38(3): 515–35.

Rohlinger, Deanna A. 2002. "Framing the Abortion Debate: Organizational Resources, Media Strategies, and Movement-Countermovement Dynamics." *The Sociological Quarterly* 43(4): 479–507.

Rothman, David J. 1966. *Politics and Power: The United States Senate, 1869–1901*. Cambridge, MA: Harvard University Press.

Sabatier, Paul. 1988. "An Advocacy Coalition Framework of Policy Change and the Role of Policy-oriented Learning Therein." *Policy Sciences* 21: 129–68.

Salisbury, Robert H. 1992. *Interests and Institutions: Substance and Structure in American Politics*. Pittsburgh, PA: University of Pittsburgh Press.

Salisbury, Robert H. 1994. "Interest Structures and Policy Domains: A Focus for Research." In W. Crotty, M. Schwartz, and J. Green (eds.), *Representing Interests and Interest Group Representation*. Washington, DC: University Press of America.

Sanders, M. Elizabeth. 1999. *Roots of Reform: Farmers, Workers, and the American State, 1877–1917*. Chicago, IL: University of Chicago Press.

Schelling, Thomas C. 1960. *The Strategy of Conflict*. Cambridge, MA: Harvard University Press.

Schlozman, Kay Lehman, and John T. Tierney 1986. *Organized Interests and American Democracy*. New York: Harper & Row.

Schneider, Mark, John T. Scholz, Mark Lubell, Denisa Mindruta, and Matthew Edwardson. 2003. "Building Consensual Institutions: Networks and the National Estuary Program." *American Journal of Political Science* 47: 143–58.

Scholz, John T., Ramiro Berardo, and Brad Kile. 2008. "Do Networks Solve Collective Action Problems? Credibility, Search, and Collaboration." *The Journal of Politics* 70(2): 393–406.

Schwartz, M. A. 1990. *The Party Network: The Robust Organization of Illinois Republicans.* Madison: University of Wisconsin Press.

Schweinberger, Michael. 2012. "Statistical Modeling of Network Panel Data: Goodness of Fit." *British Journal of Mathematical and Statistical Psychology* 65(2): 263–81.

Scott, John C. 2013. "Social Processes in Lobbyist Agenda Development: A Longitudinal Social Network Analysis of Interest Groups and Legislation." *Policy Studies Journal* 44(4): 608–35.

Simon, Herbert. 1997. *Administrative Behavior: A Study of Decision-making Processes in Administrative Organizations.* New York: Free Press.

Skocpol, Theda. 1992. *Protecting Soldiers and Mothers: The Political Origins of Social Policy in the United States.* Cambridge, MA: Belknap Press of the Harvard University Press.

Smelser, Neil J. 1998. "The Rational and the Ambivalent in the Social Sciences." *American Sociological Review* 63: 1–16.

Smith, Mark A. 2000. *American Business and Political Power: Public Opinion, Elections, and Democracy.* Chicago, IL: University of Chicago Press.

Smith, Richard A. 1995. "Interest Group Influence in the U.S. Congress." *American Political Science Review* 78: 44–63.

Smith, Ron. 1997. "Compelled Cost Disclosure of Grassroots Lobbying Expenses." *Kansas Journal of Law and Public Policy* 6(Fall): 115–82.

Snijders, Tom A. B., G. G. Van Bunt, and Christian E. Steglich. 2010. "Introduction to Stochastic Actor-based Models for Network Dynamics." *Social Networks* 32: 44–60.

Somers, Margaret R. 1994. "Rights, Relationality, and Membership: Rethinking the Making and Meaning of Citizenship." *Law and Social Inquiry* 19: 63–112.

Spence, James. 1862. *The American Union: Its Effect on National Character and Policy, with an Inquiry into Secession as a Constitutional Right, and the Causes of the Disruption.* London: R. Bentley.

Spence, Michael. 1976. "Informational Aspects of Market Structure: An Introduction." *Quarterly Journal of Economics* 90(4): 591–97.

Stigler, George J. 1971. "The Theory of Economic Regulation." *Bell Journal of Economics and Managerial Science* 2: 3–21.

Strolovich, Dara Z. 2007. *Affirmative Advocacy: Race, Class and Gender in Interest Group Politics.* Chicago, IL: University of Chicago Press.

Tarrow, Sidney. 2005. *The New Transnational Activism.* New York: Cambridge University Press.

Thomas, Lately. 1965. *Sam Ward King of the Lobby.* Boston, MA: Houghton Mifflin.

Thomas, William I., and Dorothy Swain Thomas. 1928. *The Child in America: Behavior Problems and Programs.* New York: Knopf.

Thompson, Margaret Susan. 1985. *The Spider Web: Congress and Lobbying in the Age of Grant.* Ithaca, NY: Cornell University Press.

Thurber, James A. 2006. "Lobbying, Ethics, and Procedural Reforms: The Do-Nothing 109th Congress Does Nothing About Reforming Itself." *Extensions* (Fall).

Tichenor, Daniel J., and Richard A. Harris. 2002–2003. "Organized Interests and American Political Development." *Political Science Quarterly* 117(4): 587–612.

Tilly, Charles. 1978. *From Mobilization to Revolution*. Reading, MA: Addison-Wesley.

Truman, David. 1951. *The Governmental Process*. New York: Knopf.

Tullock, Gordon. 1975. "On the Efficient Organization of Trials." *Kyklos* 28: 745–62.

Tullock, Gordon. 1980. "Efficient Rent Seeking." In J. Buchanon, R.D. Tollison, and G. Tullock (eds.), *Toward a Theory of Rent Seeking Society*. College Station, TX: Texas A&M University Press.

Ullman-Margolit, Edna. 1977. *The Emergence of Norms*. Oxford: Clarendon.

U.S. Department of Labor. 2008. *Pension Plan Bulletin, 1999–2006*. http://www.dol.gov/ebsa/publications/main.html. Accessed May 15, 2011.

Uzzi, Brian. 1996. "Embeddedness and Economic Performance: The Network Effect." *American Sociological Review* 61(4): 674–98.

Uzzi, Brian. 1997. "Social Structure and Competition in Interfirm Networks: The Paradox of Embeddedness." Administrative Science Quarterly 42: 35–67.

Vladeck, Bruce C. 1999. "The Political Economy of Medicare." *Health Affairs* 18(1): 22–36.

Walker, Jack L. 1991. *Mobilizing Interest Groups in America: Patrons, Professions, and Social Movements*. Ann Arbor: University of Michigan Press.

Walsh, David J. 1994. *On Different Planes: An Organizational Analysis of Cooperation and Conflict among Airline Unions*. Ithaca, NY: ILR Press.

Weber, Edward P. 1998. *Pluralism by the Rules: Conflict and Cooperation in Environmental Regulations*. Washington, DC: Georgetown University Press.

Weber, Max. 1978. *Economy and Society*. Ed. G. Roth and C. Wittich. Berkeley: University of California Press.

Wellman, Barry. 1988. "Structural Analysis: From Method and Metaphor to Theory and Substance." In B. Wellman and S. D. Berkowitz (eds.), *Social Structures: A Network Approach*. New York: Cambridge University Press.

White, Harrison C. 1981. "Where Do Markets Come From?" *American Journal of Sociology* 87(3): 517–47.

Whitford, A. B. 2003. "The Structures of Interest Coalitions: Evidence from Environmental Litigation." *Business and Politics* 5: 45–64.

Wilson, James Q. 1974. *Political Organizations*. New York: Basic Books.

Wilson, James Q. 1983. *American Government*, 2nd ed. Lexington, MA: D.C. Heath.

Wright, John R. 1996. *Interest Groups and Congress: Lobbying, Contributions and Influence*. New York: Allyn and Bacon.

Zorack, John L. 1990. *The Lobbying Handbook*. Washington, DC: Professional Lobbying & Consulting Center.

Index

Note: Page numbers in *italics* indicate figures or tables.

For Product Safety Concerns and Information please contact our EU
representative GPSR@taylorandfrancis.com
Taylor & Francis Verlag GmbH, Kaufingerstraße 24, 80331 München, Germany

www.ingramcontent.com/pod-product-compliance
Lightning Source LLC
Chambersburg PA
CBHW070413270326
41926CB00014B/2802

9 781138 287341